Shadows in the Light of God

Revelation to Dogma, Prophets to Priesthoods

Karl Schlotterbeck

Shadows in the Light of God: Revelation to Dogma, Prophets to Priesthoods

Published by Karl Schlotterbeck

©2020 by Karl Schlotterbeck. All rights reserved.

Cover art by R.L. Sather
http://www.selfpubbookcovers.com/RLSather

No part of this book may be reproduced, stored in a retrieval system, or transmitted in any form or means without permission from the author.

ISBN 978-1-7349203-0-7

DEDICATION

This work is dedicated
to the light that we each bring into this world,
and to those who strive to listen to the still small voice within,
and to the voice of nature of which we are a part;
to those who defy conformity and authority
and remain alive in their relationship to both nature and the inner voice.
It is also dedicated to those who showed me steps on this path:
shamans, swamis, ancestors, Druids, Christians and Pagans;
to the embodiments of the Divine Feminine,
and my children and grandchildren in the hope that they may remain
alive in their relationship with the Divine Other;
to the memory of all who have been and still are
martyred by the intolerance of hostile religions, governments,
social paranoia, political manipulation, and ignorance;
and to that persistent spirit of Divine Presence
that ever seeks to make itself known.

What Is Hidden Shall Be Revealed. (Matthew 10:26)

Table of Contents

Dedication

Prologue   1

Introduction: As a Child, I Understood as a Child   3

Chapter 1: The Land, Biology, and Relationship   9

Chapter 2: The "Other"   13

Chapter 3: Abram – A Sumerian Nomad with his Pagan God   17

Chapter 4: Ur of the Chaldees   19

Chapter 5: Queen of Heaven, Part I   27

Chapter 6: Migrations into Egypt   29

Chapter 7: Creation of the Egyptian World   35

Chapter 8: Egyptian Mythology, Metaphysics, and Magic   39

Chapter 9: People of the Pharaoh   47

Chapter 10: Egypt's Political History   51

Chapter 11: The Rise of Moses   55

Chapter 12: Moses and the Bond of Blood   59

Chapter 13: Who Was Moses?   63

Chapter 14: Invading Canaan   67

Chapter 15: The Queen of Heaven, Part II   69

Chapter 16: The Sacred Life and Temple Worship   77

Chapter 17: Catal Huyuk   81

Chapter 18: Winds of Change   85

Chapter 19: Joshua's Charge   89

Chapter 20: From Judges to the Throne of David   91

Chapter 21: The Birth of Scripture in a Divided Kingdom   95

Chapter 22: The Prophets and Baal   99

Chapter 23: Prophets, Priests, and the "D" Writer   103

Chapter 24: Babylonian Exile   107

Chapter 25: Return to the Temple and Its Priests   109

Chapter 26: Ezra's Torah of Moses   113

Chapter 27: Persian Apocalyptic Visions   115

Chapter 28: Alexander and Hellenism	119
Chapter 29: Pompey of Rome Takes Over	121
Chapter 30: The Myth of One God, One People, One Scripture	123
Chapter 31: The Roman World	131
Chapter 32: Jewish Pluralism	133
Chapter 33: Ano Domini	135
Chapter 34: The Teachings of the Master	141
Chapter 35: Writing the Word of God – Again	147
Chapter 36: A Yeshuite Secret Society?	155
Chapter 37: The Movement Splinters	159
Chapter 38: Saul of Tarsus	161
Chapter 39: The Struggle for Identity, Survival, and Power	165
Chapter 40: Be Ye Transformed	169
Chapter 41: Church Fathers and the Creation of Heresy	179
Chapter 42: The Mithraic Mysteries	181
Chapter 43: Romanization: From State Enemy to State Religion	183
Chapter 44: The Evolution of Satan	189
Chapter 45: The Dark Ages	191
Chapter 46: Crusades and the Growth of Papal Authority	197
Chapter 47: Inquisition into Heresy	201
Chapter 48: Reformation and The Bible	207
Chapter 49: New Order of the Ages	211
Chapter 50: Conclusions – Is Past Prologue?	215
Appendices	
A. Of Mind and Heart	225
B. Substance and Shadow	227
C. "The Fall" and the Psyche's Original Sin	229
D. Revelation, Fragmentation, and Integration	233
Acknowledgements	237
References	239
Endnotes	247

PROLOGUE

A Time Before

There was a time before Adam, Eve and Abraham –
    A time before Genesis.
There was a time when Satan was servant to the Divine.
There was a time before Satan.
There was a time before sexuality was taken from the Divine and given to demons,
    A time before patriarchal institutions,
    A time before matriarchy.

There was a time before relentless news and televangelists in tailored suits,
    A time before religion justified warfare, torture, genocide, and oppression.
There was a time before tools of torture and weapons of war spread the Gospel,
    A time before book burnings,
    A time before books.
There was a time before the nature of the Divine was decided by committee,
    A time before sexuality was a marketing strategy,
    And a time before Holy Fires were smothered by impenetrable ideologies.

On Earth, there was no time before land, sea, and sky.
For culture, there was no time before people.
For people, there was no time before sexuality.

We once knew our survival depended on our relationship with the land,
    Our relationship with each other, and
    The dreams and visions within us.

Out of the mysteries of those relationships came awareness –
    Awareness of an OtherWorld, and
    An ever-evolving concept of the Divine.

As spiritual movements became religious institutions
    Masks covered the face of The Divine –
    Each with its Light,
    Each with its Shadow.

Introduction

As a Child, I Understood as a Child

This book grew from childhood questions. What I remember of my early Sunday School teaching was comfortingly simple.

> In the beginning, God created everything, including Adam and Eve. They disobeyed God, were thrown out of the Garden of Eden, and had children. These children married people who came from somewhere else. Abraham and his children and their offspring became the Jews. These "chosen people" ended up in Egypt but were led out by Moses. He was the hero who miraculously persuaded Pharaoh to release them and then miraculously saved his people from the pharaoh's change of heart.
>
> The Jews came to the Promised Land which was theirs by divine right. Somehow – I couldn't remember how – the Jews were dispossessed of their country. Yet they claimed to be guided by their God.
>
> Here in my childhood narrative, Christmas stories take over. The messiah was born in a stable, performed miracles, and healings, taught, and made promises of freedom for his people; in return, he was rejected by his people and given to be killed by Rome. After his death and resurrection, his followers spread the faith that took form in the Catholic Church. This church withstood the attacks of the Roman Empire and heretics to carry the light of God until corruption brought reformers (like Martin Luther) who triggered a Protestant reformation and subsequent branches of Christianity.

Such was the memory of my childhood Sunday School lessons.

Religion has been an important part of my identity, but there were things that troubled me. Some of the most pious-sounding people advocated war, bigotry, and intolerance. I loved the teachings of Jesus. I wanted to be like him: to comfort the troubled, heal the sick, and inspire people to be as whole as they could be. The words of Paul, however, did not always sound like the same source. Even as a "sinner," I never felt degraded by the words of Jesus. Even at my best, I never felt loved by Paul. While Paul's followers said we were unworthy to enter the "Kingdom of Heaven," Jesus was always showing a way.

I was in college in the late 1960s when long-haired hippies were visible targets for social and religious hostility. Communists were valid targets, too, but they were mostly invisible or far away – and often the product of manufactured paranoia. Long hair was a good target: it was visible, rebellious, and violated some unwritten tenet of a strait-laced upright life. After all, if your hair was long, who knows what other transgressions might lurk under it? I heard preachers passionately quote a Bible passage that said long hair was an abomination on a man but, on a woman, her crowning glory. I wondered how Sampson's strength came from his long hair, but I never heard these two topics discussed in the same sermon.

Sometime in the 1970s I came across my first alternative to the King James translation of the Bible. It was nothing more revolutionary than a direct translation of the New Testament from the Greek language. I read it with interest, and there it was: the passage about long hair, but it was not as I'd heard it piously proclaimed. The writer of I Corinthians did say that "Nature" teaches these things about hair but goes on to say that "we have no such custom." Here is what I read:

> Judge for Yourselves: is it fitting for a woman to pray to God bare-headed? Does not Nature herself teach you that while flowing locks disgrace a man, they are a woman's glory? For her locks were given for covering.
> However, if you insist on arguing, let me tell you, there is no such custom among us, or in any of the congregations of God's people. (I Corinthians: 13-16)[1]

Clearly, there were two scriptures: one was written, kept in books, and occasionally referred to. The other, however, was spoken and embedded in a modern cultural context responding to current concerns and prejudices of the "faithful." The first was supposed to be a revelation of liberation but the second was being used as a weapon in a cultural war. Of course, there was also the irony that most of the hippies advocated peace and love – like the savior whose scriptures were being used against them. This devolution of spiritual revelation to a social weapon was a theme I found repeated throughout history.

Now, many years after my childish understandings, similar questions returned. How, I wondered, did Jesus' religion for rejected masses become the state religion of Rome and a tool of conquest and cultural oppression? How did prophets turn into profits?

In seeking answers, I found that what I had been taught was more myth than reality – contradicted by the Biblical writings on which they claimed to be based. I found Jesus to be an interlude in a "Judeo-Christian" tradition, having less to do with either one than with other traditions now rejected by "his" church. As I investigated, I found my questions justified, but came to admire the relentless persistence of that spiritual force that ever seeks to erupt into our structured, ideology-laden lives.

Religions are not the pure effluent of heaven's light. They reflect the land in which they are born, the social and political needs of the individuals who are their propagandists, and the intertwining of new ideas with old. Boundaries between clean and unclean, holiness and sin are not automatic but are established by social, political, and spiritual needs. Such movements are, without doubt, political because they ask people not only to *believe* in certain things, but to *behave* in ways that support, change or overthrow political structures.

In this history, the lands, languages, customs, and seasons are mostly those of the Mediterranean and European regions. Again and again, a new religion arrived, and its followers attempted to supplant the old. Buildings, holidays, and old celebrations were claimed and re-named.

In the Mediterranean religions I researched, I was surprised by the way some early religions used sexuality – and my surprise surprised me. It revealed to me how my own culture had conditioned me to view sexuality in only one way. Whether sexuality is sacred or profane (and when) is a judgment that reflects *social* mores of a particular time. To understand the culture I was studying, I had to set aside my preconceptions and, as best I could, look through the eyes and hearts of the people I wanted to know.

The foundations of the Jewish religion seemed to be rooted in the monotheism of one Egyptian pharaoh, followed by the Hebrews' struggles to separate themselves from the "pagan" religions around them. Their view of the world and Yahweh's relationship to it changed markedly under Persian and other influences, and they absorbed some of the ideas of cultures they rejected. With the coming of Jesus, we see the messiah that was not a messiah, and the way his most vociferous organizer began to depart from basic teachings and return to his own Jewish Hellenic roots.

I had to look hard to find the teachings of Jesus among all that was said about him. These efforts renewed my childhood interest in the religion *of* Jesus over the religion *about* him. The history I found showed me that the early church was not a clear entity but was one of several competing factions until the *Roman* church triumphed and became the state religion of the hated Roman Empire. This religion was useful to Constantine's Empire.

The Bible itself raised innumerable questions. Perhaps inspired, it was also brutal, primitive, and pedantic. Full of contradictions, it has been used to justify social revolution, social oppression, racism, civil rights, exploitation of natural resources, ecological responsibility, the suppression of women, and even condemnation of long hair in men. In my early years, I hadn't realized that this "book of books" had its own questionable history, was pieced together from various sources, and revised – as much from divine inspiration as for political and social purposes. I wanted to know how this collection came to be called *the* Word of God and, even if inspired, whose minds shaped the words, whose pen wrote the manuscripts, who decided which books would be included, and what was lost and added in the translations from one language to another.

Little changed as these movements swept across the lands. Rulers pitched peasants against one another in religious wars, people lived and died for mere promises while privileged classes enjoyed material and spiritual blessings. Beliefs and practices were stolen from conquered peoples as militant religious leaders sought control of their followers' minds, hearts, souls, and wealth. Today, while people suffer, wealthy churches offer piety, rituals of forgotten meaning, appeals for money and threats of damnation. Something has long been amiss in the relationship between people and their religions, between people and the Divine.

Again and again, spirited "heresies" emerged and were violently suppressed by excommunication, murder, and torture. The church of Jesus, even with its history of service and charity, developed a satanic shadow. There were murderers among the mystics, pretenders among the priests.

As I researched this evolution, I began with the teachings of Jesus as revealed in the gospels but, to better understand them and the times in which they arose, I explored the Judaism of his time. I traced backwards into the history of the Jewish people – and then sought *their* context. It was an adventure into deceptions, mistranslation, and unacknowledged debts owed one religion to another. The boundaries between Pagan, Jewish, and Christian ideologies and practices were artificial: differing masks on the same substance. Each religious revolution was as much theft as revelation.

This is the story of that evolution as I found it. This work does not present the best sides of our established religions. On the other hand, neither does it present their worst sides for, to catalogue all their excesses would have burdened my task unbearably and made this an unreadable tome of corruption, torture, and a cancerous evil of satanic forces wearing smiling masks of piety.

Not that many years ago, I might have found myself on trial for heresy for such writings, or sent to the torturer, costing me my tongue or my life. At one time, the church held such a tight grip on the minds and beliefs of its followers that even the printing of a Bible to be read by ordinary people was heretical. Often, I had to remind myself that this is the 21st century – but even now in an America that supposedly guarantees religious liberty, a resurgence of religious tyranny and intolerance has stirred that seeks freedom for some religions at the expense of others.

I have compassion for those who come to the bosom of any church hungering for spiritual nourishment. Unfortunately, it is also these masses that are left to bear the guilty burden of their churches' excesses. They come with innocence and are grateful for what fare they may be offered. They seek fellowship and belonging, a chance to offer prayers and praise, a desire to participate in something greater than themselves, with the hope of receiving a divine blessing. But there are stones in the bread. The institutions have been constructed with the planks of stolen traditions, painted with a veneer of deception, and maintained by the sweat of those it disempowers.

This book may appear to be a wholesale dismissal of all that believers hold dear, but that is not my intention. Rather, it is a call for the courage to fearlessly face the shadows of their faith's origin without having to create lies and gratuitous myths to justify the behavior of religious institutions over time. Such a truth could set us all free, based on the principle that the highest religions are those of love, forgiveness, humility, service, and truth – not conquest, propaganda, ideology, and political advantage.

Chapter 1

The Land, Biology, and Relationship

Despite the elevated pronouncements of metaphysics, theology, philosophy, biology and quantum physics, life arises from the land. Humanity arises from animal life; and culture and religion are shaped by the intersection of land, people, and time.

Our first need has always been to survive on the land on which we find ourselves. Because we had to survive, "primitive" people were in direct relationship with the elements that support or threaten life. If people were to survive, some of us must also reproduce. Life depended on the fertility of plants and animals.

"Culture" took shape in the context of our interaction with the land, the way the land nurtured us, and what it required of us. We lived in awe, fear, and gratitude of nature. We recognized forces of germination, growth, fruition, and decay, and we honored those forces as gods, devas, spirits, angels, or demons. *This relationship with the land shaped our image of the Divine.* How could it be otherwise? Nature was the face of the Divine.

"Primitive" religion may have been the earliest science for it was founded on observations of regular occurring patterns, and the recognition that there were forces behind natural events. Consequently, we attempted to influence those forces through actions, attitudes, and prayer. Everything was experienced as alive and in relationship with humanity. This was not superstition as we might denigrate it today, but it was our *experience* of the world. We have modern words for this worldview such as animism, or *participation mystique*. Naturally, modern people look at such ideas as an early stage in the evolution of consciousness as we gradually become more differentiated, but I'm not convinced that losing one capability to master another is progress. True progress incorporates and integrates both ways of being.

Developing in tribal groups, we felt an affinity for the forces that supported our well-being, whether those forces came from plants, flocks, and herds, from waters, mountains, or trees. Thus, deities were local events. They belonged to a family, tribe, or place, and manifested themselves in objects, events, animal activity, and forces of the weather and earth.

There were no "false gods" in those times but gods of other localities and times, or gods that might have been active at one time but now have withdrawn. Localized deities reflected the reality that forces supporting the people in one place may not apply elsewhere. A pertinent example here is the volcano god that manifested in thunder, fire, smoke, and lightning on the mountain but would not usually appear in farmlands, in the desert or the sea.

A group of people might admire the attributes of a particular animal, such as the high-flying falcon, or natural forces like wind and water. And so, seeking a symbol for transcendence, they might see something divine in the falcon with its keen eye, swift flight, and apparent independence from the land beneath it. Or they might admire the cunning and strength of the crocodile that lay on the threshold between land, sea, and sky. Animals – like spirits – might appear and disappear. They have an uncanny knack for survival and, by following them, we learn their secrets and expand our world.

Thus, the spirit world had its own seasons and dynamics, and wise ones watched to see what nature and their dreams might tell them. They watched for signs and cycles in the world around them – cycles of seasons, cycles of life and death, and cycles of daily living. There were distant and transcendent cycles in the movement of lights in the sky. Nile dwellers, for example, realized that the "sign" of the fertile flooding of the Nile was presaged in the rising of blue Sirius, the brightest star in the sky. The behavior of these planetary wanderers sparked mythologies. Surely the heavens were alive and related to things on Earth!

As the sun rose and set, it moved north and south across the horizon, signaling seasons of planting or harvest. At times, the sun was swallowed up by shadow and then reappeared. The moon, too, disappeared, changed shape, and lit the night with its silvery glow. It bore the signature of life: change within stillness. It was the first example of the life that died, entered darkness and, three days later, reappeared. What's more, the moon in its cycle joined the woman in hers. They may not have known what the connection was, but they knew it was there. Mythology gave that relationship meaning.

Gestation, growth, ripening and death stamped life with predictable fertility cycles. But where did life go in the winter – and after death? Myths revealed the answer. The fulfillment of each cycle gave its own experience and, to the wise, taught its own lesson. Those who learned the lessons and knew the signs became religious and political leaders – and could impose their own mythologies on others.

Life was where it was found. Differing experiences of the land and its resources lead to two main lifestyles, each with its own attitudes, approach to life, conceptions of the Divine, and social structures. Some lands were lush, giving rise to settled communities and farming. Others were barren and rocky deserts dotted with oases, encouraging a nomadic way of life.

Sedentary peoples lived *with* the land that gave them life and they learned to cultivate its resources and develop farming. The land taught them about life and its "providence." Productivity depended on working with the cycles of nature, her schedule of ripening food, and the best times to sow and harvest. Nature gave of herself to sustain the life of the people. In lush areas, nature pleased the senses with color, sounds, aromas, varieties of fruits and vegetables, and moderate temperatures. Indeed, sensory pleasure indicated that life was healthy and well.

The Divine was intimately close to these people. Its spirit quickened the soil and raised new life from the prior season's death. The power and care of deities for their people came in harvests – the true meaning of "Providence." When sacrifice became a part of religion, cultivators saw death and resurrection as part of a cycle. One aspect died so that another might live.

Those who lived on meat, on the other hand, depended on the health and fertility of their herds. Nomadic tribes could survive on the hoof as they moved from one grazing area to another. Other necessities of life could be obtained in exchange for skins, wool, or meat. They needed to be able to move, to reproduce and to kill to survive. Moving from one grazing land to another, roots were not set down into the land, and anything of use had to be portable. The wise leaders, or those engaged with the spirit world, moved their people in the direction of water, grazing land, or new herds – or else they perished.

People took control of the animals and encouraged reproduction. Sexuality, although pleasurable, served fertility – and therefore one male could "service" many females. Sexual energy was an essential force of survival and was a source of power. Sanitary methods of handling dead flesh had to evolve along with safe and efficient means of slaughter. For these people, efficiency lay not in harvest and preservation, but in slaughter and consumption.

To the nomad, death was not part of a cycle of renewal. Man, woman, child, or beast that ceased to breathe was dead. Stillness was not a sign of dormancy or the promise of eventual resurrection; it was the end. However, these people saw cycles in the distant movement of the stars, in their own reproduction and in seasonal grazing grounds. Nature was stark and intense, yet distant. The desert sun was always a threat, yet it protected them from the dangers of the night. What's more, sandstorms could come upon them at any time, or the night might light up with mysterious fires from oil or volcanoes.

Deities spoke through natural events and heavenly bodies. Thus, the gods of nomads were more likely to be distant and fierce; and more likely to be seen as a disembodied spirit separate from the world. This earth was a place of hardship and corruption, leaving hope for a better life somewhere in a spirit world. Leaders were those who could read the natural signs, remain in control of their territory, and bring productivity.

The sun, the land and water were essential players in life's survival. All of life – human, animal and plant – required water. Some areas had constant sources of water such as rivers, lakes, seas, or wells. In other places, water came only from the morning dew that formed as a mist during the night. Protected from the heat of the sun and morning winds, valleys might hold the mists of the night a little longer.

Water brought life and could also destroy. Terrible storms with thunder, lightning, and driving rain could disrupt the delicate balance of life. Or waters from a great sea might swell and flood (as occurred in Mesopotamia). Or an underground sea might come up through the earth – seen in the overflowing of rivers – to fertilize or to destroy. Life would not grow without the power of the sun, and yet that same power could wilt. Life required both the light of day and the cool mist of night.

In hot lands, trees welcomed people to rest in their cool shade. Trees were protection from harsh elements of nature, whether sun, wind, or rain. Trees, hills and mountains were also places of power for, when the storms came, the thunderous voice of a god was heard there, and great flashes of light connected earth and sky. Having chosen the high places and trees for the discharge of such awesome power, the Divine was sought in these places.

The land was not the only source of numinous contact with the Divine, however, for within each person were mysterious forces we still struggle to understand: emotions, visions, intuitions, and dreams that have a life of their own. Those who dreamed useful dreams became spiritual leaders.

I realize I've painted two extremes that may not have existed in any purity, but the trends are there. There were, of course, sedentary cultures that harvested grains and other plants, as well as hunted. What's important here is to recognize that differing ways of life arose, depending on the people's relationship with the land and how nomad and settler carried different values based on their lived lives – and consequently developed different images of their deities.

Chapter 2

The "Other"

Much of what I found in my reading has involved issues of identity, experiences of The Other, and what boundary might be needed to define the relationship between them. "The Other" might be a sacred Other, a cultural or religious other, or something inside of us that we don't grasp. So, when we engage the world around us, we have biological, spiritual, and psychosocial layers of otherness. Each of these has its developmental aspects but what is most important for this discussion is the way they come to bear on identity and boundaries – both personal and social.

A Sexual Biology with Social Ramifications

It won't be a surprise when I say that we are sexual beings and that it has always required two genders for us to create life. Not only that, our modern politics notwithstanding, many cultures have recognized a spectrum of gender expression not confined to gross physiology. Some differences were obviously physical, some attitudinal, and nearly all shaped by culture.

Sjoo and Mor assert that women, with the ability to create life, have always had a special relationship with nature. In fact, the first 30,000 years of humanity was dominated by an acute awareness of female processes in nature: menstruation, pregnancy, and childbirth. Furthermore, women shared another bond with each other and with the moon: synchronous menstrual cycles among closely knit women tended to make their menstrual period during the new moon, with ovulation at the full moon. In addition, studies have shown a possible genetic response to moonlight. The moon in those times was not associated with "lunacy." Rather, many languages assign words for cognitive activity that are related to names for the moon such as mental, measure, month, and mind.[2]

Jamake Highwater notes that the reproductive cycle of women differs significantly from that of other female animals. This has been important in the development of human culture.[3] In fact, human sexuality may have been the singular factor to humanize homo sapiens. First, the change from estrus to the menstrual cycle allowed sexual activity outside of times of reproduction. Second, the capabilities of the vagina and clitoris enhanced the potential pleasure of sex for both non-reproductive as well as reproductive purposes. Third, the erogenous quality of the breasts allowed not only another area of pleasurable interplay, but also the arousal of maternal care for the woman's *personal* lover. Finally, in the view of Sjoo and Mor, the change from rear to frontal intercourse was of inestimable value in moving sexuality from a primarily biological-reproductive activity to a personal interaction between two individuals facing one another.[4]

These differences took sexuality out of a purely reproductive function and made it an interpersonal event. Other animals mate for reproduction when the female is fertile, but humans have the option for pleasure bonding at any time. Through these changes, a *biological* need was transformed into a *social* pleasure. In addition, a face-to-face position presented the stimulus most conducive to personal bonding – the human face. Thus, the biological forces of sexuality became, through the physiology of woman, an act of *relatedness*.

Other differences between men and women shaped our collective psyche, such as the way women and men experience creation. The woman's way emphasizes the internal: to take in and to nurture life from within. For man, creation is external (except in the world of his ideas). He can fabricate *things* outside of his body, while woman creates *life* within herself. The man must hunt, gather, or grow food for his children. The mother *may* do the same, but she can also feed a child from her own body. It was easy to see the generative and nurturing nature of the feminine in both women and in nature itself. This shaped how many of the concepts of the Divine evolved. Man could hunt, build, protect, and cultivate – but woman was the "Mother of All Living."

Their blood rituals seem strange to our modern sensitivities but there is reasoning behind it. They can be traced to associations of blood with menstruation and birth, and in the cessation of life at the loss of blood. Thus, blood was part of the creation of life and its continuation; hence the importance of blood rituals.[5] As we shall see, Abraham and Moses sealed covenants with Yahweh with blood and the circumcision of male infants. And blood became part of Christian celebrations.

The essential reality was that life came from Nature through Woman. The word *nature* itself comes from the Latin *nasci* which means "to be born." People came *through* the mother from somewhere else and left life through the mysterious doorway of death.

The First "Other"

The first "other" that we encounter is from within our mother's womb. Therefore, our primal experience of otherness is female. I call this "primal" because it is before we have language but is, I believe, encoded in our earliest experiences and becomes a template for how we experience otherness and the world. This has been borne out in my own psychotherapeutic work in prenatal regression and birth memories.

Erich Neumann was not the first to point out that women and men have different experiences of their relationship with life, but his work *The Great Mother: An Analysis of the Archetype* was a hallmark in developing a deep understanding of not only our experience of the world but also the transition from matriarchal to patriarchal institutions as a developmental stage in the evolution of human consciousness. Because women gestate within another woman and emerge from a woman, their first experience of relationship with otherness is that the other is *like* them. The male's experience of otherness, however, is one of difference. That which surrounds him, gives birth to him, and gives him life is not like himself. I suspect this has several important ramifications. One is that men are more likely to feel alien in this world and more strongly suffer from the threat of being overwhelmed and re-absorbed by the feminine. This may intensify his objectification of all that is around him – including nature and women. A woman's relationship with the world is more comfortable than man's because the world is like her. For some men, mysticism has been an antidote to this alienation.

Neumann viewed the emergence of male-focused religions out of the matriarchal world as a necessary step in human collective evolution but judged that we should have transcended that stage long ago. After all, neither matriarchal- or patriarchal-dominated systems are healthy. Each does damage to both genders. Why we have not grown out of the male-dominated patriarchy is not difficult to see. Even a cursory look at today's economics and politics should give us a clue. For thousands of years, men – especially white men with property – have manipulated social and political structures for their benefit. Privileged classes in power have long depended on an underclass of poorly compensated workers from whom they could extract wealth, as well as draft into wars of conquest. Women have been one of those underclasses. They have yet to escape being part of the enslaved classes used for the advantage of the privileged elite.

A large part of America's economic engine has been literal slavery that gave way to economic slavery with upward distribution of wealth to white male overlords. Women have been one more resource for exploitation. Work is extracted from women for which they are not paid. The United States of America has yet to pass an equal rights amendment. Women only gained the right to vote 100 years ago. They do not earn the same rate of pay for the same work as men in either sports or corporate life; and gender-related activities like service professions, childcare or house cleaning are devalued. Men are more likely to be promoted into management positions or encouraged to pursue higher education. Thus, the system of white male supremacy has been effectively exploited in ways that keep men in power, *bolstered by religious ideologies* so that even in non-white cultures women are kept subservient.

These inequalities have been enshrined in religious ideology from the beginning of Christianity which, we all know, is notoriously difficult to change.

The Otherworld

Dreams, visions and apparitions of a spirit-body of the deceased suggested to anyone who paid attention that there was not only an afterlife but also another – usually invisible – world inhabited by the dead and other creatures that would occasionally make themselves known. Such apparitions are more frequent even today than is publicly acknowledged. Thus, it seemed obvious that there was/is some Otherworld from which we came to inhabit a body and to which we return when the body is done. Death may be the ultimate earthly "other."

In the 1980s I was asked to investigate a haunted family to see if they were sane, if their claims could be verified, and to assist them in writing about their experiences in *Lion of Satan, Lion of God.*[6] When coworkers asked what I was doing on the approaching weekend and I responded that I was going ghost hunting, there was usually one of two responses. One was to uncomfortably back away from me. The other was to later approach me in private and begin a conversation with, "I've never told anyone this but. . ." and proceed to tell me of some undeniable contact with a deceased relative or an uncanny, synchronistic event such as a rosary sliding off the shelf on the anniversary of its previous owner's death. Similarly, some of my psychotherapy clients confessed uncanny experiences that they felt unable to tell a "regular" therapist. This demonstrates to me both the taboo against admitting or even discussing such experiences, as well as the fact that many people have had otherworldly experiences that they keep to themselves because of that social taboo.

Because woman is the human doorway through which life comes, she had a central position in the deification of life's processes. She was akin to the Great Goddess who had given birth to the *Universe*. In addition, the "feminine" earth receives our bodies at death. We shall return to these feminine mysteries again and again but, for now, this simplified rendition of men and women's earliest relationships to one another and to their world will serve as a landscape for the emergence of *his*-story and, perhaps, hers as well.

Chapter 3

Abram – A Sumerian Nomad with his Pagan God

Abram – later renamed "Abraham" – is considered by some scholars to be the first genuine historical figure in the Bible. Previous characters – Adam, Eve, Cain, Able, and Noah, for example – are part of teaching stories. That is, they are part of a *mythological* story designed to explain something. For early peoples, it's not the characters that are significant, but the message taught by the story – like the fables of Aesop. These were stories that they used to answer basic questions of meaning, identity, and origin:

> Who are we?
> Where did we come from?
> Why are we here?
> What is our relationship to the Divine Otherworld and to each other?
> Why do we suffer, why do we have to die, and where do we go at death?

Biblical scriptures that have come down to us may appear as a loosely integrated narrative but, when we look at the history of the people, we find a diverse group of stories, each of which taught its own lesson. Stories were later combined and presented as history to establish the Jews' identity, their relationship to the Deity that claimed them, their place in the world, and a justification for their invasions into the lands of other people. It has even been suggested that the patriarchs were not Jews at all but were founders of Canaanite shrines who were later drafted into Jewish history to provide rootedness and continuity for this nomadic people. In any case, we can begin our historical chronology with Abram and his migrations.

Around the years 2000-1800 BCE, "Terah took his son Abram, his grandson Lot [who was] the son of Haran, and his daughter-in-law Sarai [who was] Abram's wife, and they set out from Ur of the Chaldees for the land of Canaan...."[7], but the family settled in a place called Harran where Terah died at the age of 205, we are told. It was then that Abram's god began to speak to him.[8]

Why Terah took his family out of Ur is not known, nor why he was headed for Canaan. Nevertheless, Abram received a call from a god named "El-Shaddai" to migrate into Canaan. To some interpreters, El Shaddai means "God of the Mountains."[9] This call was the justification of much of the subsequent political, military, and religious activity of his descendents.

At this point, Abram was not Jewish, nor did he carry scriptures with him. He came from a Pagan land, guided by the voice of a god later claimed to be Yahweh. We take for granted the presence and unalterable eternity of the Bible, that we might almost believe that Abram carried it with him. The Jewish scriptures, however, would not be written for many years, so all Abram had to bring with him was the Pagan Sumerian culture from which he came. And in that culture, we can see the foundations of his new faith.

Chapter 4

Ur of the Chaldees

The wandering Abram seems out of place when we look at the social history of his reputed homeland, Ur. But its influence on his people's yet-to-be-developed mythology becomes evident when we learn about their temples, rituals, lawgiving, world of clay, and the curious story of Sargon I.

Garraty & Gay[10] describe the land of Ur in Sumeria as a flat expanse of brown dust and mud, swept by stormy winds and unpredictable devastation from the flooding of its two rivers. The origin and prehistory of the Sumerians is lost in time. In contrast to their neighbors, they were a non-Semitic people and called themselves "the dark-headed." They were a short, heavy-boned people with long, narrow heads. They may have come into the area by water, through the Persian Gulf.

In Sumeria and Akkad, people lived in independent cities, each with its own primary deity. Neighboring cities often competed for water and cultivated land. Empires, when they could be established, were temporary. Like the ages of biblical characters, Sumerian king lists have been found that attribute incredibly long lives to their rulers. The legendary Gilgamesh was listed as one of these kings. There were also references to "The Flood" that we encounter later in Jewish mythology.[11]

Royal graves suggest a previous history of human sacrifice, particularly at the death of royalty. Human sacrifices may have been held in the temple but, over time, lambs became the sacrificial substitute for humans.[12]

Sumerian society was well organized. Sumerians used the technology of their time. They took the clay on which they lived and shaped it to create a civilized, urban life out of unpredictable weather, flooding, and dust. By about 3300 BCE, they developed the earliest known writing called "cuneiform." By then, they also had sailboats, wheeled vehicles, animal-drawn ploughs, the potter's wheel, beer, fired-clay knives, medicinal drugs, and imitation precious stones.[13] They cultivated dates, which require a five-year wait before the trees bear fruit. To cultivate their land in the face of unpredictable forces of nature, they developed irrigation canals for farming and for fishponds. Around 2700 BCE, the walls of Uruk – the Biblical "Erech" – were 18 feet thick and had a circumference of about six miles.

Each city was built around its temple, a giant ziggurat. Ziggurats were made of brick and resembled the stepped pyramids of Egypt. These ziggurats were in ruins by the time of the Jews and became the stimulus for their mythical account of the tower of Babel. Each city state also had its own history of dynasties. The First Dynasty of Ur is thought to have existed about 3100 BCE. The Third Dynasty is listed as after "the Flood".[14] In the 24th century BCE, King Urukagina of the city of Lagash boasted of having restored justice and freedom by doing away with exploitation by oppressive priests and officials – one of the earliest examples of civil authorities having to intervene to limit the corruption of religious institutions. Already, the shadows of corruption had to be purged from the light of their religion.

Sumer was not alone in the world. History shows a peculiar relationship between non-Semitic Sumeria and its Semitic neighbors to the North. The people to the north of Sumer spoke a Semitic language and called their land "Akkad." Akkadians steadily infiltrated into Sumer while they constantly had to protect themselves from nomads and people from the mountains.[15] By the time of Abram, Sumer had been politically conquered by the Semitic Akkadians, but the Akkadians absorbed the culture of the Sumerians.

Around 2350 BCE, Sargon I from the Akkadian city of Agade – a town near Babylon – subjugated Sumer. Sargon I was said to have been born secretly by a priestess or enitum, a female devotee,[16] who set him adrift in the river in a basket of rushes. He was found by a "drawer of water" who then adopted and reared him.[17]

Sargon's empire was eventually broken up by barbarians and, about 2150 BCE, rulers from Ur united the area again for another century or so. The Sumerian king Ur-Nammu, founder of the third dynasty of Ur, instituted a law code about 2050 BCE. Another law code around 1970 BCE was written in the Semitic language by another king, Bilalama. About 1900 BCE, king Lipit-Ishtar set down a law code in the non-Semitic Sumerian language. These are well before the famous Semitic code of Hammurabi of 1750 BCE. It was said that, like Moses, Hammurabi had been given a code of laws by his god, Shamash.[18]

The laws written before the time of Hammurabi had required a payment of damages for injury such as 60 sheckels for lost eye but, for the highest class, exact retaliation was applied as in "an eye for an eye." The later Semitic codes, however, were more severe than those of their Sumerian predecessors.

Sumer had a participative government with dual assemblies of elders and armed male citizens who discussed matters of war and peace.[19] They may have been the first bicameral legislature.

The difficult process of learning to read and write cuneiform resulted in a class of scribes. There was also a class that has been misnamed "slaves." These people were more indentured servants than slaves. The Babylonian word for "slave," for example, was also that for a king's minister.[20] These servants remained persons in their own right: they could own property, participate in the legal system, marry non-servants, and could also buy their freedom.

Unmarried women were independent and had most of the same rights as men. A married woman's primary function, on the other hand, was to provide sons for her husband.[21] An adulterous wife was drowned with her lover. Men might have temporary wives or concubines, and a concubine might be provided by a wife to her husband to propagate a son,[22] a custom that appears in the later story of Abram, Sarah and Haggar.

Their gods were men and women "writ large" with human needs and behaviors.[23] The ziggurat was the residence of their deity and was attended by priests and priestesses. Special classes of women, misunderstood even by sympathetic historians, were committed to the service of their god(s). Labeled by modern writers "temple prostitute," these women, in fact, lived to serve their deity. There were different classes of these "Women of the Temple." The highest position was that of "entu," or the wife of the god.[24] Little is known about her responsibilities, but high expectations were placed upon her such as staying out of wine shops. Women of the class known as "Sal-Me" were also considered married to the god and were rich and honored.[25] They often had children by an "unknown father." Unlike the entu, they could marry, but were to have no children by their earthly husband, still being married to the god.

Zikru and kadishtu were the class often called "temple harlots".[26] These classes of women and their spiritual/sexual functioning were well integrated into the Sumerian society. There was an earlier time, however, when they were the very fabric of their society, as we shall see in their relationship to the Queen of Heaven.

In Mesopotamia in general, as in Sumer, kingship was by heavenly decree, but the king was neither permanent nor without accountability. The city's god or goddess was the owner of the city and the ruler was the deity's steward.[27] (This idea appears among Celtic mythologies in Europe as well.) Kings were subject to review and charged with integrating the society, protecting the rights of its people, and promoting fertility. As part of the city's New Year festival, the king gave up his office and was humiliated by the priest after which the office could be returned to him. As I noted before, two assemblies – elders and fighting men – acted as a bicameral legislature. The Akkadian concept of well-being or "shulmu," which occurs when the king fulfills his obligations, is related to the Hebrew word "shalom".[28]

From about 6500 BCE came the celebration of the *hieros gamos*, or sacred marriage. The New Year festival, held at the summer solstice, commemorated the abundance of life through a sacred union of opposites, which called for the recognition that both male and female forces were necessary for the creation of life.[29] This ritual reenacted the union of the goddess of love and fertility with her lover, the vegetation god.[30] Thus, at the New Year festival, a holy marriage was celebrated between the king and the goddess of the city.[31] The chosen woman who became the *presence of the goddess* united with the reigning monarch who was identified as the god. This was to assure fertility of both land and womb.[32] A text from about 3000 BCE describes the rite as the king goes to the "holy lap of Inanna" where he "embraces the Hierodule" or sacred servant.[33]

Pantheons

Each city was ruled by its own deity:
- at Babylon, it was Marduk;
- at Larsa, it was Shamash, the sun god of justice;
- at Ur, it was Nannar;
- at Nippur, it was Enlil, lord of rain & wind;
- at Erech/Uruk, it was Innini or Ishtar, goddess of love.[34]

Mesopotamian deities were a group of superhuman beings who controlled the actions of the cosmos according to prescribed laws. These *dinger*, or gods, were arranged in a hierarchy with a king, seven gods who "decree the fates," and fifty who were called the "great gods".[35] There are differing Sumerian names for deities, occasioned by the fact that, in the earliest times, the people of each city had their own names for the deities and assigned importance in their pantheon based on the individual needs of their city. Over time, Marduk absorbed the functions of many of the other deities and was eventually worshipped under 50 names, each of which reflected one of his attributes.

Enlil was the earth-god of Nippur, Anu was the male sky god, and Ea the feminine water god. It was Enlil who later became known as Bel or Baal.[36] Enlil remained the chief god of their pantheon and seemed to be protective of humankind.[37]

The son of Enlil was the moon god originally called "Ur" but later came to be called "Sin." Sin remained the presiding deity of the city of Ur. The moon god was considered more significant than that of the sun, a fact reflected in the use of a lunar calendar by the later Hebrews and others. The moon god's son was the sun god Shamas (or Shamash) and his daughter was Ishtar or Venus.[38]

Deities had their responsibilities. Nanshe, who was a Lagashite goddess, for example, was expected to oversee the moral order of humankind by, in part, comforting the orphan and turning the mighty over the weak.[39] Nebo, as another example, was the patron of writing and speech whose symbol was the wedge. He was the voice of the gods. In fact, the name "Nebo" may be related to the Hebrew *nabhi* which means "prophet".[40]

The Universe

The deities had direct relevance to the lives of the people since they controlled the natural forces on which life and social order depended. A theology developed as the people attempted to explain their relationship with the deities, why they were on earth, and how the world came to be. Creative power was given to the divine word,[41] a concept that persisted into Jewish and Christian mythology, as it was in Egypt.

The major components of their universe were heaven and earth. Indeed, their term for universe was *An-Ki*, which is a compound word meaning "heaven-earth." Between heaven and earth was the substance *lil*, which was wind, air, breath, or spirit. The sun, moon, planets, and stars were made of the same stuff as lil but were luminous. Outside of this was the boundless sea.[42]

Creation

There were various creation stories from these early times. Apparently, these early people had no need for one ultimate explanation. Perhaps evolving myths also reflected earlier experiences and values of the people. For example, the relatively stable culture of the marshlands of Sumer would develop different values and stories from the more difficult lives Akkadians had in defending themselves.

One of the stories of the origin of the world began with the primeval sea. The sea engendered the "cosmic mountain" that united heaven and earth. From the personified heaven and earth – An and Ki – was generated the air god Enlil who then separated heaven from earth. The subsequent union of Enlil with his mother the earth created the rest of earthly life. In another creation story, a god bound reeds together and spread earth on them.[43] This reflects the experience of the marsh-dwellers who created foundations for their dwellings in exactly that way.

A more dramatic, violent, and misogynist creation story tells of Marduk who brought about the world through his confrontation and defeat of a terrifying goddess named "Tiamat." She represented the chaotic, overwhelming ocean and was feared by all the gods except Marduk.[44] After binding her dragons, Marduk slew Tiamat and cut her corpse into two parts, making heaven and earth. He then added the constellations, planets, and other heavenly objects.

This is the first of several creation stories like those found in Genesis and in Egypt that have in common the creation of the world by separating what was one into two parts – unity into duality.

Their creation stories tell us that humankind was fashioned by the gods from clay for the purpose of serving their needs, and various accounts are given of the creation of people. In one story, Ea and a goddess Aruru create man "from clay by the power of the divine word".[45] In each account, clay was the medium used, but it is vivified by blood, breath, or word. Humankind's fate was always uncertain because of the unpredictability of the gods who controlled natural forces. After death, the soul descended to the dreary netherworld that vaguely reflected earthly life in a dismal way.[46]

Mythology

Some of these mythological figures may have been genuine ancestors (like Gilgamesh) whose lives became magnified over time. For example, the Moon god Nanna had at one time been king of Ur, appointed by An and Enlil.[47] There can be little doubt that mythological stories reflect not only the peoples' beliefs about their place in the world, but also changes in political power over the years.

In one story, Inanna, Queen of Heaven and goddess of the city of Erech, wanted to increase her own fame as well as the welfare of her city. She went to Enki who was the lord of wisdom and, as such, oversaw the divine laws. After feasting and drinking, Enki gave Inanna the 100 divine laws that formed the basis of their civilization after which she left for her home city. After he sobered up, Enki realized what he had done and sent a servant with sea monsters to deter Inanna but, at each onslaught, she was saved by the mother goddess Ninhursag. The Queen of Heaven and the Mother Goddess prevailed, and the divine laws (as though they were things to be moved) came under the control of Inanna at the city of Erech.[48]

This may be less of a mythological story of deities than an observation of a rise in power and learning in the city of Erech. Here, as we shall find later in Egypt, a female deity used her intelligence and cunning to come into possession of the secrets of power. It was she who brought knowledge (science) out of the realm of the deities and into the world of humankind.

As noted before, the king list tells of a flood which was, of course, explained mythologically. Tablets of the legend of Gilgamesh contain an account of a flood like that in the Bible.[49] In the Sumerian/Akkadian account, the gods were angry, and decided to drown the entire human race. Enki, however, told a good man named Uta-Napishtim, or Utnapishtim, of the impending danger. Utnapishtim built an ark and so survived the flood. At the end of the flood, Uta-Napishtim sent forth birds (including a dove) to see if land had arisen from the flood waters.[50] After the flood, Ishtar swears that those days would be remembered by her jeweled necklace – the rainbow.[51]

Abram's exit from Ur would have been during the rule of Ur or shortly after its breakup. Whether this was under Semitic or Sumerian control is less relevant than the fact that it was Sumerian values and customs that prevailed there. One of the curious facts is that the nomadic life chosen by Abram was in stark contrast to the settled people of his supposed homeland. Like other people of the Near East, they referred to nomads as barbarians "who knew no grain."[52] It is assumed Abram came from Ur but, given his differences, he may have simply passed through there from somewhere else on his way to the Promised Land. Or perhaps his story is from a much earlier time or different culture, where sacrifice of the first-born was common, and women were used as men wished. In addition, since his god – El Shaddai – was possibly a God of the Mountains, Abram may have come from the mountain people against which Akkadians had to defend themselves.

Abram's family was most likely from a town called "Haran" in Turkey, which was part of the kingdom of Mitanni who were Indo-Europeans from Asia. Mitannians were people with rigid social codes, which Abram reflected more so than the conventions of Sumer.[53] Whether or not Abram's people came from or through Sumer, their traditions shared some mythological features, but also showed some strong differences, perhaps the most significant being the role of the Divine Feminine.

Chapter 5

Queen of Heaven, Part I

Feminine deities were not an isolated incident in the history of humankind. Her worship was known in Babylon, Egypt, Crete, Greece, and Canaan.[54] Goddess religions were well organized and known to exist by 7000 BCE – if not as far back as 25,000 BCE. A 4000-year-old cylinder from Sumer depicts a tree with a male on one side and a female on the other. The tree is guarded by a serpent while a woman reaches out toward the tree – a tree planted in Inanna's holy garden.[55] This image, of course, shows up later in Judeo-Christian scriptures.

The Goddess had a number of names – or represented several discrete goddesses. To the Babylonians and northern Semites, her name was *Ishtar*. Bible writers referred to her as *Ashtoreth*. In Phoenicia, her name was *Astarte*. In Syria, she was called *Athar*. In Cilicia, it was *Ate* or *Atheh*. In Akkadian, her name was *Inanna*. In Egypt, she was known as *Au Set* – or her Greek rendering as *Isis*.[56]

A 5000-year-old hymn from a Sumerian town speaks not only of the "holy house" of the goddess, but also her fertile virginity. It describes the house of Mighty Mother that "No man has entered."[57]

From the third millennium BCE, a Sumerian poem about the Descent of Inanna tells a richly symbolic story. (Semitic accounts used the name Ishtar.) Inanna decided to visit the Netherworld and instructed her female friend Ninshubur to seek help for her if she did not return in three days. At the first gate to the Underworld, Inanna was stopped and informed she must be treated as any other who enters the world of Ereshkigal, Queen of the Netherworld. Hence, Inanna must give up part of her clothing and insignias at each of the seven gates until she arrives before Ereshkigal naked. For her efforts, Inanna is judged, killed, and hung on a peg.

When Inanna did not return after three days, Ninshubur set in motion the events that would release Inanna by providing empathy for Ereshkigal's travail. A substitute, however, must be found for Inanna in the Underworld. She chose her consort, Dumuzi (later, Tammuz) whom she judged to have not been sufficiently grieving her absence. Inanna decreed that they will each spend half a year in the Underworld. In one version, Dumuzi's sister, Geshtinanna, offers herself as a replacement for him.[58]

These themes appear again and again across the mythologies: three days in death, mourning for the annual death of the goddess' consort, sacrificial substitutes, and the seven gates to approach the Divine.

We see from Sumerian mythology that the goddess was not just a consort. She was powerful in her own right, but her decline had already begun. Stories of the legendary King Gilgamesh circulated from the third millennium BCE and portrayed him as an exemplary ruler. Interest in his exploits extended even into the Neo-Babylonian era – about 550 BCE.[59] Gilgamesh's encounter with Ishtar is more than mythology, as it reflects a shift in religious power.

In one of the stories, Ishtar brings to Gilgamesh his royal robes and hints that he might have peace if he marries her. Gilgamesh, though tempted, rejects her seduction with the implication that her offer is but an entrapment. He confronts her with the fates of her previous lovers: one she turned into a mole, and another into a wolf so that his own shepherds and dogs chased him. Her days of glory waning, he complains of being tired of her promises and has become skeptical that goddesses return the love of their people. She has "left in men a memory of grief."[60]

Enraged, Ishtar convinces her father Anu, against his own better judgment, to send the Bull of Heaven to lay waste to the humans. After killing several hundred men, the Bull turns on Gilgamesh. However, Gilgamesh's loyal friend Enkidu steps in and, to protect Gilgamesh, kills the Bull of Heaven. The Bull of Heaven dead, Ishtar curses Enkidu and retires among the other women.[61]

This story places Gilgamesh at a time of transition between men's disillusionment with the goddess and waning of her power, and the assertion of masculine sovereignty. It foreshadowed what was to come of Her.

Through these Sumerian stories and customs came the first of four known exposures of prechristian Hebrews to the Queen of Heaven – the others being in Egypt, Canaan, and Babylon. Such was the Pagan Sumerian culture to which Abram was exposed during his early life and as part of his travels.

Chapter 6

Migrations into Egypt

The origin of the Hebrews bears little resemblance to the later people who built beautiful temples, professed monotheism, and argued innumerable laws of purity. They were originally a desert people and, since a desert people will honor its landmarks, they venerated stones and pillars. In addition, wells, springs, streams, and trees were evidence of creative power in the universe. Spirits were seen in trees and places, in the winds and in animals, only some of which were domesticated. All spirits of power were given the Semitic name of *el* (singular) or *elim* or *elohim* (plural), which referred to a "superhuman being" or "divinity".[62]

The early Hebrews worshipped a number of "foreign gods."[63] Early scriptures use the plural form of god – "Elohim" – for their deities. The variety of names of these elohim is hidden by later editing and translations that homogenize the differences by rendering them as either "The Lord" or simply "God." Among the elohim were El Shaddai (God Almighty), El Elyon (God Most High), El Olam (God Everlasting), and El Roi (God Seeing).[64] I noted before that El Shaddai referred to "God of the Mountains." There are other interpretations of this name, however, including "destroyer" and "breasts." One's choice of interpretation may depend on whether the interpreter wants to emphasize the god's destructive power or his care and nourishing of his people. It's not unusual for mountains to be seen as breasts, such as the Paps of Anu in Ireland and the Grand Tetons range in Wyoming. It the mountain happens to be a volcano, it would certainly qualify as a destroyer.

Gods were also referred to in the Semitic world as Adonis or Adoni ("Adonai" in Hebrew) that meant *Lord*, "Malack" or "Moloch" (Melech in Hebrew) meaning *King*, "Bel" or "Baal" which meant *Landlord* or *Possessor of the Land*, and "Rabb" which meant *Master* (Rabbi in Hebrew). These gods were not seen only as impersonal natural forces but were personal or familial.[65] Because of this personal nature, clans often adopted their own tribal deity. For Abram, it was El-Shaddai.

As a group, the Hebrews were a nomadic people, though less so than the Bedouin.[66] When we hear of Abram's people, we are viewing only one small clan of a class of people who were not then known as Hebrews. A term sometimes thought to refer to the Hebrews remains controversial.[67] There is a word – 'apiru – which generally referred to a low class in Canaan before the term evolved into "ibri" and "Ibrim," which did refer to Hebrews.[68] According to advocates of the connection between Hebrew and 'Apiru, the Sumerian word Ha-BI-ru was equivalent to the Sumerian SA.GAZ which, in Egyptian, appeared as 'A-pi-ru. The West Semitic translation means "dusty" and 'Apiru is part of a Hebrew family of adjectives that refers to a temporary condition, such as "hungry", "thirsty", and "barefoot."[69]

In fact, they were caravaneers. Caravans in those days, in which the 'Apiru were normally employed, traveled by donkey. However, as caravan trade fell with the breakdown of international commerce in the late eighteenth century BCE, the 'Apiru turned to other work. Since caravans had to be defended against raiders, they knew about arms and about fighting and so they became mercenaries, slave troops, or "slaves," which was not necessarily an undesirable condition in those days.[70] Population shifts were also common at that time and, 'Apiru or not, Abram's deity – El – told him to settle in the land of the Canaanites. Meanwhile, Indo-Iranians (or "Hyksos") pushed past Abram's descendants and moved on down along the seacoast into Egypt where they dominated from 1750 to 1580 BCE.[71]

But back to Abram: he migrated from Ur to Harran which were two of the major centers of trade in the area at that time. Both cities shared the same Sumerian moon-god religion.[72] As Abram journeyed toward Negeb, there was a famine in his promised land so he detoured into Egypt like other nomads.[73] He arrived in Egypt as an Emir, the head of a large tribe. As such, it was appropriate for him to pay his respects to the ruler of that land – the Pharaoh.[74]

Abram's wife, Sarai, was a beautiful woman. Prompted by a dream, he told her to pretend to be his sister instead of his wife because he was afraid they would kill him for her.[75] As a result, Sarai was taken into the household of the Pharaoh. She must have served admirably since Abram was richly rewarded for his charade: Pharaoh gave him sheep, cattle, asses, camels, and slaves. But then diseases came to Pharaoh's household and he (Pharaoh) divined it was on account of Sarai and Abram's deception. Pharaoh was offended at the adulterous charade and sent Abram and Sarai away – along with all they had received.

Abram's motivation was reported to be his own survival, but his means was to sell the favors of his woman. It was the spiritual vision and morality of his Pagan host that prevented a continuation of the deception. Enriched by selling the favors of his wife, Abram, Sarai, Lot, and their herdsmen left Egypt, parted ways and Abram settled in Canaan once more. Again, he heard his god promise him all the land he could see.[76]

After some local intrigues, Melchizedek, who was a priest of El and king of Salem, appeared and gave Abram a blessing. Then Abram had visions of his god promising him once more the land of the Canaanites and other peoples. After ten years in Canaan, Abram and Sarai still had no children so Sarai brought to Abram her Egyptian slave, Hagar. They lay together and Hagar conceived. However, Hagar despised Sarai's ill-treatment of her and ran away. But Hagar was found by El-Roi (God of a Vision) and told to return to Abram and Sarai.[77] So, Hagar returned and gave birth to Abram's first child, Ishmael.

When Abram was 99 years old, he had more visions telling him that his name was changed to "Abraham" and that his covenant with his god required that all males be circumcised.[78] In addition, Sarai's name would be changed to Sarah and, despite their age, she would conceive.

Abraham had more adventures, including conversations with El-Shaddai during which Abraham attempted to get his god to discriminate between the good and bad people of Sodom and Gomorah rather than destroying them wholesale.[79] Lot and his daughters escaped the cities before they were destroyed. The story of his flight from Sodom was hardly to his honor. When two angels came to the town and stayed in his house, a crowd gathered and called on Lot to give his two visitors to them that they might have intercourse with them.[80] Lot, however, protected his two guests by graciously offering the crowd his two daughters in place of his visitors. "Look, I have two daughters, both virgins; let me bring them out to you, and you can do what you like with them. . ."[81] However, Lot's daughters were saved by the two visitors themselves who pulled Lot inside and struck the crowd with blindness.[82] Lot and his family were told to leave and not look back but his wife, turning to look, was turned into a pillar of salt.[83]

Lot, now a widower, and his daughters first fled to a small town and then took up residence in a cave. The daughters, concerned that there were no men around and no male heirs, conspired to make their father drunk on two consecutive nights so each could lay with him. Thus, both became pregnant by Lot, their father.[84]

Meanwhile, Abraham traveled on and lived a while in Gerar where, once more, he pretended that Sarah was his sister. The local king took Sarah, but the king, Abimelech, was told in a dream of the true situation and threatened with death if he did not return Sarah. When Abimelech rebuked Abraham for what he had done, Abraham claimed that Sarah was his father's daughter by a different mother before he took her as wife. Again, Abraham was given sheep, cattle, and slaves and, as a result, Abimelech's household was cured of the affliction besetting them because of Sarah's presence.[85]

Eventually, Sarah bore 100-year-old Abraham a son whom they named Isaac. Sarah prompted Abraham to drive out the slave who had borne Ishmael for him, which he did. But then the god appeared to Hagar who was lost in the wilderness and about to die and showed her a well and so they lived on. Under the prompting of his god, Abraham took Isaac to an altar on a specific mountain, bound him and raised his knife to kill his son. At the last minute, however, an angel appeared who said Abraham had been tested and would be rewarded for his willingness to sacrifice Isaac. Strangely, this Lord refers to Isaac as Abraham's only son in Genesis 22:17 – as if Ishmael hadn't existed. This incident may reflect, as some believe, a transition from human sacrifice to the sacrifice of animals – an echo of what we found in earlier Sumeria.

When Sarah died, Abraham sought to buy land from the Hittites for her burial. Although they offered him a burial plot gratis, Abraham insisted on paying and a deal was struck. Abraham arranged to get a wife for Isaac and then he married again. Sarah's barrenness was apparently not Abraham's fault for, by Keturah, his second wife, and by his concubines, he had numerous children, only the sons being mentioned. Finally, at 175 years of age, Abraham died and was buried in the cave where he had buried Sarah.

Echoes of Abraham's pimping charade are heard in the life of Isaac and his wife Rebecca. In Gerar, Isaac claims that Rebecca is his sister for the same reason Abraham had. Abimelech the Philistine king figured out the ruse and challenged Isaac, aware that if any of his people had slept with Rebecca, they would owe Isaac some payment. Thus, Abimelech warned his people and forbad them to touch either Isaac or Rebecca. Again, Isaac and Rebecca were sent away after they had accumulated much wealth. They settled into the valley of Gerar.[86]

The stories then go on with contention between Isaac's sons, Jacob and Esau, and how Jacob deceived his blind father into giving him what belonged to Esau. Among Jacob's adventures was his wrestling with an angel, after which he was given the name *Israel*.[87]

As the people journeyed under various patriarchs, they built altars or set up sacred pillars in honor of their god or of an event. Their households also picked up "foreign" gods, which had to be occasionally purged.[88]

It was Jacob's son Joseph who, because of the jealous intrigue of his brothers, ended up in Egypt as an interpreter of dreams. The biblical story presents it as a remarkable thing that Joseph, using Pharaoh's dream, predicted fat years followed by lean. In fact, such cycles were commonly known in Egyptian history long before the time of Joseph. The story is also told that, because of famine, the Pharaoh came to gradually own all the land that was in Egypt because he had food that the people bought with their land. At least that was what the scripture writer believed, being ignorant of Egyptian civilization and its customs.

Joseph lived the good life in Egypt and was eventually joined by his father's household. As the writer tells it, the Jews became so numerous that a new Pharaoh feared these people and not only put them into slavery, but also ordered their male newborns to be killed. It was to prevent this carnage that a baby son of a Levite woman was put into a basket and set adrift – a reprise of the story of Sargon I. This Levite child was found by Pharaoh's daughter who adopted him – despite her father's edict.[89]

It is said that she gave him the name of "Moses" because he was drawn from the water. Moses, however, was a common Egyptian name, found in such names as Thutmose, Ahmose, and Ramesses, for example.

This folksy account of Moses' name and origin is just one of the efforts to separate Hebrew origins from the Egyptians. Indeed, Egypt has many faces in the Bible: as the land of plenty, of slavery, of generosity, of safety and refuge. In Egypt, these wandering nomads were faced with overwhelming monuments, palaces and temples, and a vast array of colorful deities. Let us, for the time being, shift our focus from the followers of El Shaddai and look behind the mask placed on Egyptian culture by biblical writers. Let's allow the people of the Black Land to speak for themselves.

Chapter 7

Creation of the Egyptian World

In a desert land with one great river, there were two elemental forces that shaped the world of the Egyptian: one was the sun, and the other was the Nile. As a result, two deities came to prominence: the sun god Re (or Ra), and the Verdure-god, Osiris.[90]

Fed by rains far upstream, the Nile swells in August, reaches its peak in October, and sinks to its lowest level in April.[91] When it recedes from flooding the land around it, it leaves behind rich deposits that renew the topsoil. Only a hoe was needed to till the ground, which yielded two or three crops in a year.[92] Because of the Nile's annual gift of black earth, they called their land "Keme" – the Black Land.[93] The dangerous, sterile desert, on the other hand, was called *Dashre*, the red land.

The rising and falling of the Nile shaped the mythology of Egypt. When the Nile overflowed each year, cultivated territory was lost to watery chaos. Then, as the water receded, the "primeval mound" emerged once more and become a resting place for large birds such as falcon, ibis, or the mythical phoenix. Rich sediment that came from beyond the known world brought regeneration, renewal – resurrection.[94] This yearly flooding reenacted their primal creation myth in the annual appearance of the mound that brought order out of chaos, as well as the idea that life may return to watery chaos if order is not maintained.

In addition to Nile inundations, Egyptians created rich farmland by draining marshy tracts that bordered the river. In addition to agriculture, there were numerous domestic animals as well, such as oxen, sheep, goats, pigs, donkeys, and eventually the horse. Cattle breeders and herdsmen lived in portable shelters and trapped animals rather than farming. These were the exceptions, however, as most of the people relied on farming.[95]

Irregularities in Nile inundations led to the Egyptian expectation of seven lean years followed by years of plenty. This tradition dates from at least the reign of Djoser around the 28th Century BCE – long before Joseph's legendary dream interpretation.[96] Also, plagues were a common occurrence as some sort of plague occurred almost every year.[97]

Many of their neighbors sought Egypt's wealth and fertility. In sharp contrast to the arid summer pastures in Palestine, the land of Goshen adjoining the Nile Delta was a land of milk and honey, rich with flowery pastures on which fed cattle and bees.[98]

Deities and Districts

The diversity of Egyptian deities arose from local surroundings, as well as from imported ancient gods from other parts of Africa, Asia, and the Mediterranean.[99] For example, hunters of the Nile marshes humanized the sun god and pictured him as paddling a solar boat through the marshes. This god, Re, displaced an ancient sun god called Atum at Heliopolis and took prominence as the pre-eminent deity. At Edfu, the falcon, comrade to the sun, represented the sun god there.[100] Thus, the sun god was often portrayed with wings flying across the sky.

Deities might also be represented by a jackal at Abydos and Suit, or a falcon at Edfu and Hieraconpolis, a vulture at El Kab, a goddess at Dendera, a god at Elephantine, or a pantheon at Hermopolis. Of special significance are the deities of Thebes, Memphis, and Heliopolis. Thebes had a trinity of deities, while Heliopolis had an Ennead – nine deities. Memphis had a special theology we'll examine later.

Over time, Thebes became the center of religion with temples at Karnak and Luxor. The Theban trinity consisted of:
- Amun, the creative hidden one;
- Mut, the maternal force; and
- Khonsu, representative of the sun and time.

At Innu (which was Heliopolis to the Greeks and On to biblical writers), the regional god was "Harakhte," or Horus in the East. During Egypt's second dynasty, Harakhte became associated with Re, who was also associated with Atum.

There was no one before Atum – the completed one. With no one to see, name, measure or limit him, he is invisible, nameless, unmeasurable and limitless. Atum created himself and sought a place on which to stand, so he caused the appearance of a hill or the primeval mound. His appearance on the hill, since he was associated with the sun god, represented the coming of light to Earth. (This is a similar motif of the ancient Irish tradition of the Divine coming to earth on the Hill of Uisneach on May 1 – the origin of our modern May Day.) The coming of light was also represented in Egypt by a Bennu bird on an obelisk, since the dawn's light would first reach the highest obelisk. This shows the meaningful use of animals' behavior to represent specific attributes of the deity, as well as integrating the reappearance of order after the flooding of the Nile.

Atum begot Shu and Tefnut. Shu was sunlight, space, and air, while Tefnut was procreating moisture. Shu was also the life principle and Tefnut was the world order.

Shu and Tefnut then had two children named Geb (earth) and Nut (heavens). Although Geb and Nut were initially together, they became separated by Shu – or space, thus establishing the space between earth and heaven wherein life could exist, as was also believed by the Sumerians.

Geb, the male Earth god, and Nut, the female sky goddess, gave birth to Osiris, Isis, Seth, and Nephthys. Osiris was benevolent and supported humankind by agriculture. Isis represented tradition and kingship. Seth personified negative forces, while the function of Nephthys is not always clear. Even with the existence of Seth, evil was not a power in itself but was a break in the cosmic order.

The Egyptian meaning behind this multiplicity was that there was one source of power in the universe, expressing itself in many forces. Unlike modern religious movements, an overriding tendency toward syncretism and synthesis in Egypt overcame Divine competition that we see arise among other religious traditions – especially monotheists. Differing depictions of the deity were not anathematized but were integrated to form compound deities with joined names like Re-Horachte, Re-Atum, or Amon-Ra.

Perhaps that's what happened with the various Hebrew Els as those people evolved toward their monotheism.

Chapter 8

Egyptian Mythology, Metaphysics, and Magic

Faces and Facets of the Divine

The syncretic Egyptian mind created an inclusive and multi-layered religion. Its apparent polytheism provided an infinite number of ways to approach an infinite deity. For some reason, when the worship of local cities spread out to meet that of their neighbors, it did not necessarily lead to friction. Instead, encounters with other forms of the Divine showed them the greatness of their gods and goddesses.

We must consider the possibility, of course, that not all Egyptians viewed their gods this way. Just like the neo-Pagan world today, some may have viewed the multitude of god-images as discrete stand-alone entities, while others viewed gods and goddesses as *expressions* of one or more larger Divinities. If there were two "competing" gods, it did not mean that there were two gods or that one was good and the other evil. Rather, it indicated different aspects of a Being that was beyond local conceptions. We are used to a god that has enemies and who can be contained in someone's dogma, but their god was always expanding. For the Egyptians, Atum was the ultimate He-She deity but remained hidden. Khoprer, the beetle, was not another god but the *visible* form of Atum.[101] Thus, they gave credit to the Deity for its complexity, not its simplicity.

Animal images abound in Egyptian art and iconography because people lived close to nature. To them, the cycles of seasons, sun, moon, and flood reflected changeless cosmic rhythms. These rhythms were set into motion at the beginning of time. Thus, animals held a special place in the worldview of the Egyptians. Their changelessness suggested that they were much closer to the Divine than humankind, and that they shared in the "fundamental nature of creation." They were not seen as incarnations but as divine servants.[102]

The sun was portrayed as traveling on a boat that sailed through the sky during the day and through the underworld at night. The daily rising of the sun indicated a constant victory over darkness and death.[103]

Life and architecture were symbolic, including temple halls which, for example, might include papyrus-shaped columns to simulate the Delta swamps where the god's boat floated.[104] Let's return now to Egyptian myth.

Egyptian Myth

The emergence of land and order from the waters of the Nile represented the coming of light, life, land, and consciousness. Thus, through creation came 1) the light that separated earth and sky, 2) spontaneous movement upward which reflects life, 3) the establishment of order as seen in the primeval mound and, 4) the coming of consciousness with "the Word".[105] Each dawn, every new moon and each flooding of the Nile became a celebration of the renewal of creation.

Alongside the High God and the emergence of the mound from the Primeval Waters was also a tradition of the Mother Goddess, whose influence declined although she still had her representatives at Dendera. Dendera was the center for devotion to Hathor. For these worshippers, Hathor gave birth to the new sun each day.[106]

As various local deities coalesced over time, each became an aspect of one grander deity. Ra, for example, tells Isis, "I am Khepri in the morning, Re at noon, and Atum who is in the evening".[107] A text dated about 1300 BCE showed the combination "Amon-Re-Atum-Har-akhti." Amon-Re-Atum-Har-akhti brought into existence people, gods, and animals through his speech.[108]

Amun, who was an invisible dynamic force associated with air, easily incorporated all the other creator gods.[109] By the 18th dynasty, he was *universal spirit*. A still later god-name combination was Ammon-Ra. Ammon, "the hidden one," was the invisible source of Ra who was the visible power of the sun. Ammon-Ra was portrayed on the walls of the temple of Luxor as the father of the pharaoh[110] who was thus the incarnation and living son of the god, presaging Christian ideology.

Maat and The Word

There was one principle that transcended the vagaries of changing rulerships and Divine combinations: the goddess Mayet, Ma'at or Maat. She symbolized *order itself* and was therefore beyond all change and was the very fabric of life. This divine order – established at the time of creation – was manifest in the orderliness of nature, as justice in society, and as truth in the lives of individuals. She – Maat – is the essence of all existence.[111] The word *Maat* meant something like "righteousness," "justice," and "truth".[112] She was the connection between the immanent and the transcendent; and the gods themselves were ruled by her as were the pharaohs.[113]

Thus, the Egyptians were immensely aware of a sense of order and pattern in the universe as well as invisible sources of existence and life that stood behind the visible form – the way ideas stand behind speech. Furthermore, the way in which words reflected ideas was evidence that mind had dominion over matter. Thus, the words of the gods, as expressed through ideas, governed the world.[114]

Their language used puns to show connections between concepts. Since words were an invisible substance, similar words indicated a similar substance. Take, for example, the words for column, eye, and cobra. The Djed column represented the risen, life-filled Osiris, and the word "Djed" means stable and durable, which is also the quality of righteousness. Thus, that which is righteous is also durable and stable. (Similarly, our modern word "upright" means not only a vertical orientation but also righteous.) As another example, the word for eye was "Iret" and the word for cobra was "Iaret" which means the *rearing* or *upright one*.[115] Thus, that which becomes upright, like the cobra, also becomes conscious (the eye).

With their highly developed abstract thought, all serpents related to one *identity* in its differing *aspects*. Similarly, all gods – *neters* or powers – must also be one. Thus, it was not necessary to reject previously held concepts[116] or gods. They were simply integrated into what evolved.

Evil

To the Egyptians, evil was not a part of the created world, nor does it come from the deity. Evil is the result of human hearts turning away from upright order toward chaos created by inaction and ignorance.[117] Pride, for example, rather than a "sin" or offense against the gods, was a loss of one's sense of proportion about one's place in the world. Misdeeds brought unhappiness not because of punishment by an angry god but because the individual had disturbed his or her harmonious integration into the world. Thus, "sinners" were not rejected by their god, but were ignorant and in need of correction[118] - that is, recovering a proper perspective of their place in the order of things.

Osiris, Isis, and Horus – A Holy Trinity

Although the worship of solar deities remained the official state religion, the family of Osiris, Isis and Horus became the most popular mythology among the people.[119] The suffering and resurrected Osiris was more immanent than distant solar deities, and he captured the hearts of the people through his struggles to bring civilization to Egypt, by his murder at the hands of his brother Set (or Seth), and his resurrection and promise of an afterlife. Isis was his devoted wife who mourned, searched for pieces of his body, and brought him back to life. Horus was their child, conceived magically by Isis after Osiris' death. Horus battled with Set for rulership of the world and, through his victory, redeemed his father and, in an act of filial devotion, brought Osiris his eye that had been lost while he battled with Set. This meant that the eye of the god exists in both the otherworld and on the earth.

Osiris was both transcendent and immanent as the source and substance of vegetation. Isis, as the sister and wife of Osiris, exhibited great powers and knowledge, and governed Egypt in her brother-husband's absence. Horus was the archetype of the pharaoh. His suffering and his recovery were to redeem the world from the darkness and misery that would have reigned had Seth been successful.[120]

Inscriptions by Amenhotep III in the temple at Luxor show the birth of the savior Horus with a process of annunciation, virginal conception, birth, and adoration by kings and people – 2,000 years before his Christian counterpart.[121] The popular rise of the Osirian religion against the old solar faiths also paralleled the later competition of the risen Jesus in the Roman Empire that worshipped Caesar as "the invincible Sun." Egyptians, however, *integrated* the two mythologies, for Osiris became the god of the dead while Ra, the sun, was king of the living.[122]

Judgment in the Afterlife

Egyptians believed that judgment after death would determine the nature of life in the hereafter. Judgment was a formal affair, attended by various deities. Papyrus paintings show the judgment being decided by a large balance scale with a small vase on one plate and a feather on the other. Osiris or Anubis presided over the judgment as the heart of the deceased was weighed against a feather. Wrong deeds would have given the deceased a heavy heart, while deeds in Ma'at (i.e., truth and order) created a light heart. "Negative confessions" were prepared to help the recently dead get through the judgment. Foreshadowing of the words of a later prophet was this "Repudiation of Sins" written for the time of judgment. . .

> I have given bread to the hungry and drink to him that was athirst, and have clothed the naked with garments. I have not blasphemed. I have not stolen. I have not made false accusation. I have not slain any man treacherously.[123]

Obvious social values are indicated by these negative confessions. One text included 36 assertions of guiltlessness – about having not committed evil against others, mistreated cattle, committed sin in the place of truth, blasphemed a god, done violence to a poor man, etc. The text then goes on naming various gods with further protestations, given here without the gods' names.

> I have not committed evil
> I have not stolen
> I have not been covetous
> I have not robbed
> I have not killed men

> I have not damaged the grain-measure
> I have not caused crookedness
> I have not told lies
> My mouth has not gone on unchecked
> I have not been abusive
> I have not blasphemed against my local god
> I have not committed adultery

There were 42 such assertions[124] and, if we arrange a few of them differently, they come out like this:

> I have not blasphemed against my local god
> I have not killed men
> I have not committed adultery
> I have not robbed
> I have not told lies
> I have not been covetous

These are remarkably like the commandments given in Exodus 20:7-17. This is not surprising, however, since these were common values in the Mediterranean at that time.

Theology of Memphis: The Word

In the eighth century BCE, an Ethiopian pharaoh named Shabaka copied an already ancient manuscript, apparently from papyrus, onto stone. It contained language that placed it around 3500 BCE[125] and became known as the "Memphite theology." Unfortunately, the stone onto which Shabaka carved the manuscript was later used as a grinding stone. Consequently, the inscription on the middle third of the stone was lost.

What was clear, however, was that *mind* was the source of everything. Mind, by fiat, created the world. As the ancient writer put it, everything "came into being through that which the heart (mind) thought and the tongue (speech) commanded".[126] Indeed, the primary god of the ancient city of Memphis was Ptah who was known as the architect god and, therefore, was called "the heart and the tongue of the gods." This was one of the earliest expressions of the idea that the *divine word* created the world according to thoughts in the mind of the deity – or as was said thousands of years later "in the beginning was the word." Clear also was the concept that the intelligence of the god pervades all of creation, giving rise to the Egyptian idea 2,000 years later – and the Christian one 3,500 years later – of the "god that is in thee".[127]

Egyptian Magic and Science

The power of Egyptian magic was believed to be nearly boundless. Words or names of power, if properly pronounced and intoned, could heal the sick, cast out evil spirits, restore the dead to life and make the body incorruptible – thus providing eternal life. Egyptian magicians are said to have destroyed their enemies by magic.[128] According to legend, the dead were sometimes raised to life to provide legal testimony.

Baiuf-Ra told a story to the Pharaoh Khufu. This story was set down about 1550 BCE about the power of a priest named Tchatcha-em-ankh. The priest was called in to cheer up King Seneferu. The priest proposed that they sail on a lake near the palace whose beauty would lighten Pharaoh's heart. To further help boost the king's mood, the priest enlisted 20 young women –attractively arrayed – who were to sing to the king, as well as to do the rowing. The king agreed to the priest's proposal and, once on the lake, his heart began to lighten until the women unexpectedly stopped rowing. A turquoise ornament belonging to one of the women had fallen into the water and seemed lost.

Pharaoh wished for the return of the ornament whereupon Tchatcha-em-ankh spoke his words of power (hekau), which caused one section of the water to pile up upon the other, doubling its depth to 24 cubits. The waters thus parted, the priest found the ornament lying upon a potshard and returned it to the maiden. Tchatcha-em-ankh again uttered words of power, and the water of the lake returned as it had been. This story of Egyptian magic is from about 3800 BCE,[129] thus predating Moses' parting of the water by over 2,000 years. Historical texts indicate that Jews around Babylon had great interest in Egyptian magic.[130] I suspect a lot of people did.

The light of Egyptian religion, magic and science had its shadows. High-minded symbolism and elaborate ceremonies may have been beyond many of the less fortunate of their society, who were preyed upon by the unscrupulous who would sell power for money, or deal in sorcery and talismans[131] – much like medieval times and today. Nevertheless, we see intelligent and creative minds ever enlarging their vision of the Divine, and a belief in a cosmic and social order that transcended personal advantage.

As I mentioned already, one of the oldest names of Egypt is Keme, Kamt or Qemt which means "black" or "dusky," referring to the mud overflowing onto the land on either side of the Nile. In addition, from the famed Egyptian skill in metalworking came a process that produced a black powder that was given mystical properties and was identified with the body of Osiris. Thus, the "preparation of the black ore" as a chemical process was described by the name "Khemeia" to which the Arabs added the article "al," thus creating the word "alchemy." We see, therefore, that early references to the "black art" referred not to some evil activity but to the powers of alloys and metals.[132]

In summary, we find in the theology and mythology of Egypt unique contributions to chemistry, metalworking, ideas of holy trinities, virgin birth, parting of the waters, resurrection, after-life judgment, creation by the word, magical spells and animal veneration – mythologies and beliefs later used by Jews and Christians while they reviled their origins.

Chapter 9

People of the Pharaoh

Maat Binds and Gives Order to All

Pharaoh enjoyed a special place in the order of things. Egyptian society was directed toward one point, the king, who was the connection between earth and heaven. Although there were a few female pharaohs, I will use the male gender for simplicity and to reflect the norm for the times. He was not an ordinary mortal. Called "Neter Nefer, the Perfect God,"[133] he was divinely conceived and divinely appointed to rule. After the 5th dynasty, the pharaoh's status changed from god himself to the son of a god. Either way, he retained authority as the living representative of the Divine.[134]

This God-King was conceived when the queen was impregnated by Amun-Ra, after which the god revealed to her the name of the new Divine Majesty[135] who would reign as the son of god on earth. Even with predominantly male pharaohs, royal lineage came through the females, and the great mother, Mayat (Maat), stood behind everything as the order of the universe.

Despite popular images, Pharaoh did not generally rule an unwilling people by tyranny but, rather, with their support as God-in-their-midst. The royal blood of the Pharaoh, having been descended from the God, was necessary for rulership – a principle found later in the biblical lineage that attempted to prove that Jesus came from the House of David.

Thus, Pharaoh was God-on-Earth, having earthly power over the lives of his subjects, and spiritual power over the forces of nature. Through Pharaoh came divine benefits to his people.[136] Through Pharaoh, the Nile rose and fell, the people were protected, and from him they drew their lives.[137]

He was not totally separated from his people. Although he, as the god, owned the people and the land, he was also a part of the order or Maat which applied to them all. The foundation stone of the Pharaonic/Egyptian system was this concept of Maat with its combination of both social and religious meanings,[138] as noted earlier.

Thus, there was a bond between Pharaoh, his people, and the land, for all were part of one cosmic order. In their view, rulership came from the beginning of time when the creator assumed *his* kingly office.[139] Priests in the temples were representatives of the pharaoh.[140] Since all beneficial power flowed into the world through him, he was the only true priest and all ceremonies were conducted in his name.[141]

Pharaohs hoped to celebrate the Sed Festival or the "Thirty Year Feast" as it was described on the Rosetta stone. This was a renewal festival for Pharaoh and may have been celebrated as an update of prehistoric rites when the failing divine king would have been slain. In this way, the ritual death of the divine king was replaced by a magical ceremony that was essentially a reenactment of his coronation ritual.[142]

An annual festival for the falcon-headed god of death and resurrection known as Sokar took place a few days before New Year, at the beginning of Winter. Thus, at the winter solstice – around the time of Christmas – the king as Sokar dies, is resurrected as Osiris, and lives on as the rejuvenated Horus.[143]

When death did overtake Pharaoh, elaborate funerary preparations for the god-king allowed the humblest servant to be a participant in "the sacrament of pharaonic immortality".[144] Over time, such sacraments were extended to common people as well. Identified with his father the sun god, Pharaoh rode with him in the solar barque after his own death.

Clearly, the theme of resurrection and eternal life pervaded much of Egyptian mythology.

The Life of the People

Massive stone structures standing heavily on the desert belie a lighthearted and luxurious life. Sanitary facilities were found in the humblest of homes[145] and recent excavations indicate that workers on the enormous stone monuments shared affectionately in the work. This is a far cry from the images of slave labor and drudgery we often see in Bible-based movies.

Egyptian women enjoyed freedom and control of their own lives and had influence in the affairs of their husbands as well.[146] Even the proper position for sexual intercourse was for the woman to be on top.[147] In the earliest times, women had religious power that allowed them to serve as priestesses and to perform the same functions as their male counterparts on occasion.[148] Hathor, for example, was served by 61 priestesses and 18 priests, while Neith was attended solely by priestesses. Yet, for unclear reasons, by the 18th Dynasty women were no longer part of the clergy, serving only as temple musicians.[149] Nevertheless, there were at least five female pharaohs, including Cleopatra and Hatshepsut, although some were temporary. At a time when

Greek women were largely confined to their homes, Egyptian women had been involved in trade for 2,000 years – and were paid equally for their work.[150]

In Egypt, as in many early societies, those who could read and write became a special class. Scribes were charged with daily administrative duties and were thus educated about the land, agriculture, architecture, arts, crafts, and foreign affairs.[151] In general, talented workers could rise to royal administrative positions[152] as the biblical Joseph was said to have done.

This historical picture differs significantly from Bible stories, especially regarding the life of the workers, the status of the Pharaoh, and their relationship. The biblical account also downplays why they left Egypt. We'll look later at their dishonorable departure. One might also wonder if, perhaps, the status of women in Egypt wasn't a threat to their patriarchal attitudes.

Chapter 10

Egypt's Political History

Perhaps Egypt's political history will be more understandable considering its mythology and world view. It is impossible to do justice to the full history in such a short space, but I have attempted to focus on Egypt in the time of Abram, Joseph, and Moses.

Two millennia before Abram, the city of On (Heliopolis) attempted to unite Egypt. For the first time known, a national organization attempted to organize a population of several million people. This union deteriorated but left On in a position of prestige, along with the sovereignty of the Sun God above all others.[153]

The pyramids were built around 2600 BCE along with numerous storehouses where grain was kept for the lean years. The people enjoyed a diet of onions, vegetables, grapes, wine, bread, barley, and beer.[154]

One of the great wonders of both the ancient and modern world, the Great Pyramid at Giza, covers an area of 13 acres with its 2,300,000 blocks which, on average, weigh two and a half tons each. The variation on a level plane is little more than half an inch. Its orientation to the cardinal points with a maximum error of 1/12th of a degree, other measurements, and lack of funerary implements or ornamentation have led to speculation that it was built for purposes other than a tomb.[155]

During the pyramid age, the sun god ruled Egypt, stood guard at her boundaries, and absorbed most of the other deities. This was about to change, however. Thutmose III expanded Egypt beyond its old borders and so the king that ruled over Egypt now ruled over other parts of the world. Certainly, their deity could have been no less. In fact, it was said of the deity that "He seeth the whole earth hourly." In this way, a form of monotheism grew along with imperialism.[156]

The 18th Dynasty and Akhenaton

The New Kingdom began with the 18th dynasty when the Pharaoh Amosis reunited the land after the Hyksos pharaohs.[157] About 1400 BCE, a sun-hymn was composed under Amenhotep III that increased the sweep of the sun god to include all people of all lands in all seasons. This movement reached its climax in a brief hour of glory under Amenhotep IV who came to power about 1375 BCE.[158]

Amenhotep IV resurrected an old name for the Solar Deity – Aton – that had originally referred to the physical disk. The traditional depiction of the Aton had been a Hawk-headed human with the sun disk on its head.[159] Amenhotep IV, however, represented his deity as a four-part abstract symbol: the sun disk, encircled by a serpent called a *uraeus*, an ankh which hung from the neck of the uraeus, and rays coming out from the sun that end in hands.[160]

Since Amon was already being worshiped at Thebes, Amenhotep IV built his new city 300 miles to the north at Tel el Amarna and called it Akhetaton, meaning "the Horizon of Aton".[161] All of the other gods had a central place for their worship and the new city and pharoanic residence at Amarna provided the Aton with a seat of its own. Amenhotep IV changed his name to Akhenaton and, in his monotheistic zeal, erased all references to Amon on monuments, along with words referring to "gods" as plural[162] [163] – as later Jewish writers would do for their gods-become-God.

By or for him were composed hymns referring to this sole deity as the source of the beauty of the land and the light of the sun, noting the way all nature turns toward it for life and light, as the creator and sustainer of humankind and of animals, and nourisher of the gardens.

> How manifold are thy works! They are hidden from the sight of men, O Sole God, like unto whom there is no other! Thou didst fashion the earth according to thy desire when thou wast alone – all men, all cattle great and small, all that are upon the earth that run upon their feet or rise up on high flying with their wings....[164]

How similar are these words of the Pharaoh in praise of his beloved Aton to those of the biblical Psalmist in Psalm 104:24.

> Countless are the things thou hast made, O Lord.
> Thou hast made all by thy wisdom;
> and the earth is full of thy creatures,
> beasts great and small. . .

Akhenaton's emphasis on truth also affected the arts. All that was natural to him was true; therefore, family life was depicted openly and naturally. Consequently, he was portrayed not as the stereotypical monarch, but in natural family life, and showing affection to his wife and children. His wife was the famous Queen Nefertiti whose bust is represented on almost anything Egyptian.

Under the Living Light of the Aton, the Osirian religious faction was suppressed. As the fervency of Akhenaton's universal monotheism soared, both internal and external enemies closed in on his empire. Calls for help from the provinces went unheeded. The "marauding Hapiru" threatened various areas but were at that time not coordinated and could easily be contained by police action.[165]

The end of Akhenaton is lost in obscurity. A spirit of compromise may have risen within the Aton religion when Akhenaton, seeking reconciliation, sent his son and daughter to the stronghold of Amon.[166] Some have also suspected a break between Nefertiti and her husband.

A conflict between Pharaoh and the established priests is unlikely on several grounds, one of them being the fact that Pharaoh *is* the god incarnate on earth and all priests were servants of Pharaoh. Thus, no such opposition would be dared as it would violate Maat, the order of things. It is only after the end of the pharaoh's reign that he might be deified or excoriated as having been of error. References to Akhenaten as the "Heretic" were only made by later pharaohs to prove the legitimacy of their own position.[167]

Akhenaton died under mysterious circumstances in his 17th year of rule. His daughter and son disappeared, and Tutankhaton became king at 9 years of age. After 3 years, Tutankhaton moved the court back to Thebes, changed his name to Tutankhamon, and began refurbishing the temples effaced by his predecessor.[168] The 18th dynasty, the line of Amosis, ended with the death of Tutankhamun.[169] He died violently at the age of 18. Unlike most Egyptian tombs which were looted over time, his remained relatively undisturbed until found in 1922 when he was dubbed "King Tut" and his artifacts were displayed to the world.

The "revolutionary" nature of Akhenaton's reign rests primarily on his insistence upon the worship of Aton only[170] whose only son, the pharaoh, was the ruler and savior on earth.[171]

Egyptians and Jews

It was common for desert dwellers to be attracted to Egypt's rich river lands and to come offering to serve the pharaoh as Abram had sought Egypt's largesse when he faced famine in his Promised Land.

Egyptian texts dated at about 2000 BCE and again in the 13th century report that Asiatic herdsmen and their cattle were permitted to enter Egypt "as a favor" to keep them alive.[172] Nomads were called "sand ramblers" and the Hebrews were likely a smaller group amongst the larger general "Habiru".[173] Hapiru (or Habiru) was a name applied to foreign unskilled laborers, displaced persons and war captives. They lived by rapine and mercenary service. These people were occasionally hired by Egyptian commanders. As mentioned earlier, whether they were the ancestors of the Israelites is still debated.[174]

The name habiru (or hapiru) in the Amarna tablets seems to be a "generic term for 'outcasts' or 'bandits' belonging to no fixed ethnic groups." Both Syrians and Jews came into Egypt and the Jews formed a colony at Elephantine where they built a temple to their god Yahu.[175]

With the biblical description of events, one might expect mention of Hebrews in Egyptian records, especially since the Exodus is said to have resulted in the death of the Pharaoh and his army. Such is not the case, however, except for minor references to the Hapiru who were more of a nuisance than a threat.

In fact, 200 years later, the son of Ramses II was to boast that "Israel is wasted, his seed is not." This would have been during the time of Judges when there was no central Hebrew government.[176] In the eyes of the Egyptians, these nomads – Jews or not – were drifters to be hired on occasion.

Derided through the centuries in Jewish and Christian literature as the land of decadence and bondage, biblical accounts put an unbridgeable rift between the Egyptian and Jewish cultures and religions. However, an examination of the Egyptian culture through eyes other than its enemies, shows a remarkable society. Perhaps the excoriation of Egypt was an attempt to hide the wanderers' debt to this "Pagan" culture. Or, perhaps, as herders wandering into a culture already immeasurably old, they simply may have failed to grasp the Egyptian world. After all, the Great Pyramid was already more than a thousand years old by then.

Chapter 11

The Rise of Moses

Although the Pharaonic line of Amosis had ended with King Tut, the fire of monotheistic zeal kindled by Akhenaton did not. Out of Egypt came a leader that was to leave an Egyptian signature on a diverse group of people who were later to become known as *Jews*.

According to biblical legend, Pharaoh's daughter found the child, like Sargon before him, in a basket and adopted him. It is said that she gave him the name "Moses" because she "drew him from the water." As I noted earlier, "mose" and similar names are often found in Egyptian names, not because they were drawn from water but because the Egyptian word means "child." (After all, *all* children are drawn from the waters of the womb.) Furthermore, Pharaoh's daughter spoke Egyptian, not Hebrew.[177] The story, however, served to make Moses Hebrew.

Raised in a royal house, Moses became learned in all the wisdom of the Egyptians. The book of Acts refers[178] to Moses being mighty in words and deeds – an epithet also applied to Isis, meaning that they were able to utter words of power. Moses' magical act of turning his staff into a snake was a common feat in the East from ancient times. The possession of a rod through which wonders were worked was another long-time tradition.[179] Moses used his staff to make waters flow red, produce frogs, etc.

Moses fled Egypt because he murdered an Egyptian who was beating a Hebrew. He escaped to Midian and married Zipporah, the daughter of a priest named Jethro. From Jethro, Moses learned of the Midianite deity Yahweh.[180] It was while tending Jethro's flock that Moses encountered the burning bush that appointed him to lead his people out of Egypt. Moses asked the god's name and was told "I am that I am" whose name is "YHWH" (usually pronounced "Yahweh"), meaning "He who causes to be".[181]

This fickle Lord, after sending Moses to Egypt, met him at an encampment intending to kill him. However, Moses' wife, Zipporah, saved Moses by cutting off her son's foreskin and, touching him with it, saying, "You are my blood-bridegroom." So, the Lord let Moses alone.[182] Thus, Moses was saved by his connection with Zipporah and her blood rite. This bizarre incident is otherwise unexplained in scripture nor is the meaning given of becoming a "blood-bridegroom." This may be a reference to some early blood rite known to Jethro's people – which Yahweh honored.

In the biblical account, Moses went to Pharaoh and produced several signs to convince the God-on-Earth to let Moses' people leave. Pharaoh was little impressed until the first-born died. Only Hebrews were spared because they smeared blood around their doors so that their Lord would know who his people were. Why this lord's angel of death did not know his own people is not explained but, again, blood is part of their salvation.

Meanwhile, the Hebrews had borrowed jewelry and clothes from their neighbors – a custom of the times when people wanted to look their finest for a special event. Rather than returning them, however, the Hebrews absconded with their neighbors' goods when they left the town of Rameses. Thus, after 430 years in Egypt, the tribes were leaving with their neighbors' finery.

When the Pharaoh found out that the Israelites had "slipped away" with the booty from their neighbors he, according to the biblical account, led the attack against them with chariots, horses, cavalry and infantry. Already Moses' people wanted to return to Egypt and save their lives, but he prevailed and, so the story goes, not one Egyptian survived the waters that closed over them at the command of Moses. However, there is no mention of the loss of an army and pharaoh to the Red Sea in historical accounts.

The Israelites may have crossed not at the Red Sea but through a straight called "Pihahiroth"[183] which Moses would have known about, having been a shepherd near there for 40 years. Furthermore, the "walls" of water may have been lake Timsha and the tongue of the Red Sea that, in effect, protected the fleeing Israelites like a wall.[184] Thus, whether the legendary parting of the waters was Egyptian magic, an act of Moses' god, a mistranslation or fabrication cannot be known except through faith, doubt or reason. In any event, Moses took absolute charge of his people and told them of their Lord's promise that their obedience would save them from the kind of suffering inflicted upon them in Egypt.

Such is the Mosaic version of the Exodus. It is not, however, the only one. An Egyptian priest, Manetho, of the fourth century BCE, alleged that the Israelites suffered from "leprosy." Consequently, 80,000 "scabby" Israelites were quarantined in a separate city and then drowned or driven into the wilderness.[185] Manetho, however, is not always considered a reliable source.[186] Also, various other skin diseases were referred to as "leprosy" rather than the more narrow meaning it has today. And we still, to this very day, hear political partisans calling various ethnic groups "dirty," "diseased" or "criminal" to de-humanize them.

Moses' people, already forgetting how bad it was supposed to have been, wanted to return to the "fleshpots" of Egypt, so manna was provided to them by their

Lord. On the advice of Jethro, Moses appointed representatives over smaller units of people so he did not have to do everything himself.

Moses was then summoned by his god who was on Mount Sinai. When Moses brought his people to meet their god, there was smoke, fire and thunder on the mountain. The people were prohibited from ascending the mountain on penalty of death, but Moses went and returned to profess the religion of YHWH who had been unknown to the patriarchs (Exodus 6:3).[187]

In my reading of this story, the religion brought by Moses to his people originated in a Midianite deity, administered under the guidance of a Midianite priest – with a background of Egyptian wisdom, magic, and monotheism.

Chapter 12

Moses and the Bond of Blood

Israel is described in the Bible as "men of every race" (Psalm 87) and "gathered out of every land" (Psalm 107). Thus, Israel was a motley group of diverse races or tribes, such as Semitic desert people, Egyptians, Canaanites and others, joined together under the direction of the Levites[188] who may have been the only "natives" of Egypt as they are the ones with Egyptian names.[189] Naturally, it required powerful leadership to unite this group, along with a ritual of blood, that we'll come to shortly.

YHWH spoke to Moses on Sinai and delivered one version of the Decalogue, including the principle of punishing the children and grandchildren for sins of the father. Also given then were rules about the sacrifice of sheep and cattle, about slavery (treating males and females differently), and the death penalty for crimes such as premeditated murder, striking or reviling one's parents, "unnatural connection with a beast," and for witches. Monetary fines as restitution were imposed for loss of time, causing miscarriage (paid to the husband), treatment of injured slaves, treatment of a daughter sold into slavery by her father, and the price paid to the *father* of a seduced virgin. Thus, we see that a father's value depended on his daughter's distance from sexuality, from which he profited.

YHWH offered to gradually deliver land to them if they made no covenant with the other inhabitants but drive them out so that his people would not be tempted to worship *other gods*. Women were property to be sold and bought, and their sexuality was owned by men.

In addition, this god demanded the first of the harvest and, what's more "You shall give me your first-born sons. You shall do the same with your oxen and your sheep. They shall stay with the mother for seven days; on the eighth day you shall give them to me."[190]

Moses "built an altar at the foot of the mountain, and put up twelve sacred pillars, one for each of the twelve tribes of Israel. Bulls were sacrificed. Moses took half of the bull's blood and flung it on the altar and then read the covenant. When the people consented, Moses flung the rest of the blood on them, saying, 'This is the blood of the covenant...'."[191] This act of throwing blood on the altar and onto the people *made* them "of one blood." This was not unique to the Israelites, but it was a practice among Semitic groups to ratify contracts with blood.[192]

Twelve of the tribes were landed but the thirteenth tribe – that of the Levite priests – had no land.[193] A group of elders was selected, perhaps under the advice of Jethro, and taken onto the mountain with Moses where they saw YHWH standing on a pavement of sapphire or lapis lazuli. The people watching from below saw a "devouring fire" on the mountain. It has been suggested that Moses, from his Egyptian wisdom, had gunpowder that allowed him to produce many of these fiery demonstrations.[194]

After their first seven days on the mountain, Moses went apart from the others and stayed forty more days to receive tablets from YHWH. On the mountain, YHWH appointed Aaron and his sons to serve as priests for the people of Israel. These passages include "Wherever hurt is done, you shall give life for life, eye for eye, tooth for tooth, hand for hand, foot for foot, burn for burn, bruise for bruise, wound for wound."[195]

This was a turning point in the loose and polytheistic worship of the Jews for, when Moses returned, he came bearing the commandment from Yahweh, "You shall have no other gods before me," along with a second version of the Decalogue.

The new commandments brought by Moses were not happily welcomed. They were offensive to his people and had to be forced upon them. Yahweh, after all, was not a familiar god to them and they persisted in the worship of their other gods. Also, one of the sets of commandments (Exodus 34:17-26) could not have been the original compact with Yahweh but must have been later since it refers to an agricultural community, not a nomadic one.[196]

In these commandments are the gift of the first fruits: "whatever first opens the womb belongs to me, any first-born son may be redeemed, however, with a sheep. First fruits of the wheat harvest are included, meaning "the very first of the first-fruits of your land, you must bring to the house of the lord your god."[197]

A Temple for Nomads

Moving his nomadic people posed a problem because, if they left his sacred mountain, how would their god speak to them? The solution to this became a portable "tent of meeting" or the "Tabernacle of the Lord." The erection and control of the tabernacle fell to the tribe of Levi who were later to become the priests. In it, Moses could listen for instructions from El Shaddai-now-Yahweh. This tabernacle and the Ark of the Covenant associated with it became objects of reverence to the people, as well as central figures in their festivals.[198]

These newly united tribes-as-Hebrews used an ancient Semitic festival of spring related to the full moon and the spring equinox to commemorate their escape from Egypt and renamed it "Passover."[199]

We might understand that a motley gathering of tribes would need to establish boundaries and rules that would make them a distinct and separate people from those around them. However, the people would have had memories of their previous worship and values that were not so different from their former neighbors and conquered victims. The thing that stands out in my reading of all this is the place of women in a patriarchal culture that was surrounded by more feminine-friendly peoples. The ramifications of this suppression of women and the feminine has dogged much of the world to this day.

Chapter 13

Who Was Moses?

The customs attributed to Moses were hardly original with him, nor does he appear to be very much like the people he led. And where did his "God unknown" come from?

The Egyptian Source

If it's true that Moses learned "all the wisdom of the Egyptians",[200] he would have learned their religion, magic, social customs, hygiene, circumcision, and prohibitions against eating pork. He imposed circumcision on his people – a practice known in Egypt for at least 3,000 years.[201] Egyptian origins of the Mosaic teachings may be found, first of all, in its monotheism, a tribal copy of what Moses must have learned when in Egypt of Akhenaton's abortive attempt a century or so earlier.

Moses' name itself belies his Egyptian origin. Hebrew mythology notwithstanding, his name is an Egyptian one, and is suggestively close to the name of the founder of the Egyptian dynasty in which monotheism originated: Amosis (or Ahmose). Furthermore, in Egyptian theology, there was, indeed, an unknown or hidden deity named Amun (or Amon). And it was Moses who taught his people to pray using the word "Amen."[202] A coincidence? Maybe.

The brazen serpent that Moses created was a common Egyptian symbol that often represented the Goddess. Moses' staff was respected with incense until the time of Hezekiah in the late 8th century BCE.[203] Furthermore, in Proverbs 21:2 we read "but Yahweh weigheth the hearts." There was only one known faith where the human heart was weighed at the time of judgment, and that was Egypt's Osirian judgment.[204]

Psalmists refer four times to protection found "under (or in) the shadow of thy wings," echoing the image of the winged deity or sun disk so common in Egyptian art and architecture. There are also parallels between the writings of the Egyptian Amenemope and Jeremiah. In addition, about a chapter and a half of the book of Proverbs is drawn nearly verbatim from the "Wisdom of Amenemope."[205] These are chapters 22:17 to 23:11.

In Egypt, some animals were "unclean" for eating. This was mythologized by the time of the Middle Kingdom when the story was told that Set – in the form of a pig – injured one of the eyes of Horus. Thenceforth, the pig was considered an abomination to the gods and their followers.[206]

Sigmund Freud surmised that Moses was "slow of speech" because he spoke Egyptian rather than the language of the Hebrews, and that he was probably an Egyptian by birth who, through legend, was made to have been originally Hebrew. Freud also notes the fiercely monotheistic parallel between Aton and Yahweh worship.[207] Given what we've seen, this is not an unreasonable hypothesis.

Indeed, both Manetho and Strabo assert that Moses was an Egyptian priest.[208] Sjoo and Mor also suggested that the religion of Yahweh may have begun in a violent revolt of these newly wealthy male priesthoods against the goddess they once served.[209]

The Midian Influence

Breasted refers to YHWH as a Midianite deity, which would have come through the influence of Jethro. In addition, Breasted, like Freud, believes that the signs of Yahweh – pillars of fire and cloud, thunder and lightning – were volcanic in nature. In Exodus 19:16 and 20:18-21 and in Deuteronomy 4:11-13, visitations by Yaweh are accompanied by the sound of thunder, trumpets, smoke, and flashes of lightning.[210] This idea is supported by evidence of volcanic activity from Sinai northward.[211]

The name "Levite" itself may refer to the *lava* of volcanic eruptions. The cognate *Yahveh* in Sanskrit means "ever flowing".[212] The punning Egyptian mind would have had no difficulty seeing a connection between the terms *serpent* and *ever flowing*. Other writers specify that there were no volcanoes in the Sinai Peninsula but that the tradition was imported with the Midianites[213] and that there was volcanic activity where Moses had tended the sheep of Jethro, his father-in-law, in Midian.[214]

Mountain of the Moon and the Levite Priesthood

Hints of goddess origins of some of Jewish tradition are found in references to Moses going to Mount Sinai, which means "Mountain of the Moon." Astarte, the Semitic Moon Goddess, was worshipped there by the Canaanites. The name of the Levites may also indicate that they were priests of the great serpent – as in "Leviathan".[215]

Levites asserted their separateness from the other tribes not only as the official priesthood but also in the prohibition of marrying a woman of another Hebrew tribe. They were also the only ones allowed to enter the Tent of the Presence. They stayed a day's journey ahead of the rest of the Israelites as they migrated, were the judges of the law, and possessed the trumpets used to sound commands during battle and to summon the Israelite community.²¹⁶ Levites resembled the war-like Indo-Europeans with their warriors and priests who invaded and ruled over indigenous peoples.²¹⁷

At times there was mention of rebellion of the other tribes who complained about lack of food and the loss of comforts they had known in Egypt, even though they were supposed to have been badly used as slaves there.²¹⁸

Who, then, was this man Moses with an Egyptian name, who turned to a center of the moon god Sinn and established a warlike priesthood with commandments, some of which reflect a nomadic and some an agrarian society? Some of the confusion may be explained by the possibility that the "Moses" of the Bible was a condensation of several strong leaders.

The *religious* identity of Moses is found in the Bible. A historical version may be speculated as follows:

> Moses of the Egyptian dynasty of Amosis took a group of priests – Levites with Egyptian names – who oversaw a group of nomadic tribes — and, imposed a monotheistic religion through a ritual of blood and through coercion. As nomads, they would be expected to spend many years in the desert before moving into the agricultural realm of Canaan. When oral traditions were finally set down in writing, sets of commandments were combined and everything was attributed to their great leader. A story like that of the Samarian king Sargon was used to make it appear that Moses came from the people over which he took control. It seems, too, that he could have been an Egyptian priest who carried on the monotheism of Akhenaton after the Pharaoh's death to preserve it from further erasure by the priesthood of Amon.

Chapter 14

Invading Canaan

These Jewish nomads wandered in the wilderness "for forty years" before entering the land of Canaan under the leadership of Joshua. Canaan was not an open territory awaiting the arrival of Yahweh's chosen people. Biblical references do little justice to the culture that was destroyed by the invaders – as is the case in any invasion in which the victors write the history of their silenced enemy. Initially the Jews settled into open country since many of the major towns had walls to protect their homes and lands. Eventually, however, the tribes of Israel, under the direction of their imperialist god and militant leaders, conquered the land in bloody massacres. They faced more than military challenges, of course. The Jews' exposure to Canaanite culture was a major threat to their identity as a people and as a religion.

The identity of the Canaanites had been clearly established before the end of the 4th millennium BCE.[219] So, as Jewish tribes moved into Canaan, they struggled against attractive local deities, especially since Canaanite deities were more suited to the common people than the distant religion of the Levites.

The Land and Agriculture of Canaan

Today's Syria and Palestine are on the land of the biblical Canaan. In contrast to lowlands and river valleys, Canaan was on higher ground and its fertility depended on seasonal rain rather than irrigation. There are heavy rains in winter and heavy dew in summer. Without a need for centralized irrigation, there were no city states as in Mesopotamia.[220]

There are five months of summer drought each year. Grapes were harvested in September and other crops were brought in at that time for winter storage. This is the "Ingathering" that was the beginning of their New Year. The main festivals in Canaan were the barley harvest, the end of the wheat harvest 50 days later, and the Ingathering.[221]

Canaanite Religion

In Canaan, the chief god was *El*, which means "the strong one" or "the leader".[222] He was also known as "The Bull." Bull-El was father and creator, but he was not active in the mythology or in the daily lives of his people except as father of the king[223] – another son of a god.

El's consort was Rabbatu 'Athiratu Yammi, which means "the lady who treads on the sea." She was also called *She Who Gives Birth to the Gods*. In the Bible, she was referred to by her shortened name: "Asherah." To her followers, she was "Holiness" which, in Canaanite, would have been *Qudsu*.[224]

Ba'al was the most active Canaanite figure and was called *Son of Dagan* which means "grain," making him a god of fertility.[225] Baal-Hadad fought to maintain order in the world.[226] His role in fertility was to bring rain. And, since thunder accompanied life-giving rains, their Lord (Baal) was known by his proper name "Hadad," which means "The Thunderer".[227] Thus, he was a storm god, as well as the king of heaven and earth.[228]

Baal's main mythological conflict was with death or sterility, which was personified as his adversary *Mot*. Baal succumbs to Mot in the summer[229] when vegetative life is overcome by heat. In Canaanite mythology, Ba'al lost a struggle with death (Mot) but was freed from the underworld by Anath, his sister and consort.[230] Anath (or Anat) was a goddess of love and war.[231] In worship, the question was asked "Where is Baal?" to which his worshippers responded, "the Prince, Lord of the Earth" still exists.

The phrase "the Prince exists" in Canaanite is "'th zbl" – or "Zebul." Thus, Prince Baal was rendered as Baal Zebul,[232] which was later corrupted by Jewish writers.

Another figure in their pantheon was Astarte or 'Athtart who related to the evening star. The masculine form – 'Athtar – was the morning star, which meant that they realized them as different manifestations of the same entity.[233] Astarte is associated with fertility. The tree of life, a common motif, is often associated with the goddess Ishtar/Inanna/Ashera[234] and, at times, she herself is placed in the position of the tree.

The prominence of these goddesses was a major challenge to the patriarchal tradition of the invading Hebrews. Hebrew women found treasures in Canaan not granted to them by their own culture, such as valuing of the feminine, female deities, and models of women's religious and political strength. Contrary to the narrow biblical view, valuing the feminine was not an isolated or new development in that part of the world.

Chapter 15

The Queen of Heaven, Part II

Moses' tribes were sorely challenged by practices of the people whose lands they invaded. Canaanites revered the feminine and celebrated sexuality. These customs were the offspring of traditions going back tens of thousands of years. Before the Deity was masculinized and exiled into the distant sky as the Father in Heaven, she was a goddess who held intimate intercourse with humankind and embraced them within the abundant folds of plant, animal, and other immanent forces of life. Let's return to some of the ideas I presented earlier.

The bounty and life-giving sources of nature were offsprings of the Divine Mother. From within the womb of the earth came forth vegetation formed in secret darkness below the soil. Humans and animals also took shape within the darkness of the womb until the moment of emergence. Thus, darkness was as sacred as light for it was there that the "Hidden One" – the Unmanifest – prepared to emerge from the otherworld into consciousness and into the realm of matter.

Relationships were seen among seasonal changes and growth cycles on the earth. Celestial events connected earth to heaven, and woman's cycle of menstruation and pregnancy with the moon. Thus, She – woman – seemed the center of all that was alive. She created life. Where there had been one person and spirit, now there were two. The milk of her breasts sustained life in the child. Like the waxing and waning of the moon, various points in her monthly cycle brought swelling to the breasts, and a yearning for union. And regularly she bled and did not die.

Men had desire for her and took pleasure in her appearance and sensuality. His phallus responded to her. Pleasure, desire, intimacy, and a blood fear came from the secret place of the woman. From the same place between her legs issued life itself. Within her womb, hidden from sight, resided the mysteries of life and death. A recognition of the life-giving and life-supporting nature of both the earth and woman naturally led to her high regard in societies aware of the origins of human life.

This realization that women held a special relationship to nature and to the creation of life brought to these people interpersonal attitudes that gave her respect, acknowledgement of her intelligence and power, and participation in most phases of biological and social life. Matrifocal societies developed that reflected the life-giving properties of the Feminine. Equality between the sexes was the norm during the Neolithic period, according to Eisler. Furthermore, their religious beliefs and practices fostered bonding rather than rank.[235] In matrilineal descent and inheritance, the woman's property remained under her control and, frequently, her husband-lover came to the female's residence. Rather than principles of dominance, the matriarchies are said to have rested on the foundations of blood-kinship.[236] Even before Neolithic times, during the Paleolithic era, women were associated with the powers that govern life and death.[237]

The civilization of Crete was the last and most technologically advanced society where male dominance was not the norm. Cultural beliefs, worship of the Goddess and even their clothing fostered bonding between men and women.[238]

"Matriarchy" is often the word used to describe these civilizations, but the absence of obvious domination or loss of male privilege makes this misleading. Women were, however, central – hence the term *matrifocal*.

Before the "Beginning"

The technology of most European and Near Eastern societies was directed toward enhancing the quality of life for the 30,000 years of the Paleolithic age and the Neolithic agricultural revolution, which began over 10,000 years ago until the fall of the civilization of Crete about 3,200 years ago.[239] This contrasts with those who have equated the beginning of civilization with the development of weapons. Images once incorrectly related to hunting were of dancing; and some objects that appeared as weapons were, instead, vegetation. Finally, earlier scholars missed imagery relating to the female genitals altogether.[240] We see first what we are conditioned to see.

Many of these cultural advances were made possible largely through the agricultural revolution dated at about 9000-8000 BCE during Neolithic times. With agriculture, people had a regular supply of food. Therefore, towns could be established. Although people busied themselves tilling, working and irrigating the land, there were time and energy left for crafts such as pottery and basket making, textile weaving and leather crafting, jewelry making and wood carving, and such arts as painting, clay modeling, and stone carving. This was not confined to the Fertile Crescent but was found in Europe also.

Far from ignorant savages, Neolithic technologies included agriculture, construction, container making, and clothing technologies; the use of wood, fibers, leather, metals and manufacturing. There were also conceptual technologies such as law, government, religion, prayer, judgeship, priesthood, dance, ritual drama, oral literature, art, architecture, town planning, trade, administration, education, forecasting the future, and oracular prophecies of the deity.

The cycles of nature and cycles of the woman danced within the needs of the society to create images and traditions reflecting their place in the cosmos that was more immediate and intimate than our modern societies are accustomed to. The separation between the sacred and the secular, so important today, did not exist then.[241]

Observed connections between moon phases and the fertility of animals led to the association of fertility with the shape of their horns, such as of cows, bulls, goats, oxen, and other herd animals. As a result, such animals were venerated well into the Christian era.[242]

Art expressed the idea that the powers governing the universe existed to give to the people. In that abundance, their social value emphasized linkage or connection among the various aspects of life. People were at war with neither themselves nor nature. What *was* found were symbols of things that sustained life, including sun and water, the heads of bulls, egg-shaped stone sculptures, serpents, and butterflies and, everywhere, images of the goddess.[243]

Typical symbols associated with Neolithic religion were the horned altar, sacred pillar, cosmic snake and egg, world or cosmic tree, swastika, labrys or double axe, a Garden of Immortality, and the bee. Tree symbolism was like that of the snake: both shed their skin, are reborn in the spring and grow rhythmically with the phases of the moon.[244]

Celebrations of death and resurrection expressed the cyclical nature of life that was also seen in the disappearance and re-appearance of the moon in these cultures, and in the journey of the Egyptian sun through the underworld and re-birth at dawn. Vegetation deities were not the only ones who died each year to fertilize crops with their blood. In cultures with a Moon God, he was seen to die each month, disappear for three days, and return.[245]

The fact that the mother of a child was always more certain and immediate than the identity of the father, matrilineal lineage dominated in these cultures. In Egypt, for example, the pharaoh's power was legitimized by marriage to a female of the royal line, even if he was also of royalty.

At bottom, we must realize that, as Sjoo and Mor put it, "*God was female for at least the first 200,000 years of human life on earth*".[246] In addition, the feminine was associated with justice, wisdom, and intelligence. She was without doubt the Queen of Heaven. Thus, in the mythology of these cultures, the Goddess was central. As any mythology, their stories explained humankind's relationship with the Divine, their obligations to one another, forms of worship, and the meaning of natural events.

Hidden creative forces that give shape to life in the dark womb and soil were revered: they were the Deity at work to bring nurturance and abundance. The processes of nature were sacrosanct. They were honored because they bestowed life. The worst crimes were those against *life* and against nature. That which was most creative was most holy. In this manner, sexuality was a divine prerogative and a process of generation. Sexuality was sacred, and flesh was a manifestation of spirit. Rites included ritual abstinence and purification before a hunt, battle, mating, birth, at puberty, or after a death.[247] Life was a great cycle that arose from the earth and returned to it. Those areas of the greatest death and decay were also usually the most fertile.

The Great Goddess, whether taking local or specialized forms as warrior, lawgiver, teacher, protectress of children or rulers, carried one common characteristic: The Divine Ever-Virgin Mother. This is a paradox to our "modern" minds only because of our narrow understanding of the word *virgin*. To these people (including those of biblical times), "virginal" did not mean the absence of sexual intercourse but referred to a young woman of marriageable or reproductive age who was free of any allegiance to another person.

Thus, the virgin mother was not a revolutionary concept invented by Christians. Rather, it was the *commonly expected station of the female Deity*. The virgin was not necessarily "chaste," but was true to her own nature and instinct and, more importantly, free of control by another, i.e., a man.[248] Her specialness is not the state of her vagina, labia and its hymen but, rather, the state of her *sovereignty*.

Associated closely with the Goddess were not only the earth, but also the moon and serpent. This association of the serpent with the Goddess, dating back to 2500 to 3000 BCE,[249] defies modern Freudian explanations. The goddess-related serpent was not phallic but represented *revelation*. It was a symbol of wisdom.

The serpent's ability to leave behind the shell of its skin spoke of self-renewal, resurrection and, thereby, immortality. Another part of the wisdom of the serpent lay in its intimate connection with the earth and its ability to move across her face without need of legs. That is, its body was not separated from the Wise Mother. The translation of this inherent wisdom into prophetic counsel and a source of magical consciousness may be the result of the hallucinatory effect of its bite.[250] Naturally, the inherent risk in the serpent's venom also spoke of the dangers of disorienting an unprepared mind for divine contact. The result could be death or madness. Nevertheless, the venom of the serpent may have been one of the earliest means of ecstatic utterances which, self-induced, became central during periods of Jewish history.

The serpent's connection with healing appears in modern times in the caduceus as a symbol of medicine. The caduceus is a winged staff with a pair of serpents entwined around it. The wings are sometimes portrayed as part of a winged solar disk or globe. In Roman mythology, the caduceus was carried by Mercury – the messenger of the gods, or that which brought divine revelation. The *original* Asclepian symbol of healing, however, was a staff with a single serpent.

Fertility associations are inherent in all these concepts for they speak of the expansion of both life and consciousness. Thus, it is short-sighted to attempt to confine the importance of the serpent to narrow phallic obsessions. The serpent was easily related to the Goddess with its meanings of wisdom, prophetic counsel, healing, knowledge of the secrets of the creation of life, and resurrection. In fact, the cobra was the Egyptian hieroglyphic sign for "Goddess." Furthermore, the terms for magic in both Arabic and Hebrew come from the words meaning serpent.[251]

With such veneration of the Great Goddess as mother, pregnant virgin, and the process and substance of life, it was only natural that mythologies expressing her relationship to humankind centered around female imagery. She ruled the universe because she embodied the processes of life and creation. Male kings may often have been left in charge of earthly matters, but *she* would rule as the heavenly Mater.

Since she was the "mother of all of life" (the meaning of the name "Eve"), all people were her children. Therefore, her consort was initially considered to be her son, as any male would have been. Although the means varied from culture to culture, her male consort died, followed by a period of mourning. His death and subsequent grieving were commemorated in an annual cycle of grief.

The form of his death varied. He might be the Sacred King who was sacrificed so that his land and people might live. He might die through an accident or, in at least one case, his death might have been punishment for defiance of the Mother Goddess. This latter story may reflect the historical change in men's acceptance of the primacy of the feminine, which would have prepared the way for patriarchy.

These myths give meaning to seasonal changes. The death of the son-lover-king brought grief and the death of nature. His resurrection, however, wrought by the Mother, brought life back to the world.[252] Always present was an awareness of the connectedness of life and humankind's dependence and intimate participation in its renewal. In this way, the male came to represent the immediate, individual, and discrete processes of life, and seasonal changes. The female, however, brought life itself. In this sense, she was the Hidden One who stood behind that which was manifest.

In any case, the mythological cycle was the ever-present and immortal Life of the Mother who received her male consort; he was then lost, grieved for and, in the spring, resurrected by Life Herself. The loss of her consort made her the original Mater Dolorosa – Mother of Sorrows. She was the prototype of Mary who became the mother of the self-begotten Deity and who suffered the grief of his death and yet was among the first messengers to proclaim his resurrection.

The Goddess sought to relate man and woman to one another and to bless their sexual connection as the physical source of human life. Cooperation with others and with nature was key. Order was more important than control. Spiritual forces were to be found within the forces of life itself. Sexuality was a sacrament – an act of honoring the great forces of the deity. The power of the female deity infiltrated even the male-dominated Jewish religion as the words for spirit (*ruach*), and for God's presence (*shekinah*) are both feminine words.[253]

That which was most valued would naturally be the processes of reproduction, of fertility, and the fruits of life. Therefore, worship was by communion, by honoring the creative and reproductive powers of the earth, and giving of the first fruits of plant, animal, and woman's sexuality. She had power – she *was* power – and through her came the blessings of natural events as well as political life. In Egypt, even after the office of Pharaoh became mostly male, its underlying structure, as we have seen, always remained the Goddess Maat.

The Mother Goddess had different names in different places but has been portrayed, in modern times at least, as the same goddess. Ishtar came closest to being universally worshipped. Her consort was Tammuz, the god of the spring sun. She gave children to women and life to vegetation. In the sky, she appeared as the planet Venus and was, therefore, Queen of Heaven and Earth. Her worship spread to the west, into Palestine and to Egypt.[254]

Her pervasiveness led to a major thrust of the Judeo-Christian tradition to outlaw in various degrees the Goddess, nature veneration, and women.[255]

Cultures of Accomplishment

In contrast to the image of hedonistic and licentiously primitive living depicted by their biblical enemies, many of the earliest societies were highly developed. Copper and gold were used for ornaments and tools. Writing was used. Indeed, some of the earliest written language was from the temple of the Queen of Heaven in Sumer, dated at 3000 BCE. Military fortifications appeared only in response to the wandering tribes who invaded their lands.[256] At Nimrud, where Ishtar was worshipped, women served as judges and magistrates in the courts of law.[257]

By 7000 BCE at the site of Jericho (which is in Canaan), people lived in plastered brick houses with clay ovens and chimneys, and sockets for door posts.[258] Jericho, evidenced by its obsidian, apparently had trade with Anatolia as early as 8300 BCE. Toward the end of the 8th millennium BCE, the original city was deserted and its remains eventually taken over by other groups.[259] Thus, the Jericho that Joshua's trumpets are given credit for laying to waste had been in ruin any number of times before Joshua's arrival.

The people of Crete, where the Goddess was worshipped, enjoyed indoor baths, as well as hot and cold water through ceramic pipes. Their plumbing in 1700 BCE was superior to that of Europe well after 1700 CE. Women took positions as priestesses, judges, doctors, artisans, athletes, business entrepreneurs and cultural leaders on all levels.[260] The nourishing life stream of the Great Mother was represented by the uncovering of the breasts as a sacred gesture.[261] Cretan figures therefore show women as bare-breasted and often with serpents in hand.

Thus, we see in these early matrifocal societies not only the foundation for many of the ideas that permeate Christianity, but also legal and technical sophistication that some "modern" cultures have yet to achieve.

Chapter 16

The Sacred Life and Temple Worship

Union with the Divine

As humanity developed "civilization," it lost its primal contact with the numinous divine. So we sought new ways to feel close to that which we worshipped. Throughout history, ritual celebrations and pilgrimages have been two ways of doing this. Reverence for Scriptures as the direct word of the godhead has been another. Personages taken as an incarnation of the divine appear in Hindu and Christian thought and in the naming of "saints." Places and things have also represented Divine imminence such as holy sites in Jerusalem, the land of Israel itself, the Kaaba in the Grand Mosque, and the Ark of the Covenant. Then, of course, are religious relics revered as a direct connection to some significant event, place, or person. We want more than words, belief, and custom in our relationship with the Divine; we want intimacy and immanence.

Ministers, priests, and other religious leaders have always been perceived – formally or informally – as the face of the god they represent. Their words and actions carry more weight than those of ordinary worshippers (a factor that has made abuse by religious authorities especially heinous: abuse by those standing in for their god is little different from abuse by the god itself).

Various practices have also been used to achieve ecstatic or meditative states through entheogens, prayer, fasting, dancing, and singing that offer an experience of a Divine presence.

My point here is this: the more our experience of divinity moved away from direct interaction with the forces of nature and inner visions, and became increasingly abstracted into theologies that pushed our god(s) into the distance, the human need for closeness and direct relationship sought any means possible to recover that numinous communion. No matter how lofty or universal we would like divinity to be, we still want some aspect of it to be personal, relatable, and close by.

We have inherited a patriarchal culture with male-dominated religions that allow male power structures to dictate how our closeness with the divine can occur through the authority of apostolic tradition, written scriptures, and pronouncements of ministers, priests, and other interpreters. This has occurred, we must remember, in a historical context that reduced women to property, diversity to heresy, and sexuality to a stain on the soul of humanity.

Our immersion in Greco-Judeo-Christian cultural heritage can make it difficult for us to grasp other ways to relate to the divine – especially where sexuality is concerned. We have become accustomed to the use of sex to sell everything from cars to toothpaste. We have been programmed by male-dominated ideologies, for whom sex was a commodity to be controlled, to reject the significance of sexuality as part of the immanence of the deity. The goddess cultures' celebration of sexuality was as spiritual as our modern rituals of communion. Both are attempts to engage in a physical form of communion: not only between male and female, but between spirit and matter and, what's more, between the human and divine.

A form of direct communication with the Goddess could be found in the sacred precincts of her temples. After all, woman was the image of the Goddess and, like the priests of today who stand for their Lord in the midst of the people, the Goddess Herself lived in Her temple and gave direct experience of Her pleasure and communion through the agency of Her Holy Servants, the Consecrated Women.

Worshippers came bearing a sacrifice – gifts of money. Unlike the Hebrew worshippers, strangers who came to her temple were received as gods. Thus, the male worshipper came to the Temple to give an offering of his own money, and to receive the communal services of one of her priestesses. This was not a sterile and disembodied abstraction, but the act of love itself. Later called "sacred prostitutes" by other cultures who misunderstood her purpose, she was, in fact, known by a title of honor – the *Hierodule*, or sacred servant.

Worship with the Hierodule began with honoring the pleasure of the senses. Sound of flute, tambourine and cymbals mixed with the fragrances of herbs, flowers, and perfume. The stranger was bathed and treated with the respect due to a representative of the god. He was The One who comes from afar, from the outside, and enters her holy presence. They shared food (fruit, nuts, dates, bread, honey) and a draught of wine.[262]

Ideally, the preparation, setting, and his anticipation helped the stranger to realize the significance of this worship. He was to see before him not only a mortal woman, but the very figure of the Goddess Herself who reached out to him and offered renewal to them both. At the same time, the mortal woman is offering the first fruits of her sexuality to the representative of the God. She opens to the stranger for her own initiation into womanhood. Through these preparations, the act of love became a penetration into her physical and spiritual depths and into the heart of the Goddess.

When all was consummated, the stranger left the temple with a very real memory of a direct experience of divine love. He could make no claims on the woman but carried his experience of her love and sexual joy into the world.[263] Far from the rampant sexuality implied by other cultures, Herodotus tells us that:

> Babylonian custom...compels every woman of the land once in her life to sit in the temple of love and have intercourse with some stranger... the men pass and make their choice. It matters not what be the sum of money; the woman will never refuse, for that were a sin, the money being by this act made sacred. After their intercourse she had made herself holy in the sight of the goddess and goes away to her home; thereafter there is no bribe however great that will get her.[264]

The rights and reputation of the sacred servants were protected by law. Hammurabi's code protected her and her children from slander and allowed her to inherit property from her father and receive income from the land worked by her brothers.[265]

Indo-European intolerance and self-serving vehemence against all forms of female deity has left us, unfortunately, without the sort of philosophical and personal rationale for such forms of worship. We are fortunate to have the writings of the patriarchs to give us their side of the story about their own culture and their reaction to this one. We do not have, unfortunately, much in the way of writings from the matrifocal side. Their words have not survived.

The Living Religions

The Goddess religions were among the *living religions of ongoing revelation.* Thus, they often turned to various forms of shamanic or ecstatic revelation or oracular utterance known as *prophecy* in the Old Testament. Furthermore, both New Year celebrations and their rites within the Temple reflected a value system unfamiliar to us. In those days, life was precious and, therefore, desire and sexual response were blessings and a source of fruitfulness. Humankind's sexual nature and religion were inseparable.[266] And so they offered up their sexuality to the Divine in its abundance and fruitfulness because it was evidence of the blessing of life from Providence.

Modern narrow patriarchal values might decry these practices as degenerate. Naturally, they undermine the foundation of male dominance, as well as the efforts to distinguish the "chosen people" from those around them and their efforts at establishing a coherent origin myth. On the other hand, the intervention of the Goddess may have been the means by which our animal instincts were transformed into a broader form of love and love-making[267] – a goal that might be seen in many traditions but whose means of reaching that goal certainly differ, not to mention how far we fall short of its realization in any form.

Practices of these Temple priestesses were not established to entrap a man, to gain favor, power, wealth, security, or social status. Rather, they were to provide worship for the renewal of herself, the stranger, and the land. The woman serving in this manner remained virginal – belonging only to herself and to her goddess.

The hierodule thus navigated a narrow course that was neither sanctimonious nor promiscuous. By surrendering herself to her goddess through her surrender to the stranger, she acknowledged that the forces of sexuality existed beyond personal attachments. Being universal, they were transcendent and impersonal and, at the same time, were also very present and personal in the union of two individuals. Thus, the Sacred Servant was not restricted to only temple life but, having made her offering, was then afterword allowed to enjoy the personal devotion of one lover-husband.

Chapter 17

Catal Huyuk

Archaeology often involves piecing together physical remnants of a people lost in time and then trying to make sense of the way they might have lived, what they valued and what they believed based on scattered pieces of information and relics. When a place is found intact, however, excavations can be done *in situ* with a much better picture of the people's architecture, art, and beliefs. Extrapolations about social norms, religious beliefs and practices remain speculative, of course, but are based on more available evidence. One of the more fascinating discoveries in my explorations have been reports of an intact settlement from 10,000 years ago. The account in this chapter rests heavily on the work of Mellaart. Although not without controversy, most of his findings have stood the test of time over the decades.

Catal Huyuk is found at a double crossroads of time and place. It existed during the transitions between hunter-gatherer and food production societies, and between nonceramic to ceramic culture. It has sometimes been considered a formative influence on the later development of European agriculture. As noted before, the transition from hunter-gatherer cultures to those of food production and agriculture was significant for the development of cities, social organization and hierarchy, the development of weapons and even individual human growth. A nomadic lifestyle, where people moved to where food could be found or hunted, required efficiency of movement. On the other hand, planting crops and domesticating animals allowed for fixed settlements, a larger number of people living in one place, and the acquisition of goods for future lean times, for trade, and for personal wealth and status. Catal Huyuk has given us a 1,000-year window into some of those changes.

Time and Place

The development of Catal Huyuk in Neolithic Anatolia is given credit for the spread of agriculture into Europe, which laid the basis for European civilization. This was not a primitive town but had made the transition from nonceramic to ceramic culture between 6500 and 6000 BCE. There are remains of domesticated plants dated at 7000 BCE which indicate a history going back to 9000 BCE. By 6000 BCE at least 14 food plants were cultivated, including grains and legumes, along with sheep and goats. They hunted bison, deer, elk, boar, and birds. Also, apples, almonds, pistachios, fish, and eggs of waterfowl could be found not far away.[268]

Architecture

Mud bricks were the main material used for building at Catal Huyuk because that's what was locally available. However, earlier houses of wooden structure suggest that the people originated in a forest zone elsewhere, such as the Taurus Mountains. This gave way to more stable and convenient construction with large bricks and sounder buildings. This settlement had no roads or walls for fortification because their houses were built adjacent to one another with an entryway in the roof. Thus, entrance was through the roof and down a ladder against the south wall in which was also placed the hearth and oven. Ovens were set into the wall, which helped to retain heat.

Built-in storage bins were filled from the top and emptied from the bottom so that none of the grain became old. Although it appeared that each family baked its own bread, there were also large bread ovens, suggesting a bakery. Individual houses were inhabited for 100 to 120 years if not damaged by fire.

L-shaped platforms were arranged along the walls with mat-covered floors. There was a small square platform in the northeast corner and a much larger one with a higher bench at the south end against the east wall. Other platforms were found against the north wall or the southwest corner near the oven. Differences in the size of these platforms is one of the first signs of a subtle inequality in this culture.

This was a conservative and orderly society with standardized house plans that showed few changes over a period of 800 years. Having houses without doors and their only entry in the roof eliminated the need for a defensive outer wall since, if an enemy broke through a wall, he entered a closed room vulnerable to defenders on the roof. This must have been effective because there is no evidence of massacre during the eight-century life of the town.

Art and Tools

Walls inside their houses were plastered and painted with various patterns and decorations. Decorative paintings could be plain red, or with geometric patterns, or hands and feet. It appears that rooms were frequently re-plastered and repainted, which has given archaeologists a window into the development of their art and cultural shifts over time.

They had such luxuries as obsidian mirrors, ceremonial daggers, and trinkets of metal, metallurgy having begun in the 7th millennium BCE. Some of their techniques are still unknown such as how they could polish obsidian mirrors without scratching, and drill tiny holes in stone beads, or how they learned to smelt copper and lead in 6400

BCE. Most of their crafts were made from materials not in their immediate region, which indicated a great deal of trade. In addition, there were weavings as well as baskets and stone industries, and skillfully woven cloth that was dyed and stamped with patterns.

Residents were equipped with slingshot, bow and arrow, lance, and spear.

Society and Religion

In addition to burying their dead under the floor of their houses, there was also a building with human remains which was probably a "charnel house" where the dead were excarnated before burial, but it's uncertain whether the charnel houses were from that time or an earlier period. After excarnation, the bones were buried under the platforms in the house. There are still many questions about these burials. Not all were buried in their houses, but the remains of as many as 32 were found in one. Analysis of the burials indicates possibly two races living there. They were seldom over 40 years old, showed no sign of violent death, but an occasional broken limb or arthritis, excellent teeth, no degenerative diseases and more women and children than men.

There were numerous religious shrines, well-decorated with plaster reliefs and wall-paintings dated between 6500 and 5700 BCE. Of the 139 living rooms that have been excavated (at the publication of Mellaart's book), at least 40 seem to have served their religion. These were larger rooms, but they included the usual furniture platforms, benches, hearths, etc. There was no provision for sacrifice, but there were offerings of various kinds. There were about two houses for each shrine.

Statues of both male and female deities were found. Also, stylized bucrania appeared in both shrines and houses. These were pillars of brick with horn cores and the front of a wild bull. Rows of such bucrania were found in the shrines. Plaster shapes decorated the walls in the form of bulls' or rams' heads, and breasts. There were also twin goddess figures and face-to-face leopards. One relief was a goddess figure with arms and legs extended and her hair trailing behind her, clearly indicating motion.

Shrines were somewhat standardized. Scenes dealing with death were on the east and north walls, where the dead were also buried. Scenes of birth were on the west wall, and bulls were only found on the north wall, thus connected to the *Taurus* Mountains. Painting was frequent, including all shades of red and brown, buff and yellow, pink and orange, mauve, gray, black and blue. As in the plaster reliefs, paintings might stand a while and then were covered with a layer of white plaster and repainted. Up to a dozen paintings could be found on one wall.

A figure of the goddess in one portrayal is shown in a birth-giving position and having given birth to a bull or to a ram. Goddess figures were also frequently found with wild animals, suggesting her position as mistress of the hunt as well as the provider of game, especially since she is so often shown giving birth to the animals.

Her symbol of death was the vulture – appropriate for their practice of excarnation. The association of life and death apparently gave rise to an odd juxtaposition of skulls of vultures or other animals embedded in breast figures. A stone plaque shows a couple embracing on the left and, on the right, mother and child. Statuettes included different ages of the deities, ritual marriage, pregnancy, birth, and command over wild animals, or they may tell part of a story.

While not glaring, the sizes of buildings, equipment and burial gifts indicated some degree of social inequality. Burials in shrines included obsidian mirrors with females, and bone belt-fasteners with males. These were not found in house burials, which suggests a class of priestesses and priests.

In both social practice and religious art, differences of status between men and women are also evident. From burial customs, it appears that the smaller platform belonged to the male and the larger one to the female. Although the woman's position never changed, the man's did. In plaster reliefs, goddess images were anthropomorphic while the male is represented by bulls and rams. There was a clear hierarchy in the divine family: mother, daughter, son, father. I am left to wonder what impact it would have had on the male psyche to be primarily represented as an animal while women had human representations. Although patterned after a human family, they worshipped two figures: The Goddess and her son-paramour. The concept of the dying god was not found here. The female deity is represented much more than the male and the male is not represented at all beyond a certain time. As hunting gave way to agriculture, the power of woman increased and there was an almost total disappearance of male statues.

Over time, shrines were filled in. When that happened, the religious paintings were plastered over, plaster reliefs were desecrated, and the statues removed. Catal Huyuk was abandoned for unknown reasons and a new site was established across the river around 5600 BCE. The new site was also abandoned about 700 years later with no signs of violence or destruction.

Mellaart considered the lower status of the male in Catal Huyuk to have been inconsequential. Today, however, we are aware how the exclusion of female representation in current portrayals of the godhead is appropriately considered to be an affront to feminine identity and a lack of wholeness of the godhead. The loss, whether male or female, whether violent or peaceful, is a loss nonetheless and a disenfranchisement in the world of gods and goddesses – as well as on earth. Such disenfranchisement may have fostered men's eventual acceptance of traditions that are more affirming to the male half of the population – just the way goddess and feminist traditions are now being invoked to balance injustices of the last few thousand years against women.

Chapter 18

Winds of Change

Disruptions

A people devoted to the cycles of nature were themselves subject to cycles of ascendancy and death. A nomadic shadow grew on the edges of their world that would arrive simultaneously with volcanic eruptions. Disruptions of goddess societies began about the 5th millennium BCE in natural catastrophes and in waves of invasions from people sometimes called "Kurgans." They came in three main waves 43-4200 BCE, 34-3200 BCE, and 30-2800 BCE. Although they came from a land rooted in goddess country,[269] they were ruled by priests and warriors who had gods of war and of the mountains,[270] like the Hebrew El-Shaddai.

The land of India can serve as one example. There was an early goddess society among the Dravidians of India until they were invaded about 3000 BCE by the Aryans, or Indo-Europeans, from the North. Aryans considered themselves "people of the sky" and called the darker skinned Dravids "people of the earth and of the serpent".[271] These "Indo-Europeans" were Asiatic and North European nomads. The name Indo-European is misleading since they were not originally Indian, but conquered the indigenous Dravidians who were the original "Indians" there.[272] These Aryans established a caste system with Brahmans on top, and relegated women to a restricted status.[273] Thus, goddess worship with its mythos of relationship and linkage began to fall to the Kurgan/Aryans with their war-like supreme father god.[274]

As if that were not enough, from 1500-1100 BCE there was also a series of violent volcanic eruptions, earthquakes and tidal waves around the Mediterranean.[275] These natural events doubtless affirmed claims of the invaders that their god was with them and acting on their behalf. Furthermore, their patriarchal traditions fostered competition, domination and ownership rules among cattle breeders who believed that the life force was in semen, and that the womb served only as its "vessel".[276]

Like the Hebrews,[277] these invaders exterminated the males of the local people and kept the women for themselves. Like the Kurgans, the Semitic people now known as Hebrews were also ruled by a caste of warrior-priests that worshipped a fierce god of war and mountains.[278]

Differences in burial practices could be seen with clear priority given to male rulers and the inclusion of weapons with the body instead of implements of birth and religious importance. Potency shifted from the power to support and nurture life to the power to destroy and dominate.[279] Metals like copper and gold that had been used by Neolithic peoples for religious purposes, for ornamentation and for tools of farming, woodworking, fishing and sewing were diverted to weapons.[280]

Direct connections between Indo-Europeans and Hebrews may be speculative but what is more significant is the similarity of their social and religious ideologies of male dominance and violence, an authoritarian social structure, and the acquisition of wealth by developing more effective technologies of destruction than of production.[281]

Internal Threats to the Goddess

The reality of warring patriarchal tribes seeking conquest and domination should not blind us to possible inherent weaknesses in the social structure of Goddess peoples.[282] Today's admirers of matrifocal societies often place their peaceful innocence against the violent male forces of the Indo-Europeans/Kurgans/Aryans who came later. The differences between these cultures were real and dramatic, to be sure, but matrifocal societies had their own inequalities as well.

It has been suggested that, once men realized their part in procreation, they no longer accepted the primacy of the woman. However, the demise of the Goddess coincided with Aryan invasions, not man's role in "opening the womb".[283] Besides, the male role had been acknowledged and honored in the presence of the son/lover of the Goddess. However, as cultural ideas have come down to us today, males, while not oppressed, still lacked the status accorded to women. The woman seems to have held the scepter of power in all areas of life, leaving little to the men but seafaring, travel, and the hunt. This is not to suggest that men were necessarily forced out of domestic roles: men may be constitutionally inclined toward seafaring, travel and hunting by virtue of the influence of testosterone.

In matrifocal societies, womankind held a monopoly on the natural and spiritual gifts of humankind, including the province of the family. Naturally, such inequities might escape the notice of writers identified with those in power at the time, the way male scholars "overlook" their own biases as they misinterpret ancient paintings and fail to realize the extent of the damaging inequality, not only in old cultures, but in our own today as well.

Furthermore, matriarchal power has not been exclusively oriented toward nurturing. The cow, for example, was revered for her milk, but the bull was sacrificed. In addition, the mythology of the Goddess placed the male as her consort whose destiny is his sacrifice for her continued life – the way that women's social and economic status have been, in our culture, sacrificed for the aggressive hording of power and wealth that many men have taken. Finally, if acts of measurement came from the woman, she might also be the beginning of comparisons and boundaries that made her superior. She could then hoard for herself the benefits of the spiritual realities in which she partakes.

It would not be difficult to imagine that, if there were a loss of gender balance, males might come to resent the small part that they played in the processes of reproduction, worship, and survival. In fact, such a situation may have sparked one of the myths. Whereas the annual grieving for the loss of the male consort was usually occasioned by his accidental or sacrificial death, we've already seen at least one myth that attributes his death to a punishment – for rebellion against the authority of the Goddess. It's not difficult to imagine that men's dissatisfaction helped weaken the matrifocal society from within and prepared the field for the male's embrace of the invading patriarchal ideologies.

Although the city at Catal Huyuk enjoyed commerce, wealth, a priestly class, and harmonious relationships, the first signs of oppression appeared at the time when farming overtook the hunt in importance. Women controlled the economy. Male figures were excluded from the shrines. A shrine to the hunt was painted over and then destroyed. In its place was put a shrine dedicated to weaving and agriculture.[284] From this time on, as noted, statues of males almost totally disappeared.

Thus, when indigenous males faced the choice between cultural values of the matriarchy and those of the invading deities, they had already been conditioned to hierarchical thinking. When the choice came, many would naturally choose the side that gave them value and status – as women are doing today. But it took a long time for goddess reverence to fall. Although invasions by Indo-Europeans began about 2400 BCE, the last goddess temples were not closed in Rome until about CE 500.[285] She persisted – and still does. Her value has not diminished despite her loss of status.

The Sacrificial King

The life-supporting traditions of Neolithic times no doubt had their dark moments for it was during these periods that ritual sacrifice was first known.[286] The mythology of the annual death of the son-lover of the Goddess appears to be a direct outgrowth of the early matrifocal religions. With this comes the idea that the Goddess' priestesses may have had annual or periodic lovers who were then deposed or sacrificed. Her consort became king through a "sacred marriage" or *hieros gamos*.[287] The sacrifice is expressed in mythologies that speak of the descent of the king into the underworld to mark the seasonal infertility of the land. Designation of grain and its deity as male is the earliest justification of the sacrifice of the male so that the culture may live.

Viewing the universe as feminine, man could never escape the womb with which woman was always identified. The man's task in maintaining masculine identity both within the womb and within the world would be to separate himself to have identity. This alienation from nature may be the single most formative and devastating condition in the psychology of men. (This is further explored in the appendices.)

I would feel remiss here if I did not once more mention the work of Eric Neumann, referred to in Chapter 2. Grossly summarized, his thesis was that the development of patriarchy out of the all-embracing matriarchy was a necessary step in developing an individualized consciousness. However, he also judged that humanity became unfortunately stuck at the patriarchal stage – much to its detriment. Thus, we find three forces bringing an end to goddess cultures as known at the time: volcanic eruptions, male-dominated invaders, and a growing awareness of social and spiritual inequality that may also have been a part of general human evolution.

Now, having looked at the historical context in which the Hebrews developed an identity, let's return to their story.

Chapter 19

Joshua's Charge

So Joshua massacred the population of the whole region... He left no survivor, destroying everything that drew breath, as the Lord the God of Israel had commanded. Joshua carried the slaughter from Kadesh-barnea to Gaza, over the whole land of Goshen and as far as Gibeon...[288]

Despite this ritualized description in Joshua of "destroying everything that drew breath" for each of the areas he conquered, it is generally accepted that the invasion into Canaan took a couple hundred years. During that time, the Hebrews mixed – sometimes peaceably, sometimes not – with the people of Canaan whose lands they today claim as their own. First, they told their story in a way to justify their invasion and dominance as the will of their god and, second, to allow them to claim as their own whatever transpired from that time forth.

When Hebrews entered their Promised Land, they met cultural clashes on two levels. First, they had to adjust from their nomadic sheep herding way of life to farming. Their second cultural challenge was with the indigenous deities who, under the circumstances, were more attractive than Yahweh. Deities of fertility were now far more useful to agricultural survival than a god of mountains, thunder, and laws.

What's more, Exodus Hebrews were not the only people troubling the Canaanites, for there were other Semitic wanderers. These were troublesome bands who also bothered Egyptian governors in Canaan who appealed to their pharaohs about 1400-1350 BCE with frantic appeals for help against the Habiru. The Habiru did not live up to the fear of the local governors until they were bolstered by the aggressiveness of the incoming Israelites. The now-Hebrews and their neighbors were further united by a common enemy – the Philistines – who threatened them until the time of David.[289]

The biblical proscription against prostrating themselves "before other gods"[290] indicates the difficulty yet again of holding Hebrews within their own religious boundaries. Indeed, Baal-Peor and Baal-Berith were two Canaanite deities *once worshipped by the Israelites themselves.*[291]

Despite prohibitions against worshipping other gods, some of those gods' customs appear to have found their way into Hebrew tradition. It may have been the Canaanite liturgy which gave Israel the idea of the kingship of God. In addition, there is a myth involving the building of the House of Baal to be done prior to his manifestation during the winter storms[292] which may be the origin of the Hebraic "Tabernacles" festival of the same season. The annual ritualized mourning for Tammuz decried by the biblical Ezekiel[293] was most likely a summer rite when Baal would have been considered to have gone to the underworld.

Hebrew writers after the fact, like any good propagandists, began to distance themselves from their origins by re-naming some of the Canaanite figures. As noted earlier, *zebul* meant "prince" in Canaanite but was distorted by the Hebrew storytellers to *zebel,* which means "dung." In another of the distortions, *Baal Zebul*, meaning "Prince Baal," was changed by Jewish writers to *Baal Zebub*, which means "Lord of the Flies".[294] Similarly, we have a slandering of *Jeze-bul* by calling her "Jezebel." We hear similar distortions to this day between contentious factions, whether they be between individuals, religious groups, political parties, or nations. Degrading name-calling seems to be a common human trait, but hardly laudable.

Israelite writers took the symbolic tree of life and placed it in the Garden of Eden,[295] along with the serpent with its association with the tree and with woman. Even Eve's name (from Hawwah or "Mother of All Living" as in Genesis 3:20) could also be a form of a divine name of a goddess who was the wife of a Hittite storm god.[296]

What I see in all this is competition to define the narrative of struggles between peoples, justifications for invasion, murder, genocide, and domination, as well as the attempt to eliminate competing religions and their gods. This was a struggle among people who claimed an *exclusive* orientation toward religious authority, rather than the *inclusive* orientation we saw in ancient Egypt. Thus, even with Egypt's multitude of god figures, it was more monotheistic than what we see in the early Hebrew orientation to the divine. Monotheism was yet an unrealized ideal for the Hebrews. At best, they occasionally achieved monolatry – the placing of one god over all the others.

Chapter 20

From Judges to the Throne of David

Over the next 200 or so years, Jewish tribes remained little more than a loose group of peoples with no central government. In times of crisis, leaders arose and then returned to their former station when danger was past. These leaders were called "judges." Initially, the Hebrews wanted no king but their god. Eventually however, dissatisfied with Yahweh and his prophets, they sought an earthly king to rule over them as their neighbors had. Samuel led the people then as judge, prophet, and priest.

Against their better judgment, God and Samuel anointed Saul as the first king of Israel. Saul was from the small tribe of Benjamin and thus posed little threat that he might dominate the other tribes.[297] However, there was bad blood between Saul and David. While Saul was king, David often had to go into hiding from Saul and his men. David hid from him for a year and four months in the land of the Philistines. He was granted a place to live and from there he raided neighboring areas. "When David raided the country, he left no one alive, man or woman; he took flocks and herds, asses and camels, and clothes too, and then came back again to Achish."[298]

Each time, David told his host he had raided foreign lands and "Neither man nor woman did David bring back alive to Gath, for fear that they should denounce him and his men for what they had done." This was his practice as long as he remained with the Philistines. Achish trusted David, thinking that David had won such a bad name among his own people that he would remain Achish's subject all his life.[299] Thus, *truth* was David's enemy, and massacre was his means of ensuring his power.

Although "Saul had banished from the land all who trafficked with ghosts and spirits,"[300] the amassing Philistine army disturbed him such that he sought guidance from his Lord – who did not answer him.[301] He then sought out a woman with a "familiar spirit" at En-dor and went to her in disguise. She realized who Saul was and, through her, the spirit of deceased Samuel was invoked who told Saul that he and his sons would die the next day because of his (Saul's) disobedience.[302]

The prophet Ezekiel had deplored the sacrifice of the firstborn, and eventually the sacrifice of infants could be redeemed through the token of the foreskin at circumcision. The sacrifice of older first born, however, was reserved for national emergencies so Saul intended to sacrifice his own son during the Philistine war.[303] He was stopped by the army that intervened to save his son.[304]

There are two accounts of Saul's death in the Bible. In I Samuel 31:4-5, Saul is said to have died by his own hand during a battle with the Philistines when he was threatened with being overrun after his sons had already died. The Philistines found him dead the next day. However, in II Samuel 1: 9-10, Saul was dying and implored an Amelikite soldier to dispatch him. The soldier reported to David, "So I stood over him and gave him the death-blow; for I knew that, broken as he was, he could not live. . ."[305] David ordered the Amelikite soldier killed for his act of mercy.

After Saul's death, David, through a covenant with the elders of Israel,[306] was anointed Israel's second king. He ruled in Hebron – the principle city of Judah – for seven and a half years before he attacked the Jebusites (a Canaanite tribe) and took their land. "The city of peace" was a city of the Jebusites, and was called "Urusalima".[307] Since Jerusalem had not been associated with any of the Jewish tribes, no one would be offended by the establishment of a new capital there.[308] "David took up his residence in the stronghold and called it the City of David. . ."[309] Ironically, from his stronghold in the former Canaanite City of Peace, the writer of Samuel boasts of David's massacres and plundering. Then, in II Samuel 7:16, the "Davidic Covenant" is declared through the prophet Nathan that established forever the throne of David. David then strengthened Nathan's position as well. David did not build a central temple and, thus, kept a balance of power between the priests and the prophets.

Their Lord's hand was seen in David's victories, but he overstepped his bounds when he took Bethsheba, the wife of Uriah the Hittite, made her pregnant and arranged to have Uriah killed in battle. His crime did not go unnoticed, however, for "The Lord sent Nathan to David. . ." Nathan revealed his knowledge of David's latest duplicity along with the "word of the Lord the God of Israel" which, among other curses, was that "your family shall never again have rest from the sword."[310]

A Divided Kingdom

David ruled Judah, which was nearly the size of all the tribes put together, while Ishbaal ruled in the north. At Ishbaal's assassination, David assumed rulership of both halves of the Hebrews. He attempted to unite the two peoples through the appointment of two chief priests in Jerusalem – one from the north and one from the south. They also represented the families of Moses and Aaron. Furthermore, he married women from several regions and established his own standing professional army separate from those of the tribes.[311]

Two of David's sons sought his throne – Adonija and Solomon. After David's death, Solomon ordered the execution of Adonija and Adonija's general, and banished one of the temple priests who had supported him. Solomon, son of Bathsheba was favored by the prophet Nathan, as well as David's army.[312] He became third king of the Hebrews. Solomon made many foreign alliances, including marriages that were not popular with some of the prophets of his time.

In 922 BCE, Solomon completed his seven-year building of the fabled Jewish temple. He taxed the tribes for governmental functions, each owing a twelfth of the year's budget. This meant that the ten tribes of the North (Israel) were contributing substantially more than the two tribes in the south where the Temple was located. The presence of the Temple also tipped the scales of power to the side of priests over prophets and reduced the custom of worshipping on the hill shrines.

Polytheistic worship continued, however. Allegedly because of the influence of his wives, Solomon worshipped other "gods" including Ashtoreth who was, as we have seen, a goddess rather than a god. She, like Eve, was blamed for her man's behavior.

Under Solomon's administration, while he was bolstering defenses against Egypt in the south – mostly with money from the north – he neglected the defense of the north against Syria.[313] The death of Solomon brought an end to the united Hebrew nation.

Thus, after nearly 1,000 years of wandering through deserts, Egypt, and Canaan, the Hebrew people enjoyed a united nation for only a few years before falling again into distrusting factions. After the death of Solomon in 922 BCE, the kingdom broke into two parts as Israel seceded in the north with its capital at Samaria, leaving Judah in the south with its capital at Jerusalem. Israel lasted about 200 more years until the Assyrians conquered it in 722 BCE. These ten tribes of the Israelites were dispersed into the Assyrian empire.[314]

Chapter 21

The Birth of Scripture in a Divided Kingdom

Let's remember that Jerusalem in Judah – in the southern province – had come to dominate this federation of tribes. Israel in the north had been hardest hit by Solomon's administrative organization since the northern tribes provided most of the financial support but reaped none of the benefits because the Temple was in Judah. Furthermore, Israel's wealthy town dwellers revered the customs and Baals of their Canaanite neighbors, while Judah – "a poor nation of farmers and shepherds" – held to Yahweh.[315] Israel also rejected the notion of automatic succession of David's family to the throne.

In Israel, Jeroboam had established two centers for worship: Dan in the north and Beth-El in the south, not far from Jerusalem. Instead of the traditional Temple symbols of two cherubs, or sphinxes, Israel used two young bulls, mislabeled as "calves." This identified the northern Yahweh with the Canaanite deity of El and gave a conceptual advantage to Yahweh because it identified him with a Canaanite deity. In suggesting they were the same, Yahweh became a god of both agriculture as well as of the desert nomads. It also suggested that Yahweh in the north was not confined to one place like in Judah but could rule an entire geographical nation. Jeroboam's new religious organization did not include the Levites who, in addition to being landless, were now disempowered.[316]

This fusion of the gods not only disconnected the Divinity from a specific place but marked a step toward a more genuine monotheism with a more universal deity, and echoed Egypt's combined deities.

Divided Kingdom, Divided Scriptures

The scriptures telling these stories did not yet exist in those times. Bible myths arose in *different areas among various tribes* – not from a moment of revelation. Let's look at how these collected works came to be the overall Jewish narrative.

During the divided kingdom, individuals began to write down their mythology: how the world was created and by whom, where they came from, why there were different languages in the world, and why they suffered, for example. This was not originally a history of the world. Rather, Jews at the time considered this the story of the origin of *their* race alone, for we see in the earliest chapters accounts of other peoples who descended from other gods. Under the press of the mythology of Jewish monotheism, however, it became necessary to suppress the idea of other people coming from other gods. Whether from truth, myth, or propaganda, *their* Scripture was *their* view of where *they* fit into the world and tells us who they believed they were.

From Judah in the South

The earliest of these various writings are attributed to someone known only as the "J writer" who used the term "Yahweh." "J" is the designation because, in German, the Y-sound is represented by "J." J was apparently from the southern kingdom of Judah and is thought to have written about 950 BCE, near the time of Solomon and David, although other sources suggest some time between 848 and 722 BCE.[317] Their scriptures began with what is now Genesis 2:4 and gave the earliest account of creation, of the flood and other stories.

Among the scandalous assertions of J was that death was not laid upon humankind because of disobedience but, rather, that all were *created* mortal.[318] Bloom and Rosenberg suggest that the writer of J was a woman and assert that the actual Hebrew does not downgrade women. Indeed, Adam is portrayed as only imitative, while Eve is curious and interactive. J gives more space to the creation of woman than of man, and men are treated less favorably than women, except for David. In the creation story of Adam and Eve, the writer of J says Eve is created "equal to" or "alongside" him – rather than the mistranslation of being created as a "help mete" or, worse, "helpmate."

All in all, she wrote as a literary exercise. She not only honored the influence of David and Solomon – to show that they took the Hebrews from an "obscure hill clan to a high culture" – but also began the transition from a cult of Yahweh to a religion of The Book.[319] Clearly, the writer of J was different from those who came to write and edit after her. Her Yahweh was anthropomorphic,[320] all-too human and, perhaps, a satire.

When the commandments were written in Exodus 34:17, there was a prohibition against making molten gods. This was the attempt of the J writer in Judah to assail the golden calves in the north that were, indeed, molten. Their own sphinxes in the south, however, were gold-*plated* wood. J was also concerned with the ruling family, hence the inclusion of Yahweh's covenant with the patriarchs. She thereby viewed Abraham as the turning point in their history.[321]

From Israel in the North

Scriptures were also written in Israel in the north between 922 and 722[322] or, by another reckoning, 850-800 BCE.[323] The author of these northern scriptures is known only as the "E writer." His designation as "E" comes from the fact that he (or she) called the deity "Elohim" until Moses at the burning bush was given another name for the god. Although plural, Elohim has been misleadingly translated as the singular "god."

There are numerous differences between the J and E writers, which is how they can be told apart. The E writer says nothing about creation or the flood and little about the patriarchs – and makes Moses (not Abraham) the turning point in history.

The E writer, probably a priest in the city of Shiloh, spoke more sympathetically about Moses than did J. He also says nothing about Abraham's covenant and focuses on the efforts of Moses to lead his people out of bondage, while J emphasizes that it was Yahweh who brought liberation.[324]

There are other differences. Joshua, a northern hero, is heroized by the E writer. Also, in Exodus 20:23, the E writer prohibits gods of silver and gold. The ark, important to Judah where it was housed, is never mentioned by the E writer in Israel, but the meeting tent of Tabernacle is given importance.[325] E refers to the Mount of God at Horeb, while J referred to Mount Sinai. E refers to Moses' father-in-law as Jethro, while J calls him Reuel.

Two Become One

These scriptural variations stood apart as long as the Hebrew nations were separate but, at the fall of Israel, a significant number of Israelites moved south into Judah, bringing their scriptures with them. Thus, at that point, although they were of the same religion, they had two versions of their sacred history. It was by a conscious effort that someone later combined these two versions into one. To simply discard one or the other would be an affront to their general regard for the written word and would, to some degree, disenfranchise the heritage of a portion of their people. On the other hand, if they were left to stand, the authenticity of either could be challenged, thus diminishing the authority of them both.[326]

Fusing these scriptures into one narrative would establish a single origin myth that could unite the tribes of Israel and Judah into one nation – the one scripture to bind them. Anything that spoke of dual authority or dual government would be a problem. Revisions presenting the story as one nation under one god with one scripture would do what their kings could not. This revision became known to scholars as "JE." And more revisions were to come.

Chapter 22

The Prophets and Baal

While patriarchal leaders attempted to establish conformity and obedience through their promises, threats and laws, another class of religious enthusiasts arose known as *prophets*. Prophets were not satisfied with ceremonial observances and began a counter movement against a strict focus on laws.

They were the shamans and oracles of the Jews. One attribute marked the prophet: as messenger of the Deity, he or she spoke forth in ecstatic utterance. It could occur through spontaneous inspiration or be purposely provoked by singing, dancing, fasting, or prayer. In "ecstasy," prophets fell into an altered state of consciousness, underwent an inspired emotional and noetic experience, and often described having "gone" somewhere and conversed with their god or angels. At times, the Deity would appear to speak through them.[327] This ecstatic state was a mark of Divine Touch.

The first prophets were known as *nebiim* and appeared during the time of Judges (before 1000 BCE). They were ecstatics and became filled with the spirit of Yahweh through singing and dancing frenzies. I Samuel 10:5 refers to such a band traveling with lutes, drums, flutes, and lyres. Eventually, around the time of Solomon, prophets were trained in organized schools to serve with greater intelligibility. Elijah belonged to such a group.[328]

Prophets were not only seers gifted with "second sight," but also used divination to advise the Jewish kings.[329] Not all prophets were of equal status, however. Some spoke more clearly to the present condition, foretold the unfolding of events more accurately, or carried more charismatic power than others. Many prophets made social commentaries and harangued people about their behavior. Both men and women – such as Miriam and Deborah – could be prophets.

The usefulness of their utterances helped to determine their "rightness." Those who were also charismatic became leaders, especially during the time of Judges. In the days of decentralized religion before common literacy, contact with the divine could be immediate through the presence of the prophet. In the absence of priests and scriptures, prophets spoke for their god. They also helped to shape the image of Yahweh.

After the time of Judges, the sanctuaries of Bethel and Dan included bull images that were regarded as symbols of Yahweh. This was a period in which a supreme god operated *through* the Baals. However, when Baalism threatened to engulf the identity of Yahwehism, prophetic tirades were made against Baal.[330]

Another threat to Yahwehism was any concept that brought the god too close to humankind and to nature. Unlike Baal, in which the functions of nature and its fruits were divine incarnations of the god, Yahweh was made to stand separate from nature. Hebrew farmers, while holding to Yahweh as their god, also made Canaanite observances such as going to the high places, giving first fruits to Canaanite deities, and making burnt offerings. They gradually came to realize, however, that Yahweh also controlled agriculture. Many of them considered that they were worshipping Yahweh *through* the form of Baal worship.

This tendency to identify Baal as an expression of Yahweh became a threat to the tradition that had separated nature and god,[331] yet this inclusive movement was another step toward the universalization of Yahweh.

Through revelations of the prophets of the eighth through the sixth century BCE, the character of the Jewish god was changed – or perhaps the prophets revealed the changing and evolutionary nature of their god. This local, tribal, and jealous god gradually became more universal: the god of all peoples. Isaiah, for example, envisioned his god as the Lord not only of the Jews, but of all nations, which then implied that the armies of other nations were doing the Jewish god's bidding, even if they defeated the Jews. Isaiah was less interested in religious observances and any hypocritical appearance of piety than he was in advocating for kindness and social justice.[332] Micah was another prophet crying against ritualism and formalism.

A shift in focus from law to an Inner Way was most strongly advocated by Jeremiah. He argued that only a change of heart would be acceptable to his god. True piety was the individual's relationship, in a personal way, with the Divine. His vision was a new covenant written on the heart of the individual as described in Jeremiah 31:31-34.[333] Jeremiah planted the prophetic seeds that were to blossom in a later prophet and his disciples: Jesus the Nazarene.

Elijah's successor, Elisha, fomented political and religious revolution through Jehu – a king of the northern kingdom. Jehu destroyed the royal house and every vestige of the Tyrian Baal. So great was his slaughter that Hosea denounced it a century later.[334] Baal worship was not eliminated, but the efforts of these prophets established Palestine as the sole province of Yahweh.

Other peoples and their gods were not the prophets' only troubles but, as others had, Isaiah cried out against the elaborate rituals of the temple with their slaughtered animals, blood, offerings, smoke, and lunar festivals.[335]

After Micah, the prophets were silent for 70 years. They may have been suppressed.[336] With the prophets of Amos, Hosea, and Second Isaiah about 750 BCE, the emphasis in Jewish religion changed from ceremonial ritual to a way of life. Then, with the destruction of Israel in 722 BCE, Isaiah arose to proclaim Yahweh as universal, omnipotent, and omnipresent.[337]

The charismatic influence of prophets and their ability to shape the image of the Jewish god was ended when the Temple was built, which resulted in the centralization of theocratic power under the priesthood – and brought further opportunity for scriptural revision.

Chapter 23

Prophets, Priests, and the "D" Writer

These are the words that Moses spoke. . . (Deuteronomy. 1:1)

Let's return to Assyria's absorption of Israel in 722 BCE. Assyria sponsored shrines to its own gods and goddesses and these were built in the Temple in Jerusalem. Six years later, however, King Hezekiah became ruler of Judah. During his 28 years, he initiated religious and political reform, which included the elimination of religious practice outside the Temple. He initiated the destruction of idols and even destroyed places of worship of Yahweh that were outside the Jerusalem Temple. No longer could Hebrews go to high places to worship. Thus, any priests who were not connected with the Temple in Jerusalem lost their authority. There was now one altar in the nation on which sacrifices to Yahweh could be made, and the people could not eat their lamb unless they first sacrificed in the Temple. Hezekiah also destroyed the bronze snake that Moses had made 500 years earlier.[338]

Part of Hezekiah's reform included revolt against Assyria and an attempt to take back some of Israel's lands that Assyria controlled. This provoked a military response from King Sennacherib that resulted in a standoff. The Assyrians were unable to take Jerusalem, but a ransom was paid to have them withdraw.[339]

Then, during the rule of Hezekiah's son, Manasseh, pagan worship was reintroduced in Judah, which included statues in the Temple again. The high places were rebuilt, and sacrifices were once more offered outside of Jerusalem. Eventually came King Josiah who, once more, destroyed the idols and high places, "cleansed" the Temple, and centralized his religion through sacrifice at Jerusalem. Priests from high places were given second-level jobs beside the Temple priests in Jerusalem.[340]

Many of these reforms were done in his 18th year of rule after the appearance of what was said to be a scroll of the Torah. According to legend, the scroll was found by the priest Hilkiah during Temple repairs. After consulting a prophetess, Josiah held a national ceremony of renewal and destroyed the altar at Beth-El where one of the golden calves of King Jeroboam had stood. This asserted Judah's control over lands that had once been Israel's.[341]

The scroll found in the Temple became known as *Deuteronomy*, the third scriptural rendition, after J and E. This was the work of the D-for-Deuteronomy writer. In this scroll, the *first commandment was to provide sacrifice only at one place: at Jerusalem.*

Deuteronomy is presented as though it were Moses' farewell speech, although it includes an account of his death.[342] In my reading, Moses' speech seems to end at 4:40 when the third person is used. However, use of first-person resumes at 5:1 but switches back and forth until the 34th chapter describes Moses' death. It ends, "There was never yet risen in Israel a prophet like Moses. . ." (34:10).

In Jewish history, according to the newly "discovered" Deuteronomy, a covenant gave the Jewish throne to the house of David forever, regardless of the behavior of whomever sits on it. The D writer judged the kings and judges up to Josiah to all have fallen short of him. In fact, Josiah is presented as the culmination of what had begun with Moses.[343] So, this scroll, "discovered" during Josiah's reign, not only gave him standing over all that had gone before, but also centralized his authority and religious hierarchy.

Deuteronomy also called for the people to care for the Levites, gave Levites jurisdiction over legal matters, established them as *the* priestly tribe, and included laws for tithes and offerings.[344] Competition was being weeded out and policies standardized.

Deuteronomy has been called a "pious fraud" because of its divergence from prior custom (including the fact that Saul, David and Solomon sacrificed in different places) and its revolutionary concept of centralization.[345] Its purpose, however, was apparently to promote the public good and to bring about reform.[346] Solomon was presented in the worst possible light and so the writer may have been someone from Shiloh who remembers the way Solomon and Jeroboam removed them from authority.[347]

Jeremiah himself may be the author of the Deuteronomic works: he had the skills, was around at the time of both versions in 609 and 587 BCE, and there is phrasing unique to the work of Jeremiah and Deuteronomy.[348]

Regardless of its origin, this "second law" was used to spearhead religious revival and reform that sought to clear away the altars and rituals of Baal worshippers. There followed an improvement in ethics, along with a new social idealism. The Jewish books were re-written to emphasize God's hand in history. The effect of this D writer was to *centralize the power and priesthood in Jerusalem.* The Divine Presence was withdrawn from rural areas and confined to the Temple.[349] As has happened so many times over the course of human history, urban centers took preeminence over rural peoples.

Thus, the leaders of the Yahweh cult were able to consolidate their power and, in the end, once more reduce Yahweh to the status of a local god who could be worshipped in only one place: the Temple in Jerusalem. This lasted only through Josiah's rule, however, because his reforms were given up after his death, and the people once more rebuilt the high places.

And again, things changed. In the sixth century BCE, Babylonians (Chaldeans) overran the land of Judah. Judah, then on the side of Babylon, fell to Egyptian forces in 608 BCE. Three years later, however, the Egyptians were defeated by the Babylonians, and Judah was once more under Babylonian rule.[350]

Jeremiah warned the nation of troubles coming. In an ill-fated political move to use Egyptian backing for their own independence, the leaders in Jerusalem withheld their tribute to Nebuchadnezzar. Nebuchadnezzar responded in 597 BCE and took complete control of Jerusalem. He looted the temple and, as described in II Kings, the king took to Babylon "all the nobles, and all the renowned warriors, and all the craftsmen, and all the smiths," as well as "all the strong men fit for war" (from II Kings 24:14-16).[351] Nine years later, there was another rebellion by those left behind in Jerusalem that was led by Zedakiah, one of Josiah's sons.[352]

Nebuchadnezzar placed Gedaliah on the throne because he was thought to be from a pro-Babylonian family, which included Jeremiah. However, Gedaliah was then assassinated by a member of the family of David. In fear of what Nebachudnezzar would do in response to the assassination of his chosen governor, it is reported that the entire population in Judah fled once more into Egypt.[353]

In 586 BCE, the Egyptians were driven back. Babylonians, Edomites, Samaritans, Ammonites, and others moved in to loot, burn and destroy all the buildings, including the great Jewish Temple. Even the city walls were torn down. Most of the inhabitants were taken away, leaving only Jeremiah and a handful of the poorest citizens.[354]

The Ark was never heard of again.

After all this, the people who were left in Judah rejected Jeremiah because their lives had been better during sacrifices to the Queen of Heaven than under the protection of Yahweh who had brought them to their current destitution.[355]

Chapter 24

Babylonian Exile

The Jewish people were split once more. Some were left behind in Judah, while nobles, warriors, craftsmen, and smiths lived in Babylon. Nebuchadnezzar's move was not meant against the Egyptian or Jewish people but against their military and political sovereignty. As a result, the resettled people were allowed freedom to follow their old ways of life. The people in exile, however, faced the question posed in Psalm 137: "How shall we sing a song of Yahweh on foreign soil?"[356] For them, Yahweh was still a national god with a local seat. How the true god would allow Babylonians to destroy Yahweh's people had to mean that their conquest by Babylonians must be Yahweh's tool to punish them for their errors.

Having been absorbed into Babylonia, the Hebrews had no country and were without the Temple that had once been so necessary. Hebrew exiles in Babylon and Egypt could no longer go to the one place where sacrifices could be offered, so they met in homes on the Sabbath to read and study their scrolls and laws, and to hear interpretations.[357]

From 587 to 538 BCE, Jews were exposed to the Babylonian culture, which was derived to a large extent from the Sumerian – a return to their own roots in Abram's travel from Ur. This captivity prompted further development of their purity laws, which may have reduced the absorption of Babylonian elements into their traditions. Nevertheless, Jews entered civil service or the trades and enjoyed large crops from the rich Babylonian soil, which was much better than the land they left in Judah.[358]

Babylonians celebrated a spring New Year that marked the triumph of Cosmos over Chaos. Part of this celebration was a scapegoat ritual in which difficulties of the community were given to a sheep that was then beheaded and thrown into the river to be swept away.[359]

Ishtar was their primary goddess and Queen of Heaven. She was worshipped with her son Tammuz whose name meant "faithful son." This goddess, as their "mother of sorrows," had to seek her son, as the story goes, in the underworld to bring him back to life. She was also giver and destroyer of life, mother and virgin, patroness of sexual love and family life, judge, prophet, healer, and warrior.[360]

A text written toward the end of the First Dynasty of Babylon (c 1600 BCE) has the king giving thanks for blessings provided by Ishtar, calling her "the greatest of the [great gods of heaven]." She was "clothed with pleasure and love" and her word was supreme over the gods.[361] Another text, the Prayer of Lamentation to Ishtar, honors her as "queen of all peoples" and as a powerful healer because "Where thou dost look, one who is dead lives; one who is sick rises up..."[362]

From Babylonians came the seven-day week honoring the seven visible "planets," which includes the sun and moon.[363] A Babylonian tablet shows a lunar calendar that gave four weeks of seven days each to the month. The seventh day of each week was designated as a Shabbatu, or day of rest.[364] The seventh day, for Shamas the sun god, was a day when taboos were most carefully observed.[365]

A seven-tiered temple was built in the city of Borsippa in Babylonia in the 12th century BCE.[366] As already noted, the (in)famous tower of Babel was one of these common Babylonian ziggurats. "Babel" in the tongue of the Babylonians meant "gate of God" – in contrast to the later Jewish writers who claimed that Babel meant "confusion." Nebuchadnezzar called the by-then ruined ziggurat the "Stages of the Seven Spheres" as each level was consecrated to one of the planets.[367] This indicates its religious and astronomical purpose.

The pervasiveness and sacred nature of the number "7," although related to the seven visible planetary bodies, has also been attributed to the seven stars in the constellation Ursa Major. This may harken back to times when the bear was one of the oldest forms of deity. What's more, Ursa Major, known also as the *Wagon of the Heavens*, was attached to the city of Nippur, which was considered Sumer's central point and religious capital.[368]

This part of their history shows the many pressures that the Jewish culture was under. There were distractions and temptations by beautiful, exalted goddesses. The people had reasons to be disaffected by Yahweh's indifference or punishment. And traditions entered Judaism that we keep alive today that originated in these ancient times and places.

Chapter 25

Return to the Temple and Its Priests

As the power of Babylon waned, Persia was on the rise and Cyrus the Great – a Zoroastrian[369] – took Babylon in 538 BCE. He sought to win the friendship of the colony of captive Jews and use them as a buffer state by allowing them to return to Jerusalem. Not only did Cyrus permit the exiles to return and rebuild their homeland and temple, he provided them with money to do so. Everything was returned to the exiles apart from the Ark.[370] However, only about ten percent of the exiles saw fit to return from Babylon to Judah.[371] These were the tribes of Judah and Levi.[372] Most Jews remained in Babylon.

From about the 40th chapter of Isaiah, an unknown prophet speaks who is given the name of "Second Isaiah." This second Isaiah tried to get his people to return home.[373] He attempted to answer the question about the evil that had befallen the Jews. The traditional answer – that it was because of their sins – was not satisfactory since people around them, judged to be worse than the Jews, nevertheless prospered. He answered that these sufferings were part of Yahweh's plan to redeem the world.[374] Trying to entice them to return, he named them a "chosen people" to be a "light to the nations," and asserted that they had completed their suffering, that no more suffering was necessary, and that they could look forward to a restoration – in Jerusalem. His teachings were later used as reinforcement for the idea of an expected messiah, interpreted then that it was not to be the nation who would redeem the guilt of the world but an individual.[375]

Those who returned immediately resumed sacrifices in the Temple but found many disappointing conditions. The city and Temple were in ruins and those who had remained behind had made their homes on lands abandoned by the former captives. In addition, returning Jews judged that those who remained had lapsed by intermarrying. Thus, the non-exiles – those who had remained on the homeland – were treated as inferiors and consequently saw little reason to cooperate in the rebuilding of the Temple that was to serve the "better" classes.[376] They were not even allowed to help rebuild the Temple.[377] Thus, they were dispossessed by their own people.

This attempt at rebuilding the Temple lapsed for about 15 years. Then, about 522 BCE, Haggai and Zachariah inspired the completion of the new temple so that, the Lord's house being in order, prosperity could come to the people.[378] This brings to mind modern mega-churches and televangelists, many of whom solicit donations for great edifices and lavish lifestyles of their leaders – to prepare the way for salvation.

This second Temple was dedicated on Passover of 516 BCE by members of the priesthood that were of the Aaronid party. Other Levites were not recognized as legitimate. Thus, the old competition between the descendants of Moses and those of Aaron was "resolved." This may have been engineered by the Persians who perceived the Mushites – those emphasizing Moses – as being pro-Babylonian and, therefore, empowered the Aaronids.[379] Politics shaped religion once more, and a foreign country promoted the party most likely to benefit it – another tradition surviving to this day.

Despite expectations that completion of the Temple would improve the Jewish situation, a century passed without improvement until the time of Malachi who complained of a lack of sincerity and zeal in worship.[380] The return to Judah and subsequent reorganization had found favor among those who directly benefited from it, but not so much from the common people.

Through the efforts of Ezra the scribe, however, a theocratic state was instituted, with priests holding the power. Judaism moved in a legalistic direction and, with priests as the foundation, they built their establishment on the Book of the Law, with traditional principles of first-fruits, tithing, sacrifices, and fixed festivals. They emphasized matters of *ritual purity*.[381] The common people, on the other hand, had little interest in legalities but, over the course of time and with pressure from the priests, they gradually gave more allegiance to the prescribed ritual observances.

Power was further centralized by these attempts at racial purity and by the return to the one temple in Jerusalem with its supreme priest. From this centralization came castes of priests, scribes and, eventually, rabbis. Scriptures were again edited and revised, and the first chapter of Genesis was added.[382] Priestly scripture writers revised the existing JE version to reflect their own concerns and interests. This writer became known as the "P writer" for "priest." The P writer used "Elohim" as the name of the deity and showed a different focus from that of the JE writers.

The main individuals in the JE version had been the prophets, but the "P" writer asserted the importance of priests. It not only designated priestly rules, accoutrements, and clothing, but also claimed that miracles had been performed using Aaron's staff instead of Moses', and that Yahweh spoke to them both rather than just to Moses as in JE. Furthermore, the P writer established consecrated priests as the sole intermediaries between Yahweh and his people.[383]

Overall, JE had denigrated Aaron while this new revisionist priestly writer, in answer, elevated Aaron and downgraded Moses. JE had assumed that any Levite could be priest, and spoke of angels, talking animals and an anthropomorphic god. P on the other hand, claimed that only the descendants of Aaron could be priests, and depersonalized Yahweh and made him a cosmic being.[384] As a cosmic and impersonal creator of the ordered universe, the only way to reach this Yahweh was through formal and ordered structures, and not through talking snakes or asses, nor meetings with angels, or dreams of prophets. There was one way, one priesthood, and one place for proper worship.[385]

The P writer omitted the earlier story of the golden calf because it reflected badly on Aaron. Whereas JE's god was merciful, gracious, and forbearing, the god of the P writer is *just*, with a specific set of rules to earn forgiveness.[386] The priestly writer also bestows a "covenant of eternal priesthood"[387] to Phineahas and his descendants. Phineahas was the grandson of Aaron.[388]

Thus, we see how two differing images of the creator appear in our modern Bible, based on scriptures from the northern and southern kingdoms and competition between the lines of Moses and Aaron. In turn, this resulted in a shift from a once-immanent god to immanent priests speaking for a distant god no longer accessible to common folk. What's more, a specific line of priests had taken power to the exclusion of other priesthoods, lineages or prophets.

Chapter 26

Ezra's Torah of Moses

In 458 BCE, eighty years after the first exiles returned, Ezra came to Jerusalem from Babylon. He brought with him not only authority from the Persian emperor Artaxerxes that gave him authority in Judah, but he also brought the "Torah of Moses," which was likely the five books of Moses as we now know them. Ezra shared authority with a governor, Nehemiah, who had also been appointed by the emperor. They rebuilt the city walls of Jerusalem, enforced Sabbath laws, and dissolved intermarriages between Hebrews and others, choosing purity over family bonds. On their fall holiday, Ezra held a public assembly at the water gate when many people had come to Jerusalem. Here he presented the scroll of the Torah to the assembly after which they committed themselves to the covenant written in this scroll.[389]

Prior to Ezra, we had four sources of scriptures: J and E writers, the Deuteronomic "second law," and the priestly writer. The final revisions had yet to be made to make the modern Bible appear as the one text with which we are now familiar. Someone now known as the "redactor" is credited with this final version.

In this final revision, priestly stories are given preeminence, and priestly documents are used as the framework for the writing. Therefore, it is likely that this redactor was someone from the Aaronid line. He not only combined the four prior strains but added stories of his own in line with priestly traditions. Since the Tabernacle was not mentioned, the Five Books of Moses must have been written in the days of the second Temple when there was no longer a Tabernacle that had been required for sacrifices in earlier times.[390]

The redactor combined the existing scriptures in a sophisticated way, putting the cosmic versions of the stories first, followed by the more homey J version, making it look as though the story proceeded from the broad cosmic view to the specific.[391] The new synthesis also placed justice *and* mercy together.

Jeremiah, however, was hostile to this torah, calling it the "lying pen of scribes"[392] because it attacked his hero Moses and excluded him and his family from the priesthood.[393]

This process of centralization, standardization, ritual and racial purity, and "revisions" of their scriptures helped to better define and clarify the identity of these people. It also established hierarchies, acceptable authorities, and boundaries, while it created inferior underclasses that were excluded from the fruits of power and prestige. Prophets, who heretofore would have been operating in their tradition of speaking for the god, would not have been happy.

Chapter 27

Persian Apocalyptic Visions

Yet another culture was to leave its stamp on the evolving worldview of the Jewish-Christian thread. When they lived under Persian rule, Hebrews were exposed to the beliefs of Zoroastrians and their predecessors. Before Zarathustra, who was called *Zoroaster* in Greek, people worshipped "Shining Ones" or daevas who were personifications of nature powers. Mithras – referred to in a Hittite inscription of 1400-1300 BCE – came into prominence and, to the Iranians, he was God of War and God of Light.[394]

Zarathustra's birth is given by tradition at about 660 BCE but he could have lived as early as 1750 BCE.[395] At the age of 30, Zarathustra received a vision on the banks of a river near his home where he encountered an archangel called "Vohu Manah" or Good Thought.[396] He rose into the very presence of his god, Ahura Mazda, who called Zarathustra to be a prophet. But his own people, the Medes, rejected him and so he took his beliefs to the Persians.[397]

He came to be known as " shepherd of the poor"[398] and miraculous powers were attributed to him. Zarathustra objected to the burden and cost of rituals and emphasized a direct contact with the deity. Only later did the fire priests arise.[399] His original principles were shaped over time so that distinctions are made between earlier and "younger" writings. He taught a highly ethical religion that advocated holy wisdom, a just righteousness, courage, loving service to others, and self-realization.[400] Humankind was a coworker with the divine Ahura Mazda. Nature was to be revered and devotees were admonished to keep the land, waters, and air diligently clean. In addition, violence was abhorred, asceticism was unnecessary, and there was equality between males and females.[401] By 500 BCE, Zoroastrianism – properly called "Mazdeism" – became the leading faith of the Persians.

Mazdeism evolved into a cosmic dualism with opposing forces of Good and Evil. Everything and everyone are subject to the struggle between good and evil.[402] This cosmic dualism, however, began as something else – an *ethical* dualism. It was only after the Arab invasions that it became a *cosmic* dualism.[403]

The Wise Lord, Ahura Mazda, who was creator of heaven and earth, is opposed by an Evil Spirit. To Mazdaists, evil cannot come from God but from Ahriman. Ahura Mazda and Ahriman contend for the loyalty of people who must choose sides. Eventually the two great armies will come together, there will be a great test by fire, and justice will be done.[404] The concept of a central power of evil took shape in the personage of Angra Mainyu, who was not only the author of death, but also a creator of many demons which assisted him, such as Akamanah, which meant *Bad Thought*.[405] The material world, as God's handiwork, was a good thing meant to be enjoyed. The devilish Ahriman, however, as an enemy to God, would naturally try to destroy his handiwork. Those loyal to Ahura Mazda go to an immortal afterlife of holiness, while the impious fall into a hell of evil thoughts, words, deeds, and physical torment.[406] Eventually, a general resurrection will take place.[407]

Also from Mazdaism came the apocalyptic vision of a change in "the ages" from evil domination into a utopian future ruled by the power of the god. In the end days, the dead would be restored by a savior named Soshyans who will be born of the seed of Zarathustra and a virgin. A battle between good and evil will take place that Ahura Mazda will win. A final judgment will be passed on all souls, Ahriman and his followers will be consumed in flames and the devotees of Ahura Mazda will live in peace in heaven.[408]

In the land of Media, a highly respected group known as Magi arose. Their origins lie in mystery and were known as far west as Jerusalem for their magical abilities. They existed before Mazdaism came onto the scene and they initially opposed it. Eventually, however, they adopted it[409] and used the Younger Avesta to introduce the rituals used today.[410]

Not all Magi were fundamental dualists. Some proposed that Ahura Mazda and Angra Mainyu both derive from one source called "Zurvan".[411] Thus, by the 4th century CE, *Zurvane Akarne* – boundless time – was seen as the parent of both Ahura Mazda and Ahriman.[412] In Zurvanism, a god who is limited by the forces of evil cannot be an absolute, all-mighty god. Thus, Zurvan was beyond duality.[413] Once more, what initially appeared as multiple forces became aspects of one greater force. Eventually, as many religions do, the life of the religion went from moral regeneration to considerations of ceremonial purity.[414]

The dualism of opposing powers of good and evil did not exist for the Jews prior to the Exile. It was Yahweh who was responsible for everything that happened – until they absorbed Persian dualistic beliefs. Ahriman became the Jewish Satan and, from the Persians, they learned of Heaven, Hell, and a Judgment Day.[415] Although Satan was elevated in power, the Jews' strict monotheism prevented total acceptance of Persian divine duality.

We will meet the Persians again when their astrologer-priests attend the birth of the herald of the New Age.

Chapter 28

Alexander and Hellenism

Ionians, Achaeans and Dorians invaded Greece over a period from 2500 to 1000 BCE. They brought with them their male-dominated social order and Zeus, their ultimate patriarch.[416] Alexander the Great conquered most of the Near East by 327 BCE,[417] and took Palestine in 332 BCE as he moved toward Egypt. He expected that the world would be converted to the Greek view of life, built cities according to Greek designs and encouraged his people to live there.[418]

After his death in 323 BCE at the age of 33, however, his empire fell to civil wars and struggles among generals. For 100 years, Palestine was overrun by armies of the Seleucids of Syria and the Ptolemies of Egypt. By the beginning of the second century BCE, Seleucids took final possession[419] and assisted the Jews in repairing their city in Judah and its temple.[420]

Tolerant treatment opened the Jews to many Greek customs. This was especially true for the priests and better-educated Jews. As usual, the common people were slow to adopt new ways, as were the scribes and rabbis.[421] Under the pressure of Hellenization, Jewish education, sports, theatres, and libraries attained a high level of Greek culture. This went so far that, in time, many Jews no longer understood Hebrew. Consequently, a Greek translation of the Torah, known as the *Septuagint*, was written to serve these Greek-speaking Jews.[422]

Greek philosophy also left its mark on Hebrew thought – and Greek culture had its shadows. We who are used to hearing Greek culture elevated as the sublime origin of philosophy, democracy and technology may miss some of the more destructive elements of this classical culture, not only to which the Jews were exposed, but elements of which have infected our modern culture to this day. These deleterious elements appear in the relationship between women and men, between spirit and matter, and between mind and body. Plato, for example, had encouraged denial of the body in a hierarchical, spirit-oriented mentality. He relegated physical pleasure, pain, the earth, and women to an inferior sphere of existence.[423] If that weren't enough, the Greek myth of Oresteia asserted a strange distortion of reality that only fathers are related to their children. Therefore, Orestes was acquitted of the murder of his mother because she – the mother – was no parent of the child.[424]

We should remember, too, that the phallic nature of masculinity in much of the early world served a function of fertility. Athenian fear of women, however, turned the phallic nature of Greece from one of fertility to that of aggression. Women were subjected to rape and, if they went out in public, were expected to veil themselves. Her only value was to bear children, and Plato believed that a sacred love was possible only among men.[425] Women were a "male womb" wherein men could sow their seeds. In fact, the creation of woman was punishment to *man*kind for the use of fire.[426] Women were not truly human and lacked the divine spirit that is present in free-born males. Beauty was virtue – and a male attribute.[427] The Orphic idea that the body was a tomb was perpetuated by some of the Gnostics.[428] To Plato, woman was inferior to man but, to Aristotle, she was a deformity.[429] These ideas were carried into Christianity and emerged in the words of Paul and of Augustine who claimed that man alone is the image of God. Woman can be so only when she is joined with man.[430]

This dichotomy of male rationality and female chaos in a controlled society resulted in a fascination with Dionysian irrationality.[431] Celebrations of mystery religions became a joyful respite from the oppressive limitations of everyday life, and attracted those least benefiting from the privileges of social status – slaves and women.[432] Through the "mysteries," these rejected classes enjoyed significance not found in the shadows of their masters. As always, whatever elements of humanity that are repressed by social authority will find expression in those least invested in the culture and often in seemingly "irrational" ways. Every orthodoxy, through its hierarchy, exclusivity, and centrality, sows the seeds of its own heresies in its conceits of universality and delusions of final authority. Every light creates shadows, especially when enshrined in dogma that rejects any part of reality.

The desire to be accepted in Greek society even complicated Jewish requirements for circumcision. To the Greeks, exposure of the glans of the penis was considered obscene. Thus, circumcised Jews could hardly appear nude in the baths and gymnasia where important business deals were made. This Greek abhorrence to the mutilation of circumcision led to the popularity of procedures that made the penis appear uncircumcised. Epispasm and infibulation surgically pulled and fixed the remaining skin of the shaft over the glans of the penis. Also, some Jews resorted to a type of circumcision that would not leave the glans exposed, but this was rejected by their orthodox brethren.[433]

Chapter 29

Pompey of Rome Takes Over

Eventually, Antiochus Epiphanes, a king of Syria who lived about 215 to 164 BCE, tried to force Jews to worship Zeus and Dionysus. He prohibited many Jewish practices and erected an altar to Zeus in their Temple where he also sacrificed pigs. The murder of a commissioner by an old Jewish priest sparked revolt.[434] A group known as Maccabees led this revolt in 167 BCE and established a small and independent kingdom in Palestine.[435] The book of Daniel, relating events of the previous 500 years, was written about this time as a response to persecution by Antiochus.

In this revolt, Jews recaptured most of Jerusalem, and the Temple was "purged." As time went on, those who resisted Hellenization gave birth to the sect of Pharisees who believed that God *meant* to destroy the world of the Sadducees who were, to them, lost souls. Pharisees also embraced messianic concepts. Aristocratic and wealthy Sadducees had been strongly influenced by Greek culture and emphasized priestly practices of sacrifice in the Temple. Eventually, there was civil war among the various Jewish factions. This prompted the Roman general Pompey to enter Palestine from Syria and take over the country in 63 BCE.[436] There's more on these factions in Chapter 32.

By the time of their rule by Rome, Jews were thoroughly entrenched in the Torah and were led by a clear priesthood with specific beliefs and commandments. Yet the people remained divided. Pharisees had little interest in Greek culture or Roman politics. They focused their attention on oral tradition, messianic concepts, and the Law.

Under Roman rule, Herod was Judea's vassal king from 43 to 4 BCE. He was a devout but ruthless Jew. He enlarged the temple in Jerusalem and endorsed Jewish religious practices, and thus won the support of the Sadducees.[437] New Jewish parties came into being such as Zealots around 6 CE, who considered submission to Rome as forsaking the God who was their only true Lord. There were also Essenes (who would be destroyed in 68 CE), and the Christian movement which, we must remember, was initially a sect of Judaism.

In CE 66, rebellion against the emperor Nero resulted in slaughter of the Jews, the destruction of Jerusalem and the burning of the Temple.[438]

Before moving on, let's take a summary look at Hebrew mythology, the Evolution of Yahweh, revisions in the "Word of God," the arrival of Satan, gender and political politics, and messianic hopes that place the Jews into their context in the Roman world.

Chapter 30

The Myth of One God, One People, One Scripture

Mythology.

Mythology has always been used to legitimize rulers' claims to their privileged place in the world. Such mythologies trace their lineage back to the Origin of Time, to creation, to a special relationship with Divinity, or simply assert that "it was this way from the beginning."

Jewish mythology tells us that, from creation, they and their god lived around the Tigris and Euphrates rivers. From that beginning, they enjoyed a special relationship with their Deity who began as a local tribal god and was eventually transformed into a universal god.

These stories were not written down until after the time of Solomon and, if they are to be taken seriously, place the origin of the world at about 4000 BCE. Although other peoples are mentioned, the biblical story fails to account for the origin of these other cultures.

Nevertheless, elements from previous times, although rewritten, still show themselves as reminders that the writers' origin story and place in history was a purposeful narrative constructed by their own beliefs and needs for unity and self-justification. Yet even the story of their origin in Adam and Eve tells of better times before humankind had to struggle to survive, a time when men and women lived in a garden of delight, when women conversed with Wise Serpents, when a knowledge of right and wrong was unimportant, and when men and women were not ashamed of their bodies. It was a time before men blamed women for the ills of the world, a time before Yahweh was afraid of what he had created, and a time of many gods, the Elohim.

It is significant that the stories were not written until after the times of Moses – after exposures to Goddess worship and to the Egyptians. Some of the stories already existed in other cultures and were appropriated by Jewish writers and, if their content was not changed, were given explanations in line with their new beliefs. Some of those distortions may seem strange to us today but, to them, it was for their efforts at conquest and religious survival.

The Evolution of Yahweh

Scriptures evolved, as did their understanding and depiction of the deity. We see, etched in stark lines, the face of the god that they worshipped with his ethos of domination, conquest, and sexual antagonism; and how these mores came not from the people themselves but from a small caste of a determined priestly aristocracy invested in boundaries, purity, and control.

In that evolution, the words "God" and "Lord" were used in place of a variety of older words. This linguistic reduction to these two words gives the appearance that these people believed in One God. This idea serves the image of Mosaic monotheism, but it neglects to tell us that they had other names for other gods. It was not until late in their history that their One God Yahweh was given the status of an Ultimate God.

This is not simply deception but an attempt to reflect their changing consciousness about the nature of their Deity. It appears to be deceptive only when we apply standards of historical accuracy to mythology. A mythological truth should not be confused with historical truth. In addition, the name of their god was too holy to be spoken and was represented by initials (YHWH) or "the Lord." Thus, if we look beneath the veneer, we find a variety of deities with different names and different natures. Only through later revisions were they made into *aspects* of one supreme god as had already happened in Egypt. In their own time, however, they were "the gods" or Elohim.

We are first introduced to the Hebrew god Yahweh as he creates in the beginning. "Yahweh" is regarded as an abbreviation of *Yahweh asher yihweh*, or "he causes to be what is."[439] He seems at times very human as, for example, when he walks in his garden, looking for Adam who has hid. At other times, he is remote. This is because of the various scriptural writers already described. In fact, the earliest god of Genesis is still but a tribal "godling." [440]

Their god was not at first known as Yahweh, but as El or its plural form "Elohim." El could be related to root words meaning "high" or above the lower kinds of gods, images and idols.[441] This is found in Genesis 46:3: "I am El, the god of your father." El had his variations, too. The Bull El was an emblem of God in I Kings 12: 28, 29 and I Kings 22:11.[442] In Exodus 6:3, the god speaks, saying that he had appeared to Jacob by the name of "God Almighty; but by my name Yahweh was I not known to them." This "God Almighty" was *El Shaddai*, or all powerful[443] (El Shaddai probably referring to *God of the Mountains* as we saw earlier). In other words, this Deity appears under different names. The myth of one people under one god had to be bolstered by the Exodus claim that Yahweh of Moses was also the god of Abraham.

English translations hide the fact that Yahweh was one of several gods. The gods speak among themselves to say they cannot allow Adam and Eve to remain in the garden for fear that they will become like the gods. Furthermore, human daughters mated with the sons of the other gods. The Song of Moses[444] refers to Yahweh's *portion* as his people of Jacob, referring to the fact that Yahweh was one of several deities.[445]

At that time, only the Hebrews were subjects of Yahweh, while other gods spawned other peoples. In the first chapter of Genesis, god's name in Hebrew is "Elohim" and in Aramaic, "Alaha." During the conquest of Palestine, Jews believed in other gods, but promoted Yahweh as the god of gods as in Joshua 22:22.[446]

As they struggled for their identity, the Jews suffered a god who became increasingly distant from their concerns – especially as the priesthood became stronger. In their attempts at combating competition with Goddess-centered and nature-based religions, and setting the boundaries that established their own identity, they pushed their god far away from them and placed in that chasm their scriptures, interpretations, and rituals. And these could only be done in one place. This led to the later necessity to rewrite the scriptures to claim their god's hand in history – to show that Yahweh was directly involved with his people.

Their concept of god, although almighty, was narrow. Yahweh was confined to the temple, his revelation had ended, he was not found in nature nor did he speak through nature. Except for mystics, the *experience of* a god was replaced with *arguments about* him, and with laws and rituals. Truth would be found in the law and its interpretation.

The Word of God

Our misperception that there was one Judaism is as erroneous as the concept of there having been one "Bible." Originally, the word of God was revealed through "oracular divination." Nevertheless, the seeds of the original meaning of Torah – "casting lots"[447] or "pointing the way" through oracular divination[448] was to flower in the emergence of the prophets.

In the beginning, various Jewish communities did not hold the same books in common. It is no wonder we find apparent discrepancies. Inconsistencies of the writers, different orders of creation, the number of animals taken onto the Ark, the length of the flood,[449] styles of writing, and differing emphases become understandable when we realize their diverse origins.

Let's look once more at four "writers" of the Torah. In JE, the god is merciful, gracious, and forbearing. Overall, JE denigrated Aaron, while P, in answer, elevated Aaron and downgraded Moses. JE elevated Moses, assumed that any Levite could be priest, and spoke of angels, talking animals and an anthropomorphic god. P on the other hand, downgraded Moses and elevated Aaron, claimed that only the descendants of Aaron could be priests, and depersonalized Yahweh, making him a cosmic being.[450]

The thrice-appearing story of the lending of the wife-as-sister to the local ruler is less perplexing when we realize that the passages in Genesis 12:10-20 and in Genesis 26:1-11 are both by the J writer, while the middle story, in Genesis 20:1-18, is by the E writer. Thus, this does not represent three different events, but one of the events is told twice.

Even after their revisions, these writings became *canon* only in response to the scriptures of a new sect. Jewish authorities had to protect their scriptures from dilution by Christians and so made a final determination about what would be official and what would be excluded from their Testament. Meanwhile, Christians, who had already included some of the excluded books, responded by setting them aside and calling them "Apocrypha." The word "apocrypha" is a Greek adjective which means "hidden." These were books of an esoteric nature which were kept from the public. After the first century CE, however, apocrypha came to represent heresy.[451]

During these revisions, anachronistic elements of contemporary concerns were written back into existing writings. On the one hand, these revisions were attempts to falsely claim preexisting divine authority for new desires of the rulers. On the other hand, they were simply the continuation of ongoing efforts to answer basic questions of life through the perspective of whomever was in power at the time.

Cain and Able show us two kinds of people: one a tiller and the other a herder. One is accepted and the other rejected and then criticized for being disappointed at being rejected. This Deity exiled the cultivator and showed favor for the sacrifice of the first-born. This story served to justify the expulsion of indigenous peoples from their homes as the nomadic Jews coveted their lands and moved in.

Thus, these scriptures did not spring into being as one revelatory whole cloth. They began as oral myths, many from other religions, that were revised and combined with new prophetic utterances. The stories were written down in pieces and then loosely combined into a narrative *as though* they were the history of the Jewish people. Moses was given authorship of the first five books, or Pentateuch.

Of Sin and Satan

Since revelation had ended, there would be no more prophets, and religiosity was found in the law. To obey the Torah meant following 248 positive and 365 negative commandments.[452] Sin to the Jews was not the result of a "fallen nature" of humankind (as later Christians believed). Rather, people have an inclination toward both good and evil as is inherent in all of God's creation.[453] Thus, the story of Adam and Eve was originally not about a mistake whose stain taints us all but, rather, of the fact that human beings enjoy freedom of choice to either obey or rebel against God's will. Adam's sin did not reflect on those of us that came after but we share, instead, his *ability to choose* between sin or righteousness. To the ancient Jews, sin violated a taboo, and reconciliation of this offense against God required an offering in the form of an animal sacrifice. This sacrificial restitution was not to redeem some inherent evil in humankind, but to rectify a bad choice – a restitution of divine order.

For Persians, the conflict between good and evil might manifest on either plane. References to Satan by the early Jews were more of a figure of speech than a powerful evil entity.[454] To conceive of a powerful satanic being would have violated the principle of monotheism. If there was another force, God would no longer be all-mighty. Indeed, beyond the assertion "Oh hear, oh Israel, the Lord your God is One God." Isaiah makes it perfectly clear in saying:

> I am the Lord and there is none other.
> I form light and create darkness,
> I make peace and create evil,
> I the Lord do all these things.[455]

Only after the Jews' sojourn under the Persians did Satan begin to take on a power of his own as in Chronicles and Daniel.

Adam's Rib and Eve's Apple

In I Samuel 21:4 it is said that men are holy who stay away from women. Women were officially treated as property.[456] Deuteronomy 22:13 asserts the value of virginity and, if a woman's virginity were damaged, she became economically worthless.[457] A woman who lost her virginity before marriage was to be stoned or burned to death. If raped, a single woman had to marry her rapist. If already betrothed or married she would be executed by stoning for having been raped, declares Deuteronomy 22:24, 28, 29.[458] These crimes were not concerned with what a man did to a woman but what his actions with a woman did to another man. Women were not yet persons.

According to Moses, it was the command of his Lord[459] to kill every male and all non-virgins and to keep the virgins for themselves. In Judges 19, we recall, a father offered his daughters to a drunken mob and in Genesis 19:8, Lot offered his daughters to a mob.[460]

The hallowed process of birth was made into a sin for the woman. Thus, she had to make a sin offering to the priests so that they can make atonement for her and she can be clean once more as declared in Leviticus 12:6-7.[461]

Although the story of the Garden of Eden was originally one of freedom of choice (and its consequences), it had to also account for the fact that there were other civilizations before them, and matriarchal civilizations at that. To counter the influence of other cultures, the relationship between man and woman was depicted as antagonistic and adversarial. They attempted to destroy the wisdom of the woman as symbolized by the serpent. Thus, her intelligence was made the source of the evils of *man*kind.

Jewish social customs suppressed women while they lived among cultures in which women were representatives of the Divine. Foreign women were free, independent, and held public office. Such customs threatened the rigid Jewish social structures of male domination and the culture they had struggled so hard to preserve.

Returning to creation, two accounts say that the gods made humankind male and female and one of those stories tells of having made Adam first and then forming Eve out of his rib. The story of Adam's rib was later used by Saul/Paul to show that woman comes from man. Its Jewish writer, however, seems to be saying to men that women are flesh of his flesh and bone of his bone; that even in these dominator times, when women were seen as property and as the source of evil, they were still of the same flesh as the man. This passage that originally asserted the unity of man and woman was re-interpreted to keep them separate.

We may today look at the Garden of Eden story as a charming explanation of a people's account of their origin but, at the time, it was an attempt to break the spirit of the power of the feminine and to "put enmity" between women and woman-centered religious beliefs. As is so often the case, the deity of the defeated culture was made into the Satan of the prevailing one.

This denigration of womankind was a devastating thrust into the heart of the Pagan cultures' principles of relationship and kinship. It created a wound that has bled for thousands of years. Even menstruation – once a sign of woman's participation in the holy processes of life and creation – was judged "unclean." The taboo of the sacred was changed into the taboo of the unclean.

In Jewish tradition, Eve was not Adam's first wife. Lilith was the first woman formed for Adam, but they fell into disaffection. Lilith, considering herself Adam's equal, took offense at his demand for her to lie beneath him. When Adam tried to force her to obey, an enraged Lilith "uttered the magic name of God, rose into the air and left him." Lilith then became the source of unspeakable demons. Her story is thought to be a reaction against the worship and privileges of Canaanite women.[462] In fact, Israelite women had once followed Canaanite practices until their custom of dedicating to God the fees they earned were expressly forbidden in Deuteronomy 23:18.[463]

Theologians of that time called woman defective because she so often did not follow prescribed religious and social demands. But what allegiance would a woman feel toward a system that made her in practice and principle little more than the receptive agent of her husband's fertility – and disposable if she did not produce? Of course, there were exceptions, as some women became prophetesses, but these are the exception as Jewish history focuses on the "patriarchs" and the way in which the race felt it had to put a misogynist boundary around itself with male priests' domination.

In addition, many of the "Jewish" wives were virgin daughters of foreign families that had been slaughtered in conquest of the Promised Land. Why would a woman stay within a system that killed her family and in which she became little more than property whose primary purpose is to produce offspring for her husband? Why would she *not* depart from such indignities and turn toward a religion that would, at least in principle, offer her self-respect; and where her female qualities were not an object of ownership but deified as holy?

It was not a fault in her character that led Woman to stray from the established order but the strength of her character, a need to correct errors of the culture in which she lived, and to claim her share of the kingdom. The male system had found a way to validate males, but much of that value was bought at the expense of womankind. With such a foundation, it is easy to see why males were threatened by feminine independence, let alone by Goddess religions. Male status did not rest on man's own value but was dependent on the devaluation of the feminine. This suggests to the psychologist in me that the male identity was frail and dependent. In many parts of the world, not much has changed in this regard.

Given their circumstances, it is only natural that it would be the women who would be the first to "backslide" away from the Jewish cult of their oppressors into the older religions that affirmed them as persons and valued the natural cycles by which they lived and from which many had come.

Messianic Hopes

The lot of the Jews seems never to have been an easy one, surrounded by competing gods and goddesses. Even under the influence of Moses, they fell back easily into their old ways. They were subjected to many hardships and ruling empires. They suffered much, worked hard, and looked forward to deliverance. They anticipated a messiah who would, as they had been led out of the bondage of Egypt, lead them out of the oppression of Rome.

Jewish kings were designated by anointing. King David had already held the title of messiah, meaning "the anointed one," which was "Christ" in Greek. This messianic hope was not symbolic or spiritual but referred to deliverance from oppression and the establishment of the Kingdom of God on the earth. This messiah was to be a mortal who would secure God's blessings for his people; provide law and justice, righteousness and peace.[464] He would defeat all enemies, and rule over the world forever.[465] [466] Messianic Jews were looking for the messiah who would not come from Yahweh but be appointed *by* Yahweh from the House of David.

Under occupation by Rome, messianic hopes burned strongly for a leader who would lead the Hebrews in military conquest against their imperial oppressors, and who could unite the Jewish people. They were, by this time, divided among the traditionalists, Hellenists, Pharisees, Sadducees, Essenes, and Gnostics.

Chapter 31

The Roman World

This takes us to a crucial place in history. After all their struggles and evolution, and after claiming their land by divine right, Judaism was split under the influence of Hellenization, and fell under Roman rule. Although their god had become one, their people had not. There were several factions, each with its own customs and belief about what was necessary for redemption. Since Rome was a "world" empire, under its province were many nationalities, beliefs, and traditions. Naturally, when we think of Rome, visions of the Roman gods come to mind: Jupiter, Venus, Apollo, Mercury, etc.

Roman Religion

Roman religion gave attention to supernatural forces called "numina." Gods possessed numen as the power that allowed them to be more than mere mortals. Numen was also found in boundary stones, groves of trees, running water, and springs. Individuals, families, and groups might also possess it. Numen, or numinous energy, was a force that could be transferred from god to human, or from a person to his possessions. The chief of these forces was Jupiter or "Father Jove."[467] He was the derivative of the Indo-European Dyaus Pitar or Zeus Pater.

The Mysteries

Rome had its share of mystery cults. "The Mysteries" were not religious institutions in themselves but were voluntary and personal initiation rites that sought a "change of mind through experience of the sacred".[468] There were many mystery cults active in those days.

The mystery cult of Bacchus was suppressed in 186 BCE by the Roman Senate. It later had a revival that was more controlled than its previous alleged orgies.[469] Other imports included Isis and Osiris of Egypt, and the Persian deity Mithras.[470] Between December 25th and the spring equinox came the mystical forty days' search for Osiris.[471] Isis was even given a state temple in CE 38.[472]

One of the more significant mystery cults was that of the "Magna Mater" or Cybele that appeared around 1000 BCE with her consort Attis. In 204 BCE, Cybele was brought to Rome from Asia Minor,[473] and she was celebrated in Rome until CE 268. Cybele's son Attis – or his effigy – was tied to a tree and then buried for three days. When a light appeared in the burial tomb, Attis rose from the dead to bring salvation.[474] Part of the ritual of Cybele involved the slaughter of a ram in whose blood the devotee was washed (i.e., washed in the blood of the lamb).[475] In another account, devotees were initiated through the taurobulium – being bathed in bull's blood.[476]

Originally, male priests of Cybele castrated themselves in a public rite and flung their genitals on the altar[477] but this practice eventually lost favor.[478] (No surprise there.) Because of the fanaticism of her devotees, a law was passed that forbad Roman citizens to enter her priesthood, although people could attend her temple and import priests from Asia Minor.[479]

Cybele was identified with Rhea, the mother of Zeus and, in pre-Christian Rome, may have been known as "Ma Rhea" – the mother of the dying god.[480] Women were naturally attracted to the cult of Cybele, as well as an exclusively female one of Bona Dea.[481]

The Mithraic Mysteries came into prominence as an exclusively male society. About 100 BCE,[482] Mithraicism came through Iran, entered Rome in 16 BCE[483] and flourished throughout the second and third centuries.[484] It was carried through the empire by soldiers.[485] For Jews, the Mithraic sacramental ritual was often preferred over temple sacrifice.[486] Mithraicism was rooted in Persian Mazdaism. We'll examine Mithraic mythology and practices in more detail later.

Because of formalism and decay, Augustus Caesar attempted to put new life into the old Roman religion. He encouraged the rebuilding of temples and strengthening the priesthoods, seeking some power or worship that might bind it together[487] – just as Jewish leaders had had to do. He erected a temple for Julius Caesar, who had already been declared a god. He also built shrines in which his own genius-spirit was worshipped.

As the empire grew, emperor worship helped bring a unifying force into popular religion. But so did the worship of the sun as Sol Invictus – the unconquerable sun. By 274 CE, Aurelian declared Sol Invictus to be the supreme god of the Roman Empire.[488] This supreme god of the sun would later help shape Christianity through the machinations of Constantine.

Chapter 32

Jewish Pluralism

To their contemporaries, Jews were oddities because of their exclusivity. Religion for most people was a personal path chosen among a variety of deities. To adopt a deity to the *exclusion* of all others was an atheistic curiosity at best or a pernicious superstition at worst. Even though the Jews had their one god, at the time of Jesus, there were four main Jewish traditions: Sadducees, Zealots, Essenes, and Pharisees. There was also a Gnostic movement that came into greater prominence as a rival of Romanized Christianity.

Sadducees cooperated with the Romans.[489] Aristocratic and wealthy, this priestly caste had been influenced by Greek culture and emphasized priestly practices of sacrifice in the Temple. For Sadducees, the kingdom of God would come through sacrifices.

Pharisees, on the other hand, had little interest in Greek culture or Roman politics and wanted nothing to do with Rome. They were scrupulous in their observance of Jewish law,[490] oral tradition, and messianic expectations. Obedience to the Torah meant following its many commandments.[491]

Zealots looked for a military leader to bring about a military victory over the Romans. To them, the messiah meant what it had always meant: an anointed leader to vanquish Judaism's foes.

Essenes separated themselves from the world so they could follow their own version of The Law. Writings within the Dead Sea Scrolls have suggested that the community at Qumran was moving toward the idea that Yahweh would beget his messiah. They celebrated a messianic banquet that prefigured the Last Supper. There are many similarities between Qumran and what Christianity became.[492]

For the Essenes, everything was determined by fate, and they expected two messiahs, one priestly and one secular.[493] In this community, males were taught to separate themselves from natural functioning by imposing severe penalties for indecent exposure, "foolish laughter," or "unnecessary self exposure." This was to reduce the danger of men falling prey to the seductive wiles of women. Harlots were women looking for opportunities to seduce the righteous man or make the perfect man stumble or to lead the upright man astray.[494]

No doubt the desert had its influence on the Essene view of the world. In the starkness of the desert, their god was envisioned as a male spirit set against flesh, the world, and the Devil.[495] Consequently, earth, body, and women posed grave threats to things "spiritual." Essenes promulgated dualistic ideas such as there being two spirits within a human, one of light and one of darkness. They followed a solar year and prayed toward the east instead of toward Jerusalem.[496] There were some Free Essenes who recognized the dangers of total celibacy and allowed marriages for the strict purpose of procreation without sensual pleasure.[497] Josephus spoke highly of the Essenes, saying they exceed all other men in virtue, minister to each other, hold all things in common, do not allow slavery because it tempts people to be unjust, and do not marry so as to avoid domestic quarrels.[498] There is much current esoteric interest in Essenes but that is not our focus here.

These Jewish factions reflected their time of occupation, ferment, and anticipation. Some people wanted a leader to free them. Others believed the end of the world was near and awaited the coming of the messiah to pronounce the judgment of their god. They argued about the resurrection of the dead, and Pharisees believed that the dead would be raised on the Day of Judgment.[499]

Jews were not the only people with expectations. For some, there was a larger drama at play – cosmic in scope. An astronomical phenomenon called the precession of the equinoxes is caused by a slow wobbling of the Earth's axis every 26,000 years or so. This was first noted by the Greeks in the second century BCE. This wobble causes the appearance of a slow backward movement through the zodiac behind the rising sun at the spring equinox. This, in turn, results in periods of about 2160 years for each of the 12 signs of the zodiac – sometimes referred to as a Platonic month. The 12 Platonic months make up the Great Year of 26,000 earthly years.

Astrologers of that time would have expected a special birth to herald the beginning of the new Platonic month – an Avatar of the Age. The Arian age was passing, and the Piscean age was upon them. We are now, in the 21st century, at the cusp of the beginning of the Aquarian Age – celebrated in song and on stage. Many have noted the "coincidence" of the symbol of Christianity being the Piscean fish, as well as the significance of the lamb for the Jews during the age of Aries. Prior to these would have been the age of Taurus, marked by the prominence of bull symbols as we saw in Catal Huyuk.

Fear, hope, factions, and anticipation of a new age tilled the soil for new seed.

Chapter 33

Ano Domini

Around 6 BCE a man was born whose life would leave in its wake renewal, death, hope, genocide, and immense controversy. Popular European images and common usage have him born of a virgin under the "Star of Bethlehem" and attended by wise men (Magi) who brought precious gifts for the child. The timing of his birth as the year "0" or "anno domini," was unsuccessfully attempted many years after his birth. The "Herod" who played a part in this man's life is known to have died in 4 BCE because of an astronomical event.

Scholars have sought to identify what might have spawned biblical references to the "Star of Bethlehem." In 1606, Johannes Kepler noted a conjunction of Jupiter and Saturn in Pisces of 7 BCE.[500] Jupiter would have appeared first in the dawn of March 16, 7 BCE, with conjunctions occurring May 19, October 3, and December 5.[501] Later scientists also suggested the possibility of an exploding supernova recorded in Chinese records of 5 CE.[502] Planetary conjunctions are periodic, however, and most occur relatively frequently – every twelve or twenty years, for example. These are hardly the harbinger of a New Age. The "star" remains a mystery.

We have come to know this man by the Greek version of his name, which is "Jesus".[503] His given name was more likely Yeshu or Yeshua, which was a shortened form of Yehoshua.[504] In his own Aramaic language, he would have been "Eshoa".[505] We shall mostly call him Yeshua but, in recognition of the reality of linguistic revisions, I may use any of them.

References to Yeshua as the "son of Mary" as in Mark 6:3 marked him as illegitimate for, at that time, if he had been "legitimate," he would have been properly called the son of his father.[506] Legends about his virgin birth sprang up: the divine fathering of a special child was a common theme in Egypt and elsewhere. Also, a mistranslation of a passage in Isaiah[507] was used by later Christians to claim the virgin birth of Jesus. The Hebrew word *'almah* means "a young woman sexually mature," not a virgin.[508] The same term is applied to the women in the harem of the Song of Songs found in the Song of Solomon 7:3; 6:8.[509]

The King James version of the Bible says that a "virgin shall conceive" whereas the better translation of the Revised Standard version refers to a "young woman." This passage was written when Assyria was about to invade Syria and the northern kingdom of Israel. Isaiah was trying to make the point that Yahweh would provide for them. He's not predicting the birth of anyone but the fact that Assyria will come and deliver them by the time that young women of the time have children a couple of years of age.[510]

There is even less evidence to support the later Roman Catholic doctrine of the ever-virgin Mary. In fact, scripture tells us of Yeshua's siblings,[511] and the fact that Joseph did not have intercourse with Mary *until* Yeshua was born.[512] Nevertheless, the cult of the ever-virgin Mary continues to be strong to this day as people long for their ever-virgin, ever-fruitful goddess who was stamped out by their own religious predecessors.

Little of the early life of Yeshua is reported in the standard Gospels although there are legends of his travel and study in both Egypt and India. After his family's flight into Egypt before Herod's death in 4 BCE, Joseph hesitated to return during the governorship of Archelaus. Since Archelaus ruled from 4 BCE to 6 CE,[513] *Yeshua spent most of his first 12 years in Egypt.*

In the conventional account, Yeshua's public activity began with a visionary experience that came upon him during the unusual baptism performed by John the Baptist. John was already thought by some to be the messiah. Like Essenes, John had a sense of the immanence of the End Times but, unlike them, he left the desert to preach his warning to the unwary.[514] John's ministry was through his baptism, and his message was repentance. To "repent" in Greek is "metanoia," which means a *profound change in attitude*. Yeshua called John the reincarnation of Elijah.[515]

After his Baptism by John, Yeshua went into the wilderness after which his miraculous nature became evident. During his public years, he became known for healings, scathing social commentary, partying, revolutionary teachings, and violation of religious laws. Although he knew well the Jewish scriptures and was called rabbi, he is said to have spoken with an authority of his own, unlike those who stood solely on the written law. As magician, healer and revolutionary he attracted the attention of religious and secular leaders who had one primary question: was he a threat to their established authority? Others wondered if he were insane, the son of God, or possessed by a demon.

People of his time argued whether Yeshua could forgive sins, challenged his eating with the profane, and his failure to fast or to observe the Sabbath as expected. They questioned by whose authority he cast out demons. Other controversies arose over his disciples eating with "defiled hands," the coming of Elijah before the messiah, the practice of divorce, whether Yeshua's authority was from God, whether taxes should be paid to the Romans, the resurrection of humankind, and which of the laws or commandments were most important. He was criticized for his fondness for eating and drinking[516] and for spending so much time with tax gatherers, with "sinners" and with women. He enjoyed laughter, eating, drinking, and the company of women and children. He showed a deep love for everything earthly.[517] His proscription against casual divorce as a male prerogative went against the Jewish tradition that procreation was the purpose of marriage.[518] He established a dual organization with outer and inner teachings. Along with references to earlier Jewish scriptures he lived with a sense of unfolding drama.

Many of the miracles attributed to Yeshua had also been done by Elisha, such as walking on water, purifying water, raising the dead, healing, and feeding multitudes.[519] However, Romans, pagans and Jews considered Yeshua to be a magician. The accusations against him before Pilate as a "doer of evil"[520] was a vulgar term applied to magicians.[521]

In the tradition of shamanic initiation and practice, Yeshua was driven into the wilderness where he contacted spirits, sometimes appeared to be possessed of a spirit himself and, more often, controlled other spirits. In addition, he ascended into the heavens – a fair description of the shamanic journey into the upper world.

The powers of Yeshua/Jesus are also seen in magical papyri such as: the power to make people follow him, exorcism, control of spirits, miraculous cures, raising the dead, controlling weather, walking on water, magically producing food, mysterious escapes, becoming invisible, foreknowledge of events to come, telepathy, introduction of new magical rites, and claims of mystical union with others and with his god.[522]

Although there would be legitimate distinctions among a divine personage, a demonologist who commands spirits, a healer who channels subtle energy, a shaman who enters the spirit world, or a magician who uses trickery, it is clear that much of the appeal and evidence of Yeshua's uniqueness was his supernatural acts of healing, control of nature, exorcism, and raising of the dead – not to mention the content of his teachings.

Despite his miracles and teachings, however, some followers began to desert him as they realized he was not the military messiah who would return their sovereignty to them.[523] He also provoked the ire of established authorities, both secular and religious, and was executed as a criminal according to Roman law. There were mixed reactions to his teachings, his death, and expectations of resurrection. His life brought divisions among his followers, among the Jews of the time, and among the political authorities.

Shortly before his crucifixion, he celebrated what is usually called a Passover meal. However, his instructions to eat his body and drink his blood reflect another, older, tradition: that of the sacred king. 'God-eating' was a tradition that had nothing to do with Passover.[524] Thus, Yeshua joined other gods of rebirth from Osiris to Mithras to Baal; and became the sacred king whose death was to compensate for the sins of his people and to guarantee their fruitfulness.

It had originally been Osiris for whom bread was the "flesh of his body." For any grain god, bread is the resurrection after the death of the seed that gives life to his followers. Consequently, Yeshua has been called the "last vegetation deity of the Near Eastern world"[525] who adapted and modernized an ancient faith.[526] A magical papyrus tells of ingredients included in a cup of wine with an invocation that identified the drink with the blood of the deity. It was given to communicants so that they may be united in love.[527]

His death is presented in Christian tradition variously as betrayal, as the dramatic fulfillment of the scriptures, as a sacrifice for his people, as one dying for the many, and as a redemption of the sins of the world in the form of the divine scapegoat. After his execution, he appeared first to one or two women (depending on the Gospel). To show he was not a ghost, he ate with his disciples as material proof of his return from among the dead. Conventional texts end Yeshua's sojourn on earth with his "ascension" into heaven. However, a nineteenth century report from a Buddhist monastery contains an account of an earlier text that reported, after a history of Israel and Moses, how a divine infant born in Israel named "Issa" came to the Punjab where he studied the Veda. His heretical assertions that the values of the caste system were not divinely ordained enraged the Brahmans and, as a result, Issa had to flee.[528]

Further legends of his travels after death and resurrection tell of a journey into Persia where he was known as "Yuz Asaf" which means "leader of the healed;" a visit to what is now Pakistan in 47 CE; and travel in India. Twenty-one historical documents witness to Yeshua's presence in Kashmir. One author refers to the burial place of Yeshua which is believed to be confirmed by a sculpture of footprints with the marks of nails.[529]

Whatever his physical end, Yeshua spawned a new religion that was hardly Jewish. There was a new God, a new Covenant, a new method of worship with baptism and Eucharist, requirements of mercy rather than sacrifice, a new relationship to the "unclean," and a new attitude toward women. While going through the formalities of fulfilling the old law, he was releasing his followers from it – that is, from the old concept of redeeming their sins by sacrifice. He negated the need for their sacrifice by his.

Differences of opinion among his followers resulted in struggles for control. His teachings were used to justify both rebellion and obedience, rejection of the world and conquest of the world, war and peace, marriage and celibacy. For some, he was a revolutionary, for others his teaching was novel, fresh and liberating. To some, it was as old as time for he came from the ever-virgin Queen of Heaven.

This analysis is not at all intended to demean the memory of the personage of Yeshua, but to show how his image has been shaped less by his own teachings than by cultural traditions. We have become lost in elements of the stories, many of which came from other traditions: virgin birth conceived by the god as found in Egypt and elsewhere; becoming the divine child of promise as from the Celts; being Emmanuel or "God among us" as was Egypt's pharaoh; a god of sacrifice as Esus of the Druids; the sacrificial lamb of the Hebrews; a sacrificial king as among the pagans; and as a resurrected god such as Osiris of the Egyptians and Attis of the Romans, to name a few.

Now, if we set aside the dramas, can we get at the heart of what he taught that turned out to be so inflammatory?

Chapter 34

The Teachings of the Master

Given the ravages of time, inconsistent sources, rewriting and editing, it may be difficult to define Yeshua's core teachings. Scholars, theologians, emperors, and popes have been attempting to do so for two thousand years without visible evidence of lessening the chasms among numerous Christian sects. Nevertheless, it is worthwhile.

As described in the previous chapter, Yeshua is given numerous identities. He was seen not only as a prophet, but also as a magician, false prophet, blasphemer, and deceiver. Part of the problem in defining him is that he defied the categories of any of the groups that would claim him. Countless people have been killed, innocents tortured, populations wiped out, cultures destroyed, and wars fought in the name of this prophet. His own followers fought with one another, and his movement (or that of his followers) appeared first as the enemy of the state and later as its tool.

Which was the real Yeshua/Jesus/Eshoa? Like Yahweh before him, there seem to be multiple versions of him. One is conciliatory toward the established order – giving to Caesar what was Caesar's and not overturning the law. The other one spoke of a "new age" and of fulfilling the law. Yet those charged with keeping the law were agast at his statements and actions. What law was it that he claimed to be fulfilling? It did not seem to be the Jewish law of that time.

A few principles seemed to define his public teachings. After looking first at those core principles, we can better examine his attitude toward the law and Judaism of his time, and his consequent religious and social commentary.

The Principle of Love

When asked directly, he quoted Deuteronomy[530] to say that the greatest of the laws was to "love the Lord, your God, with all your heart, with all your soul, with all your strength and with all your mind and [quoting from Leviticus[531]] your neighbor as your self." Similarly, one of the last instructions to his followers was to love one another as he had loved them, and that it would be their love for one another that would show them to be his disciples.

There are two corollaries to the law of love. Forgiveness and non-condemnation were the proper attitude to human slights and injuries. "Pass no judgment and you will not be judged. For as you judge others, so you will yourselves be judged, and whatever measure you deal out to others will be dealt back to you".[532]

His doctrine of love required removal of the usual qualifiers that otherwise allowed people to set it aside. Thus, challenges to his law of love resulted in the parable of the Good Samaritan to show that *all* were neighbors, as well as the admonishment to "love your enemy." In fact, we are to give love like the heavenly father "who makes the sun rise on the good and bad alike and sends the rain on the honest and the dishonest."[533]

The Nature of Allaha and How to Witness

In John 4:24, Yeshua said in his language "Allaha rookha hoo" which means "God is spirit".[534] However, in contrast to the jealous, wrathful and punitive image of Yahweh, Yeshua presented Allaha as a loving father who, like the sun and rain, gives light and nourishment to both wicked and good, righteous and unrighteous. His compassion embraced all people.[535]

Yeshua's use of the word "Abba" for his god – usually translated as "father" – is a diminutive form that would more accurately be rendered as "Papa".[536] This is in stark contrast to the formal and legalistic image presented elsewhere. It speaks of the natural affection between parent and child. Furthermore, his use of language referring to family is a far cry from the biblical creator who was a potter/fabricator.

Yeshua was clearly comfortable with nature, whether he retired to the wilderness or sailed through a tempest. He spoke of God's natural care of the birds of the air and his decoration of the lilies of the field. Yeshua's god spoke *through* nature, and what he spoke about were care and beauty.

The proper worship of Allaha was to celebrate prayers and charity in private where the heavenly "Papa" would see in secret. In Matthew he told his followers to "shed light among your fellows, so that, when they see the good you do, they may give praise to your father in heaven."[537] They are to be perfected; that is, all-embracing as the Father in heaven is all-embracing.

The Principle of Authenticity

First, plain speaking – yes for yes and no for no – is favored over oath-swearing. Furthermore, he taught the importance of letting the inner and outer selves reflect one another truthfully, because there is something greater than outer adherence to The Law. The inner condition was as important as actions.[538] Along that line, he spoke against those who nurse anger against their brothers, and that the lustful eye has already committed adultery.[539]

This is not likely to have been meant in an accusatory manner but rather to indicate that righteous acts were not enough: he expected his followers to clean the inside of their cups as well as the outside (which becomes more evident when we look later at the language he spoke). Even the Law is secondary to these inner conditions.

His Place in History

It is often said that Yeshua had no intention of starting a new religion. Nevertheless, it is clear from his statements that he was differentiating himself, his followers, the source of his teachings, and his movement from whatever had been before. In the Sermon on the Mount, he tells his audience "Do not suppose that I have come to abolish the Law and the prophets; I did not come to abolish, but to complete"[540] and then goes on to speak of the importance of the law "*until all that must happen has happened.*" This is a double message for it asserts the importance of the law while, at the same time, states that it is time-limited and that he has come to complete it. This is a most clever rendering, for to complete something is to be finished with it.

He clearly departed from the scriptures in several areas. When he said, "You have heard that the men of old were told . . . but I tell you . . .", he established himself as an authority over them.[541] This was also the case in his teaching about the Sabbath. The family and its authority of tradition also came under fire as he spoke of dividing families.

Also, he seemed to downplay the importance of ritual sacrifice in his assertion – quoting Hosea 6:6 – that he desires mercy, not sacrifice.[542] He further departed from tradition in his high regard for women, in eschewing cleanliness rules, and in the establishment of his own ritualistic eucharist. Most telling are his parables about not putting new wine in old skins and about not mending an old garment with a patch of new cloth because things would be worse.

Sometimes, he showed humility in asserting that not he, but his God alone is good, or that it is not he who does marvelous works but "the Father." At other times he spoke of being "the way" or "the door," and to pray or cast out devils in his name. In the Gospel according to John, his perception of his place is most clear: he is one with the Father. His teaching, way, and glory are not his but the Father's. "If I glorify myself," he said "that glory of mine is worthless." Hence, he was not directing attention to himself but attempting to point to the Father. Followers to this day, however, continue to stare at the finger pointing to the moon rather than raise their gaze to seek the *way* of Yeshua.

He knew that these teachings would be controversial for, as he said, "I have come not to bring peace, but a sword." There would be those who would receive him and those who would not. His teachings would divide families. And his new wine would not be held within the old skin of the Judaic Law.

The Kingdom of Heaven

Prophets had talked about the *coming* kingdom of heaven and the paradise that is to be. Yeshua, however, spoke constantly of the kingdom of heaven not as a time or place after death, but as something near, present, and accessible. He told his disciples to preach "The kingdom of heaven is upon you," and to others, he said, "[T]he kingdom of God has already come upon you".[543]

Furthermore, he berated religious leaders who obstructed realization of the kingdom. "Ever since the coming of John the Baptist the kingdom of heaven has been subjected to violence and violent men are seizing it." And later: "Alas, alas for you, lawyers and Pharisees, hypocrites that you are! You shut the door of the Kingdom of Heaven in men's faces; you do not enter yourselves, and when others are entering, you stop them."[544] *Note that this is in the present tense*. Furthermore, in logion 113 of *The Gospel of Thomas*, Yeshua is quoted as saying, "The Kingdom of the Father is spread out over the whole earth, and people do not see it."[545]

What kind of heaven is near, is upon them already, that one can enter as well as block others' entry, and is among and within them? What kind of kingdom can be both present and yet not of this world? Since it is present and it is not a physical place, it must be a state, a condition, a relationship, an experience, or some parallel dimension. For it to be *within* makes it both present and not of this world. In verse three of the *Gospel of Thomas*, Yeshua is quoted as saying directly, "the kingdom is inside of you, and it is outside of you."

Perhaps he was attempting to voice the promise articulated by Jeremiah (31:31-34) that "The time is coming, says the Lord, when I will make a new covenant with Israel and Judah. It will not be like the covenant I made with their forefathers when I took them by the hand and I led them out of Egypt.... But this is the covenant which I will make with Israel after those days, says the Lord; *I will set my law within them and write it on their hearts*; I will become their God and they shall become my people. No longer need they to teach one another to know the Lord; all of them, high and low alike, shall know me, says the Lord..."

Social Commentary

"Always treat others as you would like them to treat you: that is the law of the prophets."[546] Yeshua taught his followers to love and respect not only each other but also their enemies. Again, he stressed forgiveness and mercy over sacrifice and revenge.

His treatment of women deserves mention. Like Mohammed after him, he attempted to improve the lot of women who were largely treated as property and inferior, if not cursed, creatures who could be owned, divorced, or bought if their marriageability had been impaired by rape. Yeshua quoted the J writer's version of creation to say that male and female were *in the beginning* created male and female and, once the two were married, they become one. She could not be disposed of at the husband's whim.

Celibacy was not for everyone but only for those "for whom God has appointed." Yeshua's statement – "Blessed is the woman who has not given birth" –is often interpreted as a reference to the end of times, but it has also been viewed as a revolutionary statement of the value of a woman despite not fulfilling her traditional role of child bearer.[547] In other words, women who were childless by choice or fate were blessed and valuable. They were not simply a male womb.

In spite of his comments that he came to "fulfill the law," he appears to have had a different law in mind than what was practiced and perceived by the educated of his time, for he often spoke of the way they followed their law and how that was not adequate. He said they miss the point and attend to the insignificant.[548] He decried the slavish use of the law that made it a burden and fostered hypocrisy. He decried the cup that was polished on the outside but full of defilement within.

He complained that the "least of these, my brethren" were being judged by others instead of being fed, clothed, and comforted. He asked that they resolve their differences in a way that put human harmony ahead of even some of their religious observances by asking that people correct issues between them before sacrificing on the altar. Repeatedly, it was not the demands of sacrifice or of the law or of personal status, but mercy that he asserted. He put the Law *below* humankind in saying that the Sabbath was made for man (Mark 2:27-28), rather than man for the Sabbath.

Thus, instead of the values of hierarchy and *king*ship, which would be expected in a messianic drive, Yeshua voiced values of *kin*ship. He called others his brothers and sisters which also made them children of his Father. Perhaps God-the-Father – "Papa" – was less a patriarchal reference than it was an attempt to pull the transcendent Yahweh from his distant heavenly throne and bring him into more intimate contact with humanity – his children. It also made Yahweh less the fabricating creator than an organic begetter.

The tension engendered by expectations of the immanent end of the age was defused by his teachings because "the essential thing to him was present unbroken union with God."[549] As Mitchell says, he taught one thing only: presence.[550] Unfortunately, the nature of his teachings about the kingdom of heaven and application of his social commentary have been lost under expectations of the apocalyptic end of time – the way sensationalized media coverage today often overshadows more substantive news and ideas.

What has happened to these sublime teachings? How have we come so far away from them despite our books, translations, and good intentions? One reason is the simple circumstance of having to translate ideas from one time, place, and language into the words and culture of another time and place: they are immediately shaped by language, culture, and politics. Another factor is the destructive shadow that grew from the new church itself when it sought to establish its own kingdom in this material world. Yet another reason was simple practicality and an accident of circumstance. When the ideal meets the real, vexing problems must be handled in the real (political) world. Communication of even the best ideas and inspiration comes through human beings to other human beings, each side with its expectations, limitations, and agenda.

Interpretations of his provocative and authoritative sayings and the charismatic stories about his life have been shaped by his followers and by the movement's struggle for identity. He has been a religious Rorschach test: observers see him through their own emotional filters and ideological preconceptions, and project their own inner condition and needs onto his words. And that, of course, includes me.

Gospels relied on oral traditions and were not written for decades. And then they were filtered through translations and revisions. That said, these writings are what we have and what our Western Christian churches claim to have been built on.

With this in mind, let's turn our attention to these sources from which our knowledge of Yeshua comes, like we did with the earlier scriptures.

Chapter 35

Writing the Word of God – Again

Over and over, the question arises in my mind: how did what we read in the Gospels turn into institutions that justified war, slavery, misogyny, political domination, torture, murder, protection of sexual predators, genocide, and all manner of denigration and exclusion of social groups? I'd like to look first at the process of scripture writing to understand the way in which they were products of their time, and then the problem of translation from the original spoken language to the limited version left to us.

Gospel Writers Play to Their Audiences

As far as we know, there are no surviving writings of the immediate apostles. Since literacy was common even among the lower classes in the Roman world, it is extremely unlikely that something was not written. One might surmise that it was intended to remain secret and perhaps was orally transmitted. Perhaps they had no need of writings since their inspiration came directly from their ascent into heaven. Or maybe they were suppressed. It seems more likely, however, that expectations of the immanent second coming with the apocalypse made writing things for the future superfluous. By the time Luke and Acts were written around 85 CE, there was also a need to explain why the end of the world had not yet taken place.

In any event, it is well-known that other "gospels" were written besides those accepted as canon. In fact, the *Gospel According to Thomas* is believed by many scholars to be the source used by the canonical gospel writers.[551]

The officially accepted gospels were written between 70 and 100 CE to strengthen the movement that was under intense persecution. Naturally, they turned toward the Jewish tradition of scripture writing. Gospel writings circulated anonymously until the second century when names were attached to them to give them authority. Differing sources are evident in variations among the gospels.

Ninety-one percent of Mark's Gospel is paralleled in Matthew and Luke. There are stories in Matthew and Luke that are not in Mark such as the birth of Jesus. There is thought to be a lost "Quelle" source from about 50 CE that consisted of the sayings of Yeshua[552] from which the other gospels may have been written.

Mark, the earliest of the gospels, was written between 60 and 70 CE, and Matthew between 70 and 80 CE. Luke was written about 85, and John between 90 and 100. It was not until the year 367 when Athenasius, Bishop of Alexandria, determined which 27 books were to be read in his diocese.[553] Thus, the "New Testament" was born.

While all the gospels had the general purpose of spreading the faith and presenting Yeshua as the messiah, each was written for its own reason, with its own viewpoint and for its own audience. This alone will explain some of the apparent inconsistencies. The synoptic gospels of Matthew, Mark, and Luke show Yeshua's earthly origin, while John presents his divine origin. Matthew and Luke give different genealogies for Yeshua's ancestors – through Joseph – to show him to be of the House of David and thereby in line for the throne of Israel. If, however, Joseph was not the biological father of Yeshua, Joseph's lineage would have been less relevant than Mary's.

Matthew was written for Jewish Christians and attempted to fit Yeshua into the Judaic context. Thus, the writer of Matthew makes the case that Yeshua was the messiah foretold by the prophets, makes him a descendant of Abraham, and tailors his story to be like Moses', such as the massacre of the innocents and flight into Egypt. He speaks of Yeshua coming to fulfill the law, not to abolish it.[554] Matthew notably deleted magical references.[555] The writer of Matthew also has Yeshua telling his disciples to avoid Gentile and Samaritan lands and go to the lost sheep of Israel.[556]

In Matthew's genealogy of Yeshua, he mentions four women besides Mary: Tamar, whose children were born of incest; Rahab, who was the madam of a brothel; Ruth, who was a non-Israelite who obtained her second husband by solicitation; and Bathsheba, whose adultery with David resulted in Solomon.[557] It is also the writer of Matthew who quoted Isaiah that a "virgin will conceive and bear a son. . ." to show Yeshua as the fulfillment of their Law.

Mark, on the other hand, was written for a wider audience and emphasized miracles to show that the healings of Yeshua were superior to those of the pagans. Perhaps also appealing to the pagans around him, the writer of Mark indicated that Yeshua's teaching is a departure from what has been – referring to patching an old garment with new cloth and putting new wine into old skins.[558]

Matthew and Mark both register the despair that their savior could not save himself from execution. Luke is more hopeful, however, framing it as a union between son and father. John suggests that nothing more was needed: the task was complete. John mentioned seven miracles as "illustrations of an underlying spiritual truth".[559] The gospel of John seemed to differentiate between the Christos or Logos, and Yeshua the person.

The book of Revelations was written around 90 - 95 during persecutions by Domitian and it sounds like some drug-induced vision – open to wide interpretation. One of the references in Revelations is to "The Beast." Modern readers often believe this a reference to a satanic being but, at the time, this "beast," known by the number 666, was a numerological reference to the emperor Nero[560] who waged persecutions against the Christian movement. Speaking or writing openly about the beastly Nero was too dangerous and, therefore, this coded reference was used.

Language

Scriptures were written *in response* to earthly situations and reflect human attempts to put human concerns into the wider context taught by Yeshua. The scriptures did not exist in their present form, with their present "books," nor in our language. Thus, potential problems of translation are obvious. Yeshua did not speak English – nor did he speak Latin, or Greek, from which most Bibles are translated. He spoke the colorful and psychologically sophisticated Aramaic language. But let's first take a brief look at the Greek language.

Greek

Perhaps the best-known example of the problem of translating from Greek to English is the all-important word "love." The Greeks had several words for love, each of which referred to a different kind of love. There was a word for universal love, another for the love between a woman and man, another for the love between parent and child. All were translated rather vaguely as "love."

Furthermore, some translations become *interpretations* that confuse the meaning of the passage. For example, in Luke 17:21 where Yeshua addressed a question about the kingdom of God, he is quoted in the Greek as using a word that is usually translated as "among" – rendering the saying as, "the kingdom of God is among you." The regular meaning of the Greek word, however, is "within" – the word used for the inside of a cup.[561] Thus, the meaning of the passage is more accurately translated as "the kingdom of God is within you." This would seem to have revolutionary theological implications in terms of the nature of our world, and the conditions necessary to experience heaven. Rather than an ephemeral place for us in the future if we behave properly, this heaven is imminent and accessible.

Some translations affect the *tone* of a passage. For example, the Greek word that we see translated as "sin" is *hamartia*. Hamartia is an archery term that means "missing the mark." We hear sin so often spoken of as if it were a permanent stain upon humankind that, once infected, there is no salvation except by the grand sacrifice. As an archery term, however, our "sins" are simply inaccurate trajectories that offer us a chance to try again. Thus, the Greek version of sin is not some inherent quality of our being but, rather, a behavior to be corrected to more effectively follow our intent.

Similarly, as I noted earlier, Yeshua's admonition to "Be ye therefore perfect, as your Father in heaven is perfect" would more accurately be rendered as "Be ye therefore *whole* (or all-embracing), as your Father in heaven is whole." Thus, this "perfection" is not an admonition to attempt to live up to a nearly impossible external standard, but the expectation that we make ourselves all embracing. I am reminded of Carl Jung's statement to the effect that being good is no substitute for wholeness. This seems an eminently more life-affirming and growth-inducing way to move through the ever-expanding experience of ourselves and the world, rather than trying to fit into a set of limiting, if well intended, imitations based on another's idea of goodness. One of the implications of this difference in focus suggests that the Yeshuite teachings were about developing more whole people, rather than about conformity to laws, rituals, and external expectations. That, in itself, is both profound and revolutionary

Aramaic

But neither Greek nor Hebrew was the primary language of Yeshua. He spoke the Aramaic tongue, which was a widespread language of the time. What little I understand about the Aramaic language suggests a world view that is difficult to grasp if clouded by the preconceptions and prejudices inherent in our own language and the perspective it both reflects and creates. I will offer some examples found in the work of Errico, Douglas-Klotz, and Lamsa. Although we would be hard pressed to find much reference to them in mainstream religious writings, I have found their translations to be illuminating.

The Aramaic language encompasses working relationships among mind sets, perception, judgment, attitude, and behavior. Also, Aramaic does not verbally distinguish between the mental and the physical worlds, or between a cause and its effect. The same words signify *both* the cause and its effect.[562] Thus, Yeshua was speaking from within his linguistic tradition to say that internal anger is akin to murderous actions, or that lust in the heart is equivalent to the action of adultery. Thought is action.

Language not only expresses thought but also helps to shape it. One can think most easily about concepts for which there are words. Similarly, words and their tone can direct our attention differentially as is seen once more in the example of "sin." The word "sin" directs attention to the wrongful action. The Greek "hamartia" directs attention to the mark that was missed.

As in Greek, the Aramaic words for sin and evil – *khata* and *bisha* – are also archery terms meaning "missing the target" and "off target" respectively.[563] Similarly, the word translated into English as "repent" is often coupled with suggestions of human sinfulness. In the Aramaic, however, "repent" means to turn back to one's source.[564] Again, the focus is on the goal, not the person or error.

The ability of language to form thought is also evident in the Aramaic view that means and ends, as well as inner quality and outer action, are *part of one another*. Consequently, various dualisms and boundaries in Greek between 'mind,' 'body,' and 'spirit'[565] have little meaning. The "self" that is directing is a part of the action and the body doing the act.

The schism between heaven and earth that we find in Greek and English is not found in Aramaic. Heaven and earth are related to one another, and the words are used alternately in the Beatitudes. Furthermore, "heaven" is not confined to a metaphysical concept in Aramaic but refers to the "light and sound shining through all creation".[566] This makes heaven intrinsic to all that exists – including earth and people.

One Aramaic word deserves special attention. Translated variously as "self," "life," "soul," or "itself," the Aramaic word "naphsha" has no direct English counterpart. Naphsha reflects the Aramaic philosophy that places life, thought, and physical health in the same concept as the harmonious interaction between human activity and divine direction.[567] Thus, naphsha suggests an agent of control that is connected to, but behind, actions, thoughts and body – much as Jung conceived of the Self. Thus, to "seek ye first the kingdom of heaven" means to align the will, consciousness and naphsha with the kingdom,[568] that is, with the light and sound shining through all creation.

What follows are further examples of translation from the Aramaic to show what light might be shed on the meaning of the passages.

"Jesus of Nazareth" is an incorrect translation of what is properly "Jesus the Nazarene," which is from an Aramaic word *nazar* indicating one who was "a keeper or celebrant of the sacred rites." The term is related to that of the Nazarites such as Sampson (in Judges 13:5-7) who did not cut his hair or drink wine.[569] Thus, "Yeshua the Nazarene" referred not to a place but to his role.

Returning to the word *perfection*, "Be ye therefore perfect. . ." as in Matt 5:48 comes from the Aramaic word *gmera* and refers to the concept of being complete, comprehensive, or all-inclusive.[570]

"Blessed are the poor in spirit, for theirs is the kingdom of heaven," found in the Beatitudes, suggests that poor folks still have value in the eyes of this God. "Poor in spirit," according to Errico, however, refers to those who surrender everything to God.[571] Thus, this is not about poverty but about devotion.

The "love" we are to have for our enemies[572] is rendered as *khooba*. This is different from the love to be held for God, which is *rakhma*. Khooba indicates a mindset that asks that our perceptions be oriented toward the good of the other.[573] To love the enemy refers to an impersonal force that admonishes us to look beyond the enemies' actions to their higher inner state and relate to that.[574] *Rakhma*, by the way, has a dozen English equivalents that include "womb," "bowels," "testicles," and "compassion." Thus, what is sometimes translated as "bowels," as in "my bowels stirred within me"[575] or "sounding of thy bowels,"[576] is intended by the writer to indicate a tender love being engendered – not the intestines.[577]

"Let thine eye be single and thy whole body shall be filled with light"[578] is rendered in direct translation from the Aramaic to say that "The lamp of earthly life is perception. Therefore, if your perception is without fault. . ., your whole life shall be enlightened. . . If your perception be evil. . . your whole life shall be darkened. . . by it. . ."[579] In other words, Yeshua is giving us the psychological truth that our attitude determines how we perceive the world: if we perceive light in the world, our perception is clear and, if we perceive darkness in the world, that perception will color our experience. Again, the boundary between the inner and outer worlds is illusory.

Perhaps these renderings tell us why the teachings of Yeshua were so different from those of "the law." He turned his listeners toward the ideal. He taught that fixing attention on the negative will have negative results, whereas a focus on the good and the true – the kingdom of heaven – will help align our consciousness and our will so that we are less often off the mark, and more frequently aligned with the light and sound shining through all creation.

In addition to translations, mistranslations and linguistic-based concepts, there is also the problem of idioms, for there are over 1,000 idioms in the Bible.[580] Idioms, of course, are understandable in their context by those who know what they mean – which is not necessarily what they say. In English, for example, one might say "I was so embarrassed, I just died." No one literally dies of embarrassment. Or one might be so angry as to "bite off someone's head." Thus, the words indicate a meaning that is beyond that of the words.

Aramaic and the other languages of the Middle East are rich with idioms. An easily transparent idiom is the admonition to cast no pearls before swine,[581] referring to pearls of wisdom. Lamsa tells us that the "Seven devils" in Luke 8:2 means seven bad habits.[582] In Matthew 5:29-30, Yeshua says "If thy right eye offend thee, pluck it out..." and "If thy right hand offend thee, cut it off..." Rather than a literal meaning of deforming the body, this simply means to "stop it"[583] in the way the we might say in English "cut that out" to a misbehaving child.

Finally, for centuries, the name "Jesus" has been used as part of prayers and as a word of power in exorcisms. This reflects a misunderstanding of one of the most significant idioms of the scriptures. To do things "in my name" would have been rendered "Beshemi" which does not refer to the use of the name itself as a magical invocation or word of power but, rather, "in my way, method, or system of doing things".[584] Thus, Yeshua was not saying to invoke him as one would a spirit but to follow his way of doing things.

As people have realized the depth of the Aramaic language, along with the fact that this was the language spoken by the Christian Savior, there has been a growing interest in Aramaic. There are at least two Aramaic Bibles,[585] and other books explaining Aramaic idioms.[586] This interest has also given rise to recordings in the Aramaic language, and dances set to music with Aramaic sayings of Yeshua. Many people yearn to be closer to The Holy than can be found in emotionalism, ritualism, and theology. The prospect of saying the very words that Yeshua may have said allows them to, in a real way, worship "in his name," that is, with his method.

What I've presented here are the works of individuals. Biblical scholarship often takes a dim view of the interpretation of individuals, especially when they violate a consensus of accepted meaning. Although something can be said for having multiple "experts" of scriptures, I would give first credibility to those closest to the language in question so that, even if they err in some details, their overall worldview – the worldview of a native speaker – will offer us a higher likelihood for understanding the original perspective, idioms, images, and figures of speech.

As a final example, the "Lord's Prayer" begins in our conventional usage as, "Our Father, who art in heaven." Douglas-Klotz, however, renders his translation from the Aramaic as "O Birther! Father-Mother of the Cosmos." Later in the prayer he says, "Loose the cords of mistakes binding us, as we release the strands we hold of others' guilt."[587] We hear in this rendition the divine "Papa" of Yeshua rather than the potter-creator shaping his clay.

Contemplation on these more direct translations could provide many layers of meaning and take us closer to this teacher's intent before it became a casualty in religious and political power struggles.

Chapter 36

A Yeshuite Secret Society?

Conventional tradition places Yeshua within the circle of his twelve apostles who were the overt connection between him and the rest of the world. Some writers have placed Yeshua among the Essenes, noting similarities between his teachings and those attributed to that separatist and austere group. The link, however, between the writings at Qumran and the Essenes has been questioned. Furthermore, contrasts with the Essenes are evident regarding his activity and teaching. For example, his admonition to love one's enemy was not Essene. He not only rejected separation from the world but reached out to the wealthy *and* to the rejected peoples of his society. He opposed religious elitism and used oil in anointing.[588] Yet his connection to *some* organized group is hinted at.

We often think of the Twelve as blessed men receiving divine wisdom and yet, in the gospels, they appear as doubting, contentious, and competitive. They failed to comprehend their master's teachings and missed completely the idea of the resurrection. And when soldiers came, they scattered, leaving the women to receive the "good news." But there were others beyond the Twelve.

Who were these others? Women, of course, were present enough to create controversy. Even in the Gnostic writings Simon Peter is quoted as saying that women "are not worthy of the Life" (Log. 114),[589] but Yeshua intervened on their behalf there, as well as when he protected the adulteress from being stoned. After his execution, women became the messengers of his return.

Beyond the Twelve and these women, we also know of 72 who were sent to heal and cast out spirits.[590] There are also events reported in the Gospels that indicate planning by Yeshua with people other than the Twelve, such as the man carrying the jug of water who was to lead them to the place of the "last supper." Since carrying water was normally a job done by women at the time, it indicates an unusual event, as well as a pre-arranged signal. Similarly, the donkey was given to the apostles when they gave the password as prearranged by Yeshua. These events show an inner circle helping Jesus to arrange experiences or to expedite what he needed to do with the apostles. In addition, it was to the Twelve "and others" that Yeshua said "To you the secret of the kingdom of God has been given; but to those who are outside everything comes by way of parables..." (Mark 4:10-11). Thus, there were more layers to this movement than 12 apostles and those nearby by happenstance. This gives us a tantalizing picture of greater complexity than that of a rogue Jewish rabbi with revolutionary teachings.

A letter by Clement of Alexandria indicates the existence of a gospel that was probably written earlier than even Mark, the earliest of the known gospels. It points to a secret rite of baptism and mystery of the Kingdom of God. Unlike the immersions to cleanse ritual impurity,[591] this was an *initiatory* rite that has come down to us in a diluted form as both a cleansing and admission to the church. In fact, two kinds of baptism are suggested in these writings. The primary one was an initiatory rite. This initiatory baptism by Yeshua was performed individually at night. The initiate, after preparatory purification, wore only a linen cloth over the naked body, and often received a mystical experience described as the "ascent into heaven." Through this act, the initiate was freed from the law.[592] As the Yeshuite movement grew, such private initiatory rites could not be offered to the masses so a public baptism was performed that would still leave the recipient subject to the laws of the church. The letter by Clement also indicated the existence of a second gospel by Mark that had been written after he returned to Alexandria from Rome. This esoteric Gospel was written solely for initiated Christians.[593]

If, for a moment, we take these various writings seriously, a three-tiered structure emerges. First, the conventional gospels were taught to the public at large. The second, or secret, scriptures were reserved for initiated devotees. A third set of oral teachings was kept for the innermost circle.[594]

The implications of a secret baptismal rite with its powerful inspiration are tremendous. Consider the possibility: Yeshua initiated his 12 apostles and a few others who, in turn, initiated their own lineage. Initiatory lineages spread out like tendrils, taking root in others who then have their own ecstatic experiences. This would be a possible explanation for the proliferation of so many variations of belief and practice as well as Gnostic sects, each deriving from the unique experiences of an initiate. Furthermore, if he lived and taught secretly after his "ascension," he would have created yet another lineage.

These various lineages would also account for some of the apparent "contradictions" in the gospels among Yeshua's libertine teachings, such as extreme legalists who called for the maintenance of the law, the party of James who called for the *appearance* of obeying the law, and Paul who said there was no need to obey the law unless disobedience would lead another Christian into sin.[595]

Barring some archeological find, we may never know for sure. One thing is certain, however: such initiatory lineages would threaten the authority of any established institution, especially the church in Rome and any of the fundamental literalists that have built their ideological structures on English versions of The Word.

Chapter 37

The Movement Splinters

Divisions began long before Yeshua's departure from the Twelve. Apostles sought an exclusive right to service and divine power. For example, the apostle John saw a man who was driving out devils in Yeshua's name. Since he was "not one of us," they tried to stop him. Yeshua, however, said to let him go for "anyone who is not against us is on our side."[596]

Yeshua, by his own account, had come "not to be served but to serve."[597] His admonition that whoever wished to be great must be the "willing slave of all" seems to have been lost in political and dogmatic struggles as each follower attempted to assert his vision of what was proper.

There were also divisions in Jerusalem among those followers who maintained their Judaism by continuing to sacrifice and honor the Mosaic laws, and others, particularly those who traveled, who were inclined toward more libertarian aspects of the teachings. The rift began as apostles lost touch with Greek-speaking radicals.[598] At the same time, there were complaints that Greek-speaking widows were neglected in the distribution of food. As a solution to this prejudice, non-apostles were given charge of the distribution of the food and the keeping of accounts.[599]

Because of their backgrounds, Jewish Christians saw the coming of their messiah to be the herald of the worldly Jewish kingdom that was to come. Gentiles, who were more Hellenistic, thought of a more present influence – an influence from events already occurred. These two factions struggled with one another over a final interpretation. James, the brother of Yeshua, became prominent in the Jerusalem church along with most of the apostles. The extremists among them insisted on obedience to all the laws of Moses as a prerequisite to baptism. They were called "Judaizers."

On the other hand, Peter's vision that is reported in Acts 11:5-18 did away with the division between Jews and Gentiles when a voice from heaven said, "It is not for you to call profane what God counts clean." Peter had seen the Spirit descend upon both uncircumcised foreigners and upon liberal converts. His dream of the cloth with unclean animals was said to be a message to take their gospel to all people. However, it referred more directly to Jewish dietary laws – and it was a message to ignore them.

His vision told him to take and eat. But he was criticized by the Judaizers, and thereafter was unable to make a clear stand.[600]

Of course, there was controversy as to whether Gentiles should be admitted into the church at all, or whether Yeshua's message was intended only for the Israelites. By this time Saul (a.k.a. Paul) had become involved in the movement. On his return from his first missionary journey, he engaged in this controversy at the Jerusalem council. Peter, Paul, and Barnabas spoke in favor of admitting the Gentiles. James, the brother of Jesus, agreed. James, who was by then head of the church there, gave a letter to Paul to that affect.[601]

Paul's very participation in the movement was opposed by the original disciples saying he distorted the word of God. They rejected Paul as neither competent nor qualified to be an apostle, and of being insane. It was the pre-conversion Saul/Paul, after all, who watched with approval as Stephen was brought before the Council, accused of speaking against the law, and was stoned to death.[602] Paul responded to the apostle's objections to claim that they were on their way to destruction.[603]

During persecution by Herod Agrippa I in 41-44 CE, Peter was driven out of the city. Leadership of the church was then taken over by James who had come into the church only after Yeshua's death. He was famous for his "traditional Jewish piety." With James and Paul in leadership positions between 45 and 60 CE, the Christian movement swung toward Pharisaic Judaism.[604]

Thus, it seems the legalistic interpretation of Christianity can be traced to its roots in the Jerusalem church while "libertine" interpretations went back to Yeshua himself.[605]

Chapter 38

Saul of Tarsus

One of the greatest forces in both the spread and splintering of the Yeshuite movement was the man who became known to the world as "Saint Paul." A number of writers have noted differences between the Yeshuite and Pauline teachings.[606] Yet he stands as a bridge between Yeshua and the church that came after him. He was a non-apostle who, nevertheless, shaped and defined the young movement according to his own vision.

"Saul" was his given Hebrew name.[607] He was a thoroughly Hellenized Jew[608] who came from Tarsus where the philosophies of Stoics and Cynics were taught. He probably became acquainted there with Greek mystery cults and their ideologies, along with practices of identifying with the dying and resurrected savior-gods[609] we found in other Pagan cultures as well.

Saul ignominiously entered the Christian story by his support and approval of Stephen's stoning. While Stephen was being given burial, Saul "was harrying the church; he entered house after house, seizing men and women, and sending them to prison."[610] With uncommon zeal, Saul breathed "murderous threats against the disciples. . .and applied for letters at the synagogues at Damascus authorizing him to arrest anyone he found, men or women, who followed the new way, and bring them to Jerusalem."[611]

On his journey to Damascus, however, he had a visionary experience that turned him from persecutor to proselyte – at least in some respects. A flash of light blinded him, and he heard the voice of Yeshua who instructed him where to go. Saul, following the instruction, was led to a house where Ananias, also responding to a vision, healed Saul's sight.[612] Ananias' vision also pronounced that Paul would be the "chosen instrument to bring my name before the nations and their kings. . ." This is thought to have been written by the same author who wrote the gospel attributed to Luke. He supported Saul's leadership, whereas the writer of Mark was more closely aligned with Peter.[613]

Saul embraced his new task with the same fervor and dedication with which he carried out his previous persecutions. He forged an agreement with the Judaizers that acknowledged his calling to work with the uncircumcised. The Judaizers agreed that Gentiles need not be circumcised but they must be chaste and obey some of the Jewish dietary laws.[614]

Because Saul was considered a Roman citizen, he was able to change his name to Paulus.[615] In the same biblical passage[616] where Saul's name changes to Paul, he is credited with becoming filled with the Holy Spirit – and blinding a "false prophet."[617] He is thenceforth known as Paul.

Paul's conversion on the road to Damascus was one of focus and not of personal transformation. He remained "arrogant, self-righteous, filled with murderous hatred of his opponents, terrified of God, oppressed by what he felt as the burden of the law, overwhelmed by his sense of sin."[618] His teachings still bore the stamp of his own breast-beating personality with its self-righteous humility. He may have suffered from temporal lobe epilepsy with his compulsive writing, sexual preoccupations, and seizure-like vision. This does not invalidate his efforts or even the source of his inspiration, but it might add perspective to his way of life.

Paul appears as the author of several books in the biblical canon. Not all the Pauline letters, however, were written by Paul. The usual ones accepted as genuine are First and Second Corinthians, Romans, Galatians, Philippians, First Thessalonians, and Philemon. First Thessalonians is considered the oldest of the letters and earliest book of the new testament, dated at about 50 or 51 CE.[619]

Paul's contribution to Christian ideology was his interpretation of the nature of Christ as the Divine Being who assumed human form, died, and was resurrected. Paul's rendition of the passion of Yeshua appealed to the Gentiles who lived in the shadow of Greek mystery religions that *already taught union with a resurrected savior-god*.[620] In fact, Paul's interest was less in Yeshua the person than in his vision of the Christ.

His Jewish-Hellenic background shows through his teachings in the way he, on the one hand, emphasized the dualistic split that pits a struggle between the spiritual and material worlds, and placed woman as inferior to man. On the other hand, he wrote beautiful passages of mystical union in which male and female would be one in the spirit, if not in the physical world. Unlike Yeshua, Paul separated the material world from heaven and made it a problem for the spirit, rather than an expression of spirit, and a home for the kingdom of heaven.

Paul complained that Gnostic elements appeared in the church at Corinth – while his own writings have Gnostic features. In fact, the Roman church was never able to overcome Gnostic influences.[621] Paul's claim that "we war not against flesh and blood, but against the dominions, the powers, the lords of the darkness," etc., was a common Gnostic epithet.[622] He seemed to take a middle road between extremists on both ends (libertarian and puritan) but, nevertheless, made marriage but a substitute for celibacy.[623]

The meaning of "messiah" was given a new face as well. This revolutionary departure from traditional Judaism is often overlooked. The new definition made Yeshua the Divine Incarnation: Emmanuel, God-Among-Us, Christ-Within. It was an echo of the *willing* sacrificial king – and an infusion of Hellenic mystery cults into Christianity. Or, perhaps, it suggests that the Christian movement began as a new incarnation of a much older lineage of "the Mysteries."

Yeshua taught the presence of the kingdom, whereas Paul taught that "flesh and blood can't inherit the kingdom of God."[624] With Paul's omission of the principle of the presence, he transformed Yeshua into the traditional Jewish sacrificial lamb, saying that he had taken on the sins of the world and would return to be our judge.[625] Paul echoes a history of past human sacrifice – the sacrifice of the first born so that the people might be spared punishment for their errors and, as a result, their lives might be fruitful. For the ancient peoples, it was a blood sacrifice for rebirth, resurrection, and renewal. Such had been the wishes of Pagans, Hebrews, and now the Christian church.

Paul presented a judging Christ with whom he sought mystical union. There can be no doubt that the image in his mind of God as a punitive master and Christ as the coming judge reflects his own psychology as well as formed his ideas about what was necessary for proper living. With his violent turn of mind, visions of cosmic warfare, an image of a punitive God,[626] antagonism toward women and sexuality, and his history of self-righteous persecution, the psychologist in me wonders what his earlier background had been.

The divine intimacy that Yeshua taught, referring to Allaha as "Papa" and showing affection to men, women, and children, was lost in Paul's emphasis on not only his own authority, but also with his focus on a transcendent and distant Christ. Consequently, the grace that came through Yeshua's resurrection became the central theme of all of Paul's letters.[627] Paul aligned with the attitude of the scribes who were shocked by Yeshua's association with "sinners," as he (Paul) admonished *his* followers to not mix with unbelievers (II Corinthians 6:14).[628]

From another view, no longer would Yeshua's teaching be for a *realization of the presence of the kingdom* and a way of entering it, but the passive receipt of redemption through the shedding of another's blood – a return to the sacrificial lamb. Paul's intent may have been to reveal a genuine and inspired ideal of the Christ, but his Judeo-Hellenic education, combined with a violent personality, led him to a sometimes murderously righteous entitlement of the right to impose his views on others. His "conversion" only changed the one he served. It did not change him.

While he seems to have rescued Christianity from its early chaos and shaped it into a functioning organization in the face of great persecution, he also irrevocably uprooted it from its source. Ironically, he may have enabled the Christian movement to survive, but it was no longer the movement of Yeshua.

As a man of his time and culture, perhaps Paul was simply attempting to integrate, as best he could, competing principles that were taking shape in the Yeshuite movement. There are two sets of admonitions, seemingly inconsistent, with a third set attempting to bridge the two. On one hand are passages referring to freedom *from* the law. On the other hand are admonitions for an ethical, decent, moral, law-abiding life. The letters of Paul attempt to bridge this schism with his conservative, law-abiding, attempts to not rouse the animosity of one's pagan Roman neighbors. Indeed, he wanted his followers to be praiseworthy as examples to the world. Thus, one was not bound to the law but may choose to follow it for appearance's sake.

And there may be yet more to Paul. His writings are sometimes referred to as being Gnostic in nature. Whether from his Greek background or possible Gnostic leanings, Paul used technical Greek terms not so obvious to us today. For example, such terms as "Illumination," "Seal," "Perfect," "Fully Grown" (meaning initiated), "I have learned the secret" (meaning I have been initiated), and the word "gnosis" itself were from Greek mystical traditions.[629]

In the end, Paul remains a mixed and enigmatic figure. He is both a firebrand who organized and nurtured the survival of the earliest Christian churches, a usurper of the movement begun by Yeshua, as well as the author of some poetically beautiful writings. Clearly, since he was not himself transformed, he transformed the world around him in his own personal image. Like all teachers, he taught what he knew, and those teachings were shaped by what he was.

Chapter 39

The Struggle for Identity, Survival, and Power

New Focus, New Messiah, and Elimination of Factions

At the time of Paul, the movement's celebrations were of two kinds. There were synagogue-like meetings with scripture readings, prayer, singing, and preaching that anyone could attend. There was also the love feast, open only to believers in which the "Last Supper" was commemorated by sharing the body and blood of Yeshua.[630] In this way, both Judaic and Hellenic roots found expression.

Admission into the community became gradually formalized to include instruction, baptism, confirmation, laying on of hands, anointing with oil, the sign of the cross, and a vow to give up old practices. The Holy Spirit might descend upon the new member.[631]

Followers of the new Christian movement separated themselves from Jews by refusing to struggle against the Romans in Jerusalem in 70 CE, by not supporting messianic leaders in the revolts against Rome of 115-117 and 132-135, and through the teachings of Paul that offended many of the Jews.[632]

Traditional Jews lost interest in the Yeshuite/Christian movement over the failure of their hoped-for messianic deliverance. Since Jews were still under another's yoke, Yeshua could not possibly have been their messiah.[633] Even the apostles were faced with this "failure." Their concept of sacrifice did not include resurrection of the sacrificial lamb and so their messianic expectations died on the cross with him. They were forced to redefine the nature of the messiah – at least for them. The fact that the language was now Greek, and the messiah was called "Christ," helped to blur the distinction: but it is not just a difference of language. The Jewish messiah was to have been an earthly leader from among them. This new messiah/Christ was not a warrior leader appointed by their god to lead the chosen people but was now the *incarnation* of their god. He was embedded in the material world as a human life. He taught by example, asserted the blasphemous claim that "I and my Father are One," and "saved" his people not by military victory but through his own death. This left Jews in a political status quo. Through all this, Yeshua's identity was taken over by Greek mystery traditions that included the earlier Jewish and Pagan sacrifice of the first-born. What he *was* took precedence over what he *taught*.

The separatist Essenes were lost with the abolition of Qumran. Jewish military and political hopes fell with the downfall of the Zealots at Masada. The priestly Sadducees lost their influence in the rebellion against Nero, which resulted in a slaughter of Jews, the destruction of Jerusalem and final burning of the Temple in 66 CE.[634] This left the legalistic Pharisees to carry Judaism into the future and, ironically, the Christians to carry forth the priestly doctrine of the first-born who is sacrificed to redeem the sins of the people through his blood offering.

Rome and Christianity

Christians were not at first popular with Rome. Since the time of Augustus' rule as emperor from 27 BCE to 14 CE, there had been a move to repress social dissidents along with astrologers, magicians and followers of foreign religious cults and philosophers.[635] The Roman historian Tacitus described the Christian movement as a "deadly superstition".[636]

A fire in Rome in 64 CE was blamed on Christians. Their refusal to acknowledge any lord but their own resulted in charges of atheism, and their secret meetings were imagined to be sexual orgies and cannibalism.[637] Under Roman law, servants of Christians were tortured until they eventually "confessed" that Christians committed these sexual atrocities and cannibalism.[638] One of Nero's "reforms" was to impose penalties on the Christians because they were judged to be practicing a superstitious magic.[639] Christians learned these lessons well for they were to use the same odious methods and accusations on those who later came under *their* power.

Disasters falling to the Roman Empire indicated to Romans that the gods were angry because of the atheism of the Christians. (We hear similar accusations today by Christians toward those they judge.) In the year 249, the emperor Decius began persecutions but was soon killed himself. Persecutions were renewed by Valerian in 257, but he was captured by the Persians in 259. Persecutions were renewed in 303 but, by then, there were so many Christians that persecution was an expensive prospect.

While Christians were being persecuted by the State, they were also splintered among themselves – each faction claiming to be the true lineage. None, however, better knew the uses of power than the church at Rome. Clement, Bishop of Rome (c.90 - 100) warned that whoever disobeyed the authority of the church would be put to death.[640] This shows a total departure from the teachings of Yeshua and began a satanic shadow that would dog both Roman and Protestant Christian sects into modern times.

The sect at Rome modeled itself after the despised Roman government. and adapted the model of a Roman political and military organization[641] (including the torture and killing of dissidents). By the beginning of the second century, its growth led to the hierarchical stratification of the congregation, with a bishop at its head who had elders and deacons as subordinates. As the Church became formalized and centralized, itinerant preachers and prophets gradually disappeared.[642] The "word of God" would no longer come unpredictably from among the people and prophets but was more and more confined to the central authority at Rome. So, by 200 CE, Christianity had ranks of bishops, priests, and deacons. Bishop Irenaeus and his followers insisted that there was no salvation outside of his church.[643] We saw this same centralization of the Hebrew faith as authority was exclusively claimed for the priests and Temple in Jerusalem. Priests replaced prophets.

Nevertheless, there were any number of vigorous movements that had arisen out of the Yeshuite experience. There were the secret societies of initiates, the lineages of each of the surviving apostles, and others who claimed the same sort of authority as Saul/Paul did: declaring their revelation of the true Christ. With these divergent sects came additional gospels.

Then, about the year 200, another boundary was drawn between the Jews and Christians. Jewish law was codified by Rabbi Judah the Prince.[644] This establishment of Jewish cannon was at least partly in response to the growing number of Christian scriptures. It allowed Judaism to disinherit the Christian movement and its new scriptures. Christianity had finally become its own religion.

Chapter 40

Be Ye Transformed

Like ripples in a pond, the impact of the Yeshuite movement spread in many directions and took different forms. One of the most vigorous sects was that of the Gnostics. Despite the efforts of those who opposed them, libraries of Gnostic writings have survived to speak for themselves.

Gnostics shared one common desire: a search for deeper insights based on direct spiritual experience. They yearned for an immanent experience of the Divine. Standing on the foundation laid by Yeshua, they had trouble accepting Yahweh's treatment of his chosen people. Nor did they accept the idea that laws would take humankind to a better state. Laws were for "maintenance," not growth. At their best, Gnostics sought a personal realization of the Divine. Perhaps more than any other group, they sought to practice the prophecy of Jeremiah that the law would be written on the heart, thereby eliminating the need for teachers. They reflected Yeshua's promise of a *realization of the Presence* – to know and experience directly the kingdom of heaven – not as a past or future event, but as a present reality.

Despite their diversity, an examination of what identified Gnostics as such will show us why the establishment opposed it with such vehemence. The Gnostic movement was a way of looking at the world that was larger than a specific religion. Thus, Christians, Jews, and others could continue their prior traditions and still be "Gnostic"[645] – at least for a while.

Gnostic belief made an implicit call for return to visionary experiences and implied that those beyond the small circle of apostolic successors would also have visions of the Lord and receive divine teaching. Gnostics spoke of secrets and esoteric teachings that came from Yeshua and the apostles. These secrets were taught privately to those who were "spiritually mature".[646]

Gnosticism, despite its reliance on the teachings of Yeshua, had roots that extended into pre-Christian times. It reflects diverse threads that included Indian principles absorbed in Babylon, various mysteries,[647] the emphasis on inner qualities professed by the Greek Stoics,[648] and Greek cosmic dualism.

The Christian Gnostics, however, claimed apostolic succession directly from Yeshua and from his disciples which would, of course, compete with Paul's claim of appointment by Yeshua.

Creation by the Demiurge

For the Gnostic, the behavior of Yahweh – the god of the Old Testament – was too inferior to be considered the absolute Deity of the Universe. In addition, they had a more complex view of the creation of the world. In the fullness or pleroma before creation, they thought there were 15 pairs of male and female emanations or "aeons" the youngest of which was Sophia (Wisdom). She brought forth a daughter from whom came the demiurge, YHWH.[649] The world was created by this foolish demiurge who then boastfully proclaimed himself to be the supreme god when, in fact, the true god stood far behind him. The Old Testament itself proclaimed this demiurge's guilt by virtue of his treatment of humanity.[650] For example, Yahweh and his followers claimed there was nothing before him, told a false story about the origin of things, cast blame elsewhere for the source of evil in the world, showed fear of his creation, and set up barriers to knowing the truth. This demiurge came to be the god of Israel, established his laws, and judged those who violated them.[651] In addition to the emanations of the deity known as aeons, there were also "archons" who were active evil forces.[652]

The Unknown God

The True God for the Gnostics was a dyad of masculine and feminine, father and mother. It did not seem, however, to come from Pagan traditions of the Mother Goddess, for the language used was specifically Judeo-Christian.[653] Gnostics themselves differed on some of the conceptions of this male-female view but the fact that it existed at all is notable. One Gnostic text refers to the Holy Spirit as being "the Mother." Thus, the trinity was comprised of Father, Mother and Son, as in Egypt; yet one of the texts from the Valentinian school taught the *oneness* of the heavenly father.[654]

A strong dualism placed the True God well apart from the created world. In fact, the world is the product of lower powers who themselves lack adequate knowledge of the absolute God.[655] This comes from the Gnostic view that the Unknown God "created" not by fabricating something apart from itself but through "emanations" of its own divine attributes.[656]

The True God is unknown and yet yearns to be known.[657]

Genesis

The Garden of Eden story had a special meaning to the Gnostic mind. In the Garden, Yahweh reveals his fear of the man and woman, and his inability to know where they were when they hid. And he lied to Adam and Eve by saying that on the day they ate of the fruit, they would die.[658] The serpent, however, told them the truth: "Of course you will not die. God knows that, as soon as you eat it, your eyes will be opened and you will be like gods knowing both good and evil".[659] Thus, the serpent was a primal earthly intelligence – the voice of divinity speaking through nature[660] and was more reliable than Yahweh.

The opening of the eyes of Adam and Eve was not a "fall" but, rather, liberation from unconsciousness, ignorance, and irresponsibility. Thus Eve, rather than a gullible temptress of Adam, initiated him into conscious life.[661] In another interpretation, Ptolemy, a follower of Valentinus, interpreted the story of Adam and Eve to indicate the way in which humanity *fell* into their *ordinary consciousness*, losing touch with the Divine.[662]

In any event, the serpent in the Garden of Eden begins the process of salvation as it attempts to awaken Adam and Eve who are benumbed not by Edenic pleasures but by the commandments of the demiurge. The awakening of the primal couple began Gnosis.

The Way of Transformation

Human problems have often been seen to arise from attachment and ways of thinking that are distorted by the material world – hence the need to detach from it. This led some Gnostic sects to renounce the world, but this was not the norm. They sought liberation from a false world of conditioned minds. It would be more accurate to view Gnostics as anti-system rather than against the world, since the Greek word 'kosmos' and the Hebrew word 'olam' are frequently mistranslated as 'world' when, in fact, they refer to the concept of systems. It is never *ge* – the earth – that is condemned.[663]

The status of humanity is greater than any system and more than the created world or materiality (*hyle*). Beyond our materiality is the complex of mind-emotion-image (the *psyche*), and beyond that is the spirit of the indwelling soul (*pneuma*). The Gnostic quest was to effectively awaken that indwelling soul.[664]

Neither faith nor obedience to the law were adequate for achieving gnosis. In general, the transformation of the mind was accomplished by detaching from the world, turning toward a direct knowledge or "gnosis" of holiness, and by the union of opposites.

The Virtue of Non-Attachment

Humankind is immersed in the material world and is "asleep" or "intoxicated" by the poison of the world caused by ignorance.[665] Humanity needs liberation through knowledge of its true origin and destiny. Thus, the inner self is to be released from the bonds of the world.[666] Gnostics' denial of the world was the most radical of the ancient belief systems.[667]

Some extremists expressed their contempt for the world by either asceticism or libertinism. Ascetics attempted to remain uncontaminated by worldly affairs while libertines tried to achieve freedom from the world. Most of them preferred celibacy since offspring would increase this world and its suffering.[668]

Even love was considered a "great seduction"[669] that threatened to trap humankind in the material world – and more so for sexual love and sensual pleasure.

To Go Beyond Opposites

In the *Gospel of Philip,* we see the Gnostic quest to take the struggle over good and bad actions from the external world and place its moral significance inside the individual. Therefore, an act is neither good nor bad, but its significance rests on the situation, intentions, and level of consciousness of the participants. Thus, the paths of the legalists, whose roots originate in the pronouncements of Yahweh, are distractions from the true way of goodness that calls us to remove the moat from our own eye.[670]

To attempt to resolve opposites requires us to go beyond "conflicting dualism"[671] toward a "complementary dualism." The former reflects the Parsiian concept of the Wise Lord against the Evil Lord and its parallel of Yahweh against Satan. It's a step beyond this dualism to reach the transcendent God, recognizing that the two are of the same reality as is stated in Isaiah 45:7.

> "I am the Lord, there is no other; I make the light, I create darkness, author alike of prosperity and trouble. I, the Lord, do all these things."

Rather than disparate antagonists, "the light and the darkness, life and death, the right and the left, are brothers to one another. It is not possible to separate them from one another. Because of this, neither are the good good, nor the evil evil, nor is life a life, or death a death. Because of this each will be resolved into its origin from the beginning." (*Gospel of Philip*).[672]

Direct Knowledge

Humankind is a mixture of material and spiritual elements. Spiritual elements create the yearning to return to the god.[673] Thus, direct knowledge of ultimate realities is not only possible but is our destiny. This was not meant as a theoretical or theological idea but the "Gnosis cardias" – the knowledge of the heart. Hence, gnosis was not a profession of faith, or obedience to a set of laws, nor justification by faith or works, but insight and transformation.[674] Such knowledge would have a liberating effect[675] and would free people from laws intended for the uninitiated. Faith for most Gnostics was but an intermediate step, as it opened the way to true gnosis.[676] The Gnostic Kingdom of God resided inside the transformed consciousness of the knower,[677] as indicated in Luke's rendering that "the kingdom of God is within you."

While the Pauline Roman sect separated their god from his creation and spoke of sin and repentance, Gnostics, on the other hand, considered the self and the Divine as identical. Instead of sin and repentance, Gnostics spoke of illusion and enlightenment. For Gnostics, to intuitively know oneself at the deepest level, is to know God.[678]

Since a part of us is of the divine nature, a profound knowledge of self will lead the Gnostic toward knowing God. Consequently, their writings contain such psychological insights as "if you bring forth what is within you, what you bring forth will save you. If you do not bring forth what is within you, what you do not bring forth will destroy you" which was a saying of Jesus in the Gospel of Thomas. Also, in the gospel of Philip, we find, "you see yourself, and what you see you shall [become]".[679]

Expanding on Yeshua's admonition that lust within the heart or anger unspoken is still an act, Philip says "as for ourselves, *let each one of us dig down after the root of evil which is within one, and let one pluck it out of one's heart from the root.* It will be plucked out if we recognize it, but if we are ignorant of it, it takes root in us and produces its fruit in our heart; it masters us... It is powerful because we have not recognized it".[680] We find a recognition of this reality today not only in psychodynamic and psychoanalytic psychology, but in shamanic writings as well.

Thus, redemption was attained neither through adherence to the law nor by sacrifice nor through the grace of the resurrection – all being external – but through a direct realization of gnosis.

Yeshua

In Gnostic thinking, Yeshua was the emergence of the *true* God's son – not Yahweh's. Yeshua never referred to his deity as Jehovah or Yahweh.[681] Rather, Yeshua came to teach people the Way to gnosis that would set them free from the errors of this world. As we have seen, Jesus/Yeshua told his disciples that they had been given the "secret of the Kingdom of God" which was kept from the others.[682] In Matthew, he is quoted as saying "to you it has been given to know the secrets [mysteria; literally, "mysteries"] of the Kingdom of Heaven, but to them it has not been given." Yeshua went out to meet those who wander away from the fold – the prodigal son, the lost sheep, the sinners, and the tax gatherers.

Marcion, one of the Gnostic leaders, took the crucifixion of Yeshua to be not for the remission of sins but "for the cancellation of the creator's claim to his property".[683] Some Gnostics believed in Docetism, and asserted that, since the material world is impure, the perfect Christ could not have had a physical body.[684] Regardless of the Docetist's view, it was the non-material Christ that was the true divine representative.[685] Others, however, believed that Yeshua was a good person who became an instrument of the Christ spirit that united with him at John's baptism.[686] Indeed, a document called "Melchizedek" states quite clearly that Christ was born, ate, was circumcised, lived in the flesh and suffered.[687]

Gnostics rejected any repetition of the eucharist, saying it was a sacrament that could be received once in a lifetime. They also had a death rite, to give a view of what happens after death.[688] Gnostics spoke of Jesus having appeared to them after the crucifixion in a spirit body. They were accused of fraud by the orthodox.[689] Gnostics, however, were not the only ones who considered that we receive spirit communications directly from the deity. To this day, Baptists, Quakers, and some charismatics have the same idea. Paul's entire significance and authority rests on such a visitation.

Variations of Gnosticism

Although most Gnostic sects shared such concepts as the corrupt nature of the world and a need for direct gnosis, they were neither unified nor consistent among themselves. Ten to twenty Gnostic sects have been identified, but one fourth-century writer reported 60.[690] One of the complaints of Roman Church Father Tertullian against the Gnostics was that they maintained harmony with one another. The writings of the heresiologists, however, are not supported by evidence from the Gnostic texts themselves.[691] Of the various groups, the followers of Valentinus were one of the most prominent.

VALENTINUS

A spiritual teacher named Valentinus joined the Christian church at Rome. Prior to that, he had established himself among the Christians in Alexandria as a poet, visionary and spiritual teacher.[692] He went to Rome about 140 CE where he taught until he was accused of heresy. Since he already had his own school, he was able to continue his activity in Rome. He is thought to have died about 160.[693]

Valentinus called for spiritual illumination over faith and baptism. His followers claimed access to deeper mysteries from Paul not available to the public at large.[694] He claimed that his tradition came from Theudas who was initiated by Paul himself.

Theudas initiated Valentinus.[695] The followers of Valentinus referred to themselves as "Disciples of Christ".[696]

In this way, Valentinus affirmed what was already in place and then encouraged his followers to take the additional inward step. The purpose of the Valentinian initiation was to allow the candidate to reject the creator's authority and affirm the True God from which comes our spiritual origin. To these Gnostics, laws and church structure instituted by the demiurge were necessary only for the uninitiated. Those who were initiated had no such need.[697]

Valentinian groups celebrated five ceremonies or sacraments: baptism, anointing, eucharist, "redemption," and "bridal chamber".[698] Because he viewed the creation of the world as pairs of emanations of a sexual nature, a Valentinian celebration was enacted on the evening preceding the day of the Roman Lupercalia, which was on February 15. Valentinians witnessed and imitated the coming together of divine aeons in the bridal chamber.[699] This rite of the bridal chamber was to recognize that the developed Gnostic is bride to the angels.[700] This love ritual, begun on the evening of February 14, is now celebrated as Valentine's Day. The Church later needed its own "St. Valentine" to turn attention away from Valentinus and found or invented a Roman martyr called Valentine of Terni and placed his death on February 14, 269.

BASILIDES

Basilides (85-145) claimed his lineage from Peter.[701] The writing of Basilides is distinguished from other Gnostic writers in ignoring any Evil Principle. The source of the Basilidan theory may have been Egyptian.[702]

MARCION

Marcion became prominent in the Roman Church's affairs after his arrival there in the year 140, but he was excommunicated in 144.[703] To him we owe the terms "Old Testament" and "New Testament." In response to Marcion's "canon," the Roman church created its own, which included both Old and New Testaments.[704]

Marcion was rare among Gnostics in asserting the importance of faith.[705] He endorsed asceticism in order to reduce the amount of the created world through the prohibition of sexuality and marriage.[706] His church was the greatest danger to the Roman sect in the second century. Eventually, legislation of fourth-century emperors against heresies brought it down.[707]

Political Ramifications

Gnostic beliefs and practices posed tremendous threats not only to the religious authority of the growing church at Rome, but also eventually to the Roman government. The importance of internal motivation rather than external commandments[708] and their rejection of all systems placed Gnostics outside of the laws of church and state. Not all commandments came from the True God, they said. Law is for the unenlightened and does not apply to Gnostics.[709] What's more, Gnostics accused the church of setting up an imitation organization which violated the true brotherhood,[710] and of becoming more and more like the Roman government.

Since only personal contact with the Divine has authority, there can be no institutionalized structure of authority. And, since Gnostics generally rejected ranks and hierarchies, they found a practical way to maintain their services: they drew lots. Therefore, anyone could be selected to serve as priest, bishop, or prophet. Not only could there be no establishment of permanent hierarchies, but human influence was taken out of this choice since the chance of the lots was determined by God.[711]

Gnostic rejection of systems also included cultural conventions. Although some considered marriage, children, and employment as inferior to the realization of Gnosis,[712] others rejected it all: money, power, families, government, and taxes. Nor were they interested in social reform since, in a fundamentally corrupt world, it would not cure the soul of its entrapment.[713]

Gnostics also challenged church and state in their valuation of women. Gnosis, with its emphasis on wisdom, presented Sophia as a feminine power. The implications are, like their interpretation of the Adam and Eve story, that it is feminine power which gives rise to knowledge.[714] Among Valentinians, women were not only equal to men but might serve as prophets, teachers, traveling evangelists, healers, and priestesses. However, not all Gnostics were supportive of women. One Gnostic text calls for disciples to avoid women because of their power of sexuality.[715]

The image of the Gnostics as amoral is in direct contrast to their sober doctrines and ethics[716] as found in the Nag Hammadi Texts.

Summary

To Gnostics, there was a supreme being, absolute and all powerful. It was sometimes known as Abraxus or Abrasax. Beneath this all-powerful being were other powers who could act with relative independence. Because of their relative distance from the center of absolute being, however, they shared progressively less in the perfect light and, therefore, could be subject to error.

Many Gnostics judged the creator of the world to be full of error because the material world was a place lacking in light, intending to seduce them to forget who they were and from where they came. Yahweh, if he were the creator of this sin, error, and darkness, must himself be wrong. Christ, however, was the son of the *Supreme* Deity sent to show the light, to show his followers the way of liberation from the hypnotic seduction of the world and lead them back to the light that had been humanity's ultimate origin.

In short, the overall, the goal of human life was to escape from this world's enchantments for the eventual hoped-for realization of direct Gnosis.

The Gnostic Obituary

Three primary factors contributed to the demise of the Gnostics as a viable movement. The first came from suppression by the church at Rome and the Roman government. The other two came from the beliefs of the Gnostics themselves. So, the second factor was their diversity. One of their initial strengths – the inspiration to create new and varied expressions of their own system of beliefs – contributed to their demise since they lacked a firm identity that could be replicated and passed on.

Third, their beliefs did not encourage earthly permanence of any kind. Although part of their appeal rested on a recognition of worldly corruption and a yearning for a higher form of relationship with a god of better character than that shown in the Old Testament, their hatred of the world was too antagonistic toward life, toward hope and toward common experiences. After all, if one were unable to reach the elevated experiences of direct *gnosis*, there was no god to be found. Under Gnostic teachings, even small pleasures became snares to entrance people into attachment to this world.

In short, Gnostics offered grand promises of heavenly visions but could not reliably produce them; and called for rejection of any other pleasurable experiences of life. Their shadow was created by part of their own ideology that confined how the light of the True God could come to them, and subsequent interpretations of the emanations of creation.

Gnostic Gifts

Despite their extremes and negative world view, fertile ideas arose from Gnostic precepts. One may look at the varieties of admonitions from Gnostics not necessarily as world denying but a means to alter consciousness that we may attain a different perspective of the habits of thought that tie us to the ordinary perception of things. Those who espouse faith and belief, rather than a direct knowing, are *agnostic*.

Indeed, why a group of sects whose beliefs and practices gave them little if any chance of competing with the physical organization of the church should draw such vehemence is an interesting question. One answer might be that human beings, indeed, contain within their hearts a yearning for direct spiritual inner experience that transcends human-made dogmas and external pleasures. This would be a threat to any establishment.

Over time the Christian sect and the Roman government had common cause to suppress Gnosticism because it challenged the totalitarian authority of both. The

Roman cult and state prevailed, of course, but not without being influenced by their struggle with the Gnostics.

Chapter 41

Church Fathers and the Creation of Heresy

Heresy requires a canon of orthodoxy, of course. A boundary must be laid out by some authority to determine what will be accepted inside the boundary and what will be relegated to the outside. This, along with acquisition of temporal power by religious authority, led to one of the greatest intellectual and moral straightjackets in history.

Marcion, although not considered Gnostic by all writers, downgraded Yahweh of the Old Testament as being of inferior moral quality. To Marcion, the True God had created an invisible and spiritual world and was not known by the old prophets. Christ was the first to reveal the True God. Like Gnostics, Marcion held that humans were in bondage to their bodies because they came from the god of the Old Testament, but their souls may be freed through their faith in Yeshua/Jesus. Because of these beliefs, Marcion broke off from the church at Rome.[717] As a result of similar differences among Christian factions, various churches began to set their own boundaries by establishing canons and creeds.

About the year 180, Irenaeus, Bishop of Lyons, complained about heretics who said that there were other gospels that had been widely circulated. These other gospels were, according to him, heresies. Eventually, Irenaeus decreed that Valentinians and other Gnostics were agents of Satan.[718]

The Gnostics, as we've seen, who questioned whether all suffering and death comes from sin, included a feminine element in the divine, celebrated the godhead as father and mother, suggested Christ's resurrection to have a symbolic meaning, and denounced Catholic Christians as the heretics.[719] Thus, to other sects at the time, the Roman Church was the heretical deviate.

By the year 200, any feminine imagery in orthodoxy was eliminated[720] by the Roman sect. This was in stark contrast to the Gnostic Sophia, the gospels' "Wisdom," and recognition by most of the Pagan world of the feminine values of relationship and family over celibacy and hierarchy. But "church fathers" were not content with eliminating any feminine presence from their organization and dogmas. They also took a militant stance against woman, sexuality, and freedom. Tertullian, who died in 230, used Genesis 3 to warn women that they were "the devil's gateway",[721] and also described woman as "a temple over a sewer".[722] He admonished women that they should wear mourning clothes since they are descendants of Eve who was the source of human misery,[723] as though men did not also descend from her.

Not only did the orthodox Origen (185 to 254) castrate himself, but one of his disciples founded a castrant sect.[724] "Every woman should be overwhelmed with shame at the very thought that she is a woman," said St. Clement. "To be fully developed as a human being is to be born a male," said Thomas Aquinas.[725]

The misogynist tone of Christian religion has been attributed by some to a fear of the Goddess religions. If we were to view Christianity as a person with traumatic early experiences, it is only natural that those experiences would infect the church with an automatic fear years later. The Roman church and some Protestant sects still fear anything resembling goddess veneration because it provokes hidden memories not only of Jewish exile and punishment by Yahweh for their temptation to participate in the local Goddess religions, but also these threats to early Christianity.

Of primary importance to the Church was the need to claim total and irrevocable religious authority centralized into one human organization. Church fathers were already forming their boundaries in response to Gnostic and Roman threats along political lines that reinterpreted scriptures. They made their Deity a limited and exclusive commodity accessible only through the established hierarchy and its rituals. The teachings of Yeshua were already lost in this return to old structures of domination, law, and violence.

Chapter 42

The Mithraic Mysteries

Out of the various mystery cults in the Roman world, another almost-hidden force influenced the Roman church that was mentioned earlier. A remarkable set of symbols of the Mithraic Mysteries suggests yet another tendril of the multiple sources for shaping the evolving Christian church.

Mithras and Mythology

The name *Mithras* is from Indo-Iranian and means "the middle one." Mithras was not the sun but related to it.[726] In fact, he stood higher than the visible sun but lower than Ahura Mazda. He was considered a creator and orderer of the universe and, therefore, the logos or word.[727] Ahura Mazda (or Ormuzd) was the spirit of good, and Mithras or light was his helper. The evil spirit was called the "Lie Demon." Therefore, the opponent of Mithraic light was not darkness but the lie.[728]

December 25 was the date of the Mithraic festival honoring the end of the winter solstice[729] and was celebrated as the date of Mithras' virgin birth,[730] an event witnessed by shepherds.[731] There were elaborate rituals and celebrations with bells, hymns, candle lighting, gift giving, and sacraments of bread and water administered to initiates.[732]

Mithras' life reached its climax in a struggle against a great bull that represented the forces of darkness. Mithras, exhausted by the battle, was laid on a bier and mourned for as if dead. He was then placed in a rock tomb called "Petra" where he lay for three days after which he was removed from his tomb with great rejoicing. He held a last supper with his disciples and returned to heaven.[733] The bull's death and its blood fructified the earth. On Black Friday, the Taurobolium, or bull-slaying, was represented. At this festival, the sacrament could include blood drinking.[734]

Mithraic initiation and sacrificial meals – for men only – occurred in "caves." The symbol of the slaying of the bull by Mithras was central. This male Mithraic religion was favored among soldiers, merchants, and officials of the Roman Empire.[735] In fact, Mithras became the most popular god of the soldiers.[736] The activities were secret and never intended to become a mass movement. Their "caves," or Mithraea, would only hold about 20 men. When membership increased beyond that, a new Mithraum was established.[737]

There was a 12-day initiation into the Mithraic mysteries.[738] Neophytes came into Mithraism through a rite of baptism and celebrated a eucharist of bread and water[739] or wine in which the priest personified Mithras.[740] The bread in this eucharist was a round cake symbolic of the solar disk. It was called Mizd, which may be the origin of the word missa, or mass.[741]

Three Mithraic holy days correspond to Christianity's Christmas, Easter, and Epiphany.[742] Sunday was referred to as the "Lord's Day" because of its sacredness to Mithras and, no doubt, its association with the Sun.

Mithras will return at the end of the world to fight a final victorious battle over evil, to judge people, and lead his own to immortality. Believers prepared for these end times by sacraments, initiation,[743] and adherence to their strict moral code.[744]

This remained a secret society of men governed by a sacred order and seven grades of initiation.[745] A man might be a Mithraicist and yet accept the doctrines of other sects, including Christianity.[746]

Mythologies of Mithras and Christ bear many similarities. Both carried titles of being "The Way," "The Truth," "The Light," "The Life," "The Word," "The Son of God," and "The Good Shepherd." Both were portrayed as carrying a lamb on their shoulders. Both were said to be born of virgins. Mithras' literal rock named "Petra" paralleled Yeshua's symbolic *Peter*.[747] Mithras had a one-piece robe like Christ's seamless one.[748] References to Mithras as the "unconquered sun"[749] become even more significant when we reach the time of Constantine.

Despite Mithras' name, his Iranian connections have been questioned. Furthermore, it has been suggested that the images of the slaying of the Bull suggest an awareness of the precession of the equinoxes known by at least 128 BCE and used to indicate the death of the previous age.[750] Thus, through identification of the precession of the equinox, Mithras was given a power greater than sun and stars. Although it was the time of transition from Aries to the Piscean Age, the death of the bull to mark the transition from the age of Taurus to Aries would have been from two millennia earlier.

The similarities of Mithraic practice to developing Christianity did not go unnoticed. Justin Martyr and Tertullian both remarked on the similarity of the Mithraic sacraments to their own Christian ones but claimed that the pre-existing Mithraic ones were imitations of the later Christian ones.[751]

Chapter 43

Romanization: From State Enemy to State Religion

We remember from Chapter 39 that, when disasters struck the Roman Empire, the "atheism" of Christians was blamed for making the gods angry, and various persecutions followed. However, Constantine the Great, who lived from about 280 to 337, was the second ambitious opportunist to take advantage of the momentum of the Christian movement and usurp its resources for his own purposes. A mythology of Constantine as the first Christian emperor has been fed by his elimination of the ancient sanctuary of Ashtoreth at Ephaca and suppression of the worship of Ashtoreth throughout Canaan.[752] In a move on Italy in 312, a legend tells of his vision of a cross on the sun.[753] Constantine let the persecution of Christians lapse and, also in 312, he made an official edict for the tolerance of *all* religions but especially patronized Christianity.[754] His mother, Helena, was a devout Christian who promoted the establishment of churches. After his vision, he did not, in fact, abandon Paganism, either publicly or privately.[755] He did, nevertheless, empower the Christian movement toward homogenization and unification.

Constantine was said to have been initiated into a sun cult just before his famous vision, which is generally interpreted as Christian but was marked by the symbol of *Sol Invictus* – the unconquerable sun. To establish unity in his country and consolidate his power, he encouraged the blurring of boundaries among the most prominent groups of the Christians, Mithraicists, and Sol Invictus. In 321 he ordered Sunday to be the day of rest – as was the custom among Mithraicists.[756] He eliminated his co-emperor in 324 and took for himself the estates and treasures of most, but not all, of the Pagan temples. He gave enough to Christians to build large churches.[757]

He left his mark on Christian orthodoxy by convening the Council of Nicea in 325. By declaring that Yeshua/Jesus was a god, Yeshua could then be identified with Sol Invictus. With Yeshua officially declared as *the* Son of God, Constantine was protected from the emergence of other potential messiahs. Meanwhile, he built churches for Christians as well as statues of Cybele and Sol Invictus.[758] Thenceforth political considerations shaped Christian orthodoxy.[759] The council of Nicaea, incidentally, ruled against castration.[760]

In 326 Constantine ordered heretical books to be destroyed[761] which included not only Christian "heresies" but also "pagan" authors that referred to Yeshua/Jesus. Further unification of church and state under his power came with a fixed income paid to the church and by installing the bishop of Rome in the Lateran Palace.[762]

In 331, he financed the production of new copies of the Bible that had been largely hidden or destroyed in persecutions by Diocletian in 303.[763] This allowed a singular opportunity to revise and edit fine points of doctrine, suppress disapproved scriptures, and further consolidate his power over church and state. Thus, Constantine became the sponsor and controlling interest in the Christian Bible.

Church organization and its wealth meant there were two powers in the empire in a symbiotic relationship. Bishops accepted Constantine's patronage and followed his directives.[764] Church authorities sought to use the government against their enemies.

The Christianity of Constantine is questionable. He had his wife Faustia boiled alive and his son murdered.[765] When he dedicated his new city of Constantinople in 330, he did so with Pagan rites.[766] Coins and banners of the realm retained images of Sol Invictus, and Constantine was not baptized until he lay on his deathbed in 337.[767] His real importance to Christianity was the way in which he nurtured its growth while shaping it to serve his needs.

Christianity was thus made acceptable as it was blended with other cults – in a structure that was palatable and nonthreatening to the Roman emperor. Thus, Christianity gained "world" domination at the expense of its revolutionary origins. What's more, the enlightened and charismatic nature of Yeshua was drafted into the service of temporal powers. Christianity thus survived in name by its adaptability, its capacity for changing its face, by its firm boundary and canon, and finally its absorption into the Roman Empire. In adapting, it dispensed with its original teachings and became the ally of its greatest persecutor, the Roman Empire.

The meaning of the original creeds, meant to establish Christian canon, also suffered under translation. The Nicene Creed, shaped by Constantine's need to prevent new messiahs from threatening his rule, was adopted in 325 and expanded in 381. It asserted that the Father, Son, and Holy Spirit were "one in essence" but showing itself in "three hypostases" meaning individualized manifestations. When the translations went from Greek to Latin, however, the word for "manifestations" became more concrete by the use of the word *persona* and, as a result, distinct personalities were suggested instead of the original point of the unified substance.[768] Christianity has ever since struggled with a polytheistic trinity in a nominally monotheistic religion.

With this incestuous blending of church and state, each was safe from the other. Leaders arose, driven by their private obsessions to further shape the growing body of church doctrine. Here is a sampling of some of those leaders and their impact.

LIBERIUS

Liberius, became Pope in 352. During his tenure, the Emperor Constantius proclaimed, "My will is the canon" reflecting the danger of this marriage of church and state.[769] Liberius fixed December 25 as the celebration of the birth of Yeshua because it was the Roman celebration of the solstice.[770] He died in 366.

JEROME

Jerome (c 347 - c 420) renounced his Pagan learning in 373 and spent four years as a hermit after which he was ordained and became a favorite with Roman ladies. He translated the scriptures from their original languages into Latin. Using the writings of Paul, Jerome claimed that "all sexual intercourse is unclean".[771] Marriage had little worth to Jerome except that virgins were produced.[772]

AUGUSTINE

Augustine (354-430), who became a bishop in North Africa, left an indelible mark on the development of the Roman church and consequently on the psyche of much of the western world through his doctrine of "original sin." He had studied Cicero and, for a while, was a follower of Manichaeism but could not give up his pleasures of the flesh. In his Confessions, he prayed "Grant me chastity and continence, but not yet".[773] His faltering on ascetic strivings reinforced his Manichean idea that flesh was evil. This, however, seems to have been tempered by his brush with Neo-Platonism which, after the philosophy of Plotinus, claimed that all reality is a series of emanations arising from one perfect form. Thus, although matter was at the outer edge of these emanations and was least pure, it was not inherently evil.

He found comfort in New Testament admonitions to put aside lusts of the flesh, eventually converted to Christianity, and became celibate. He claimed humankind was "bound by original sin".[774] Thus, he overturned Jewish tradition and the first 400 years of the Christian movement by transforming the meaning of Genesis from freedom and self-mastery to that of bondage to sexual sin. For him, Adam's sin, blamed on Eve, corrupted all of nature and, since sexual desire is of itself sinful, infants automatically share their parent's sexual nature and are consequently infected with "original sin".[775]

Augustine's tortured doctrine of "original sin" was not universally accepted. Among others, a monk named Pelagius took issue and said that, although Adam erred, it did not reduce humankind's aptitude for goodness. Augustine prevailed, however. He also claimed divine representation for his church, saying that no one could be saved outside of the church.[776] Augustine also claimed that the church was the visible kingdom of God, thus making it a physical reality rather than what Yeshua had taught.[777] He persuaded many bishops and several Christian emperors to help drive out of the church those who held to the original traditions of Christian freedom by calling them "heretics".[778]

Augustine's views were debated even after his death in 430 until the Council of Orange in 529 when he was finally endorsed. Those who disagreed with Augustine, claiming that he repudiated the goodness of God's creation and the freedom of humanity, were condemned as heretics. While Augustine saw death as a punishment for sin, Julian saw it as natural but not voluntary and, therefore, not having to do with choice. It is our choices, Julian said, that determine our spiritual destiny, not suffering or involuntary situations.

There were political reasons for imposing such ideas but there is always a question in my mind of why anyone would accept a perverse doctrine such as Original Sin. One reason may well be that people would rather feel guilty than helpless; another may be that the burden of bad behavior no longer rests fully on the individual because it is inherent in his or her nature. Whatever the reasons, Augustine's jaundiced view of human nature left its mark on Christianity, and thereby on much of western culture[779] – a wound yet to be healed.

ATHANASIUS

Augustine's work ended intellectual liberty[780] but he was not alone in his quest for the control of ideas. In 367 Athanasius, the archbishop of Alexandria, ordered that all heretical books be purged. Possession of heretical gospels was made a criminal offense and all possible copies were burned. Someone in Upper Egypt, however, took the banned books and hid them in a jar[781] to be found 1500 years later.

PRISCILLIAN

Priscillian (340-386) has the singular honor of being the first Christian martyred by Christians. He had been ordained as bishop of Avila in Spain but was later charged with heresy in the form of Gnostic doctrines and behaviors.[782]

THEODOCIUS

In C.E. 380, the emperor Theodocius is remembered for closing the temples of the Goddess – and for his massacre of 7,000 people in Thessalonica.[783] Under Theodocius I, a fanatical Christian mob made one of the greatest attacks on knowledge and wisdom by burning the library at Alexandria that contained priceless and irreplaceable writings from the known world.[784] I should note that there were other assaults on the library at Alexandria and other versions of its destruction.

Orthodoxy versus Heresy

Books were not their only enemy. Aided by a man named Cyril in March of 415, Christian monks used oyster shells to cut to pieces one of the greatest scholars of history. Hypatia's crime was that she was a woman who had taught men. Cyril was canonized as a saint.[785]

The orthodox church, to make itself "catholic" or universal, had to include as many people as possible. Tests of spiritual maturity, if they were even possible, would be cumbersome. Therefore, they fell to the Outer Way: external criteria of doctrine, ritual, and loyalty to political structure.[786] Having become the official religion of the Roman state, Christianity used Augustine's arguments to show that humans needed governing.

Meanwhile, Romans, especially the intelligent, paid homage to their gods because they represented natural forces and, in revering them, showed their proper relationship to them. Marcus Aurelius, for example, called these forces *providence*, *necessity*, and *nature*. Justin and some of the other Christians, however, decided that, whatever they were – gods or natural forces – they were demons.[787] Any forces, people or ideas these church leaders could not control were judged to be satanic and thereby lost any right of consideration.

Part of the Romanization of the church obviously involved the suppression of all else. Some scriptures were taboo and burned, people were persecuted or murdered for their beliefs, and doctrines were invented to consolidate power and render the church servant to the state. Furthermore, legends were invented to draw attention away from a threatening reality. As noted before, the Gnostic leader Valentinus posed such a threat that the Roman sect invented a St. Valentine of Persia who was claimed to have been martyred on February 14[788] in order to detract from the Valentinian Rite of the Bridal Chamber.

Many Pagan festivals were ingrained in the traditions of the people who had been celebrating them for eons because they related to archetypal experiences of life, to their survival and affirmation. Since these traditional Pagan celebrations were not easily erased, the church established many of its feast days at times of pre-Christian festivals. What's more, Christian motifs were not entirely foreign to Pagan peoples. The Virgin Mother Mary was to them another form of the Pagan ever-virgin Mother of God. And, since the story of Yeshua parallels other resurrection motifs, he became one more expression of a belief they already held: the resurrected god of their own mythologies.

My point is that the religious principles espoused by the "new" church had already existed from earliest times. Hence the need to destroy "Pagan" practices and beliefs because their very existence showed that the "Christian" rendition in its "New Testament" was but a mask on already existing and pervasive traditions. They took an idea, rite, or feast, called it "catholic" and thereby tried to destroy the evidence that they were imitators. Again and again, the practices and principles of other cultures were assimilated and then the cultures themselves or their writings were destroyed.

In 381, Mary's perpetual virginity was formally established to counter Arianism which had claimed that Yeshua was human. Mary's virginity was a way to allow Yeshua to be both divine, as some Gnostics claimed, and human, as Arians professed. Opponents to this idea were excommunicated.[789]

The religion *of* Yeshua was lost in the struggle over who would control the religion *about* him.

In these early years, as Christianity realized its ambition to become a social and political institution, we see disturbing trends that have continued into recent decades, some of which are very alive today. There is its long history of suppression of heretical writings that have also included the findings of science, suppression of women, and a willingness to excommunicate or murder anyone they saw as a threat. Doctrines were crafted to justify actions of the state. To be fair, early Christians were initially subjected to much of the same oppression – before they adopted the same measures toward *their* enemies and heresies.

This all-too-brief history of the absorption of the early Christian church into the Roman establishment through Constantine's ambition somewhat answers my early question about how the teachings and life of Jesus/Yeshua became the fractious factions, dogmas, rituals and formalities we see today. But I am left with still more questions. What were those other gospels or writings that were so threatening to church and state? What if a Pelagian doctrine of *human goodness* had prevailed instead of Augustine's assertion of the inherent sinfulness of humanity – blamed on Eve? And, what would Christianity have become if it kept the centrality of love, service, mercy, and forgiveness?

Chapter 44

The Evolution of Satan

The post-Yeshua years that gave rise to the church-state symbiosis also spawned another element foreign to earlier Jewish and Yeshuite teachings: the power of a Satan who competes with Yahweh and inspires evil-doing. The Satan we hear about in the discourses of many preachers of the last few centuries was an invention of the early church. Even before the time of Yeshua, Satan's "satanic" character did not appear until the time of Chronicles in the 3rd century BCE.[790]

Lucifer was originally Helel ben Shahar, meaning "Son of the Dawn," and referred to the planet Venus, the last "star" to defy sunrise.[791] To the early Jews, Satan was only a "devil's advocate." His role was to expose the foibles of people and accuse them before God. This Satan was an instrument of God to help teach the people. He was to bring the hidden darknesses of the people into the light of awareness to receive God's teaching and judgment. As such, he was the subordinate servant of his god, charged with bringing shadows into the light.

To expose lies, to uncover deceit, and to accuse evil doing are movements toward the Truth, toward God. He was not God's competitor but an assistant in the way modern court systems use a prosecutor. To them, God was truly all-powerful. Remember the words of Isaiah: this god was the author of all that was in the world, whether of good or evil, light or dark.

Indeed, if there is only one power in the universe, God must be the ultimate source of all that is. Thus, Satan was only a shadow cast by humankind's errors. He was the Mephistophelean spirit who, although intending evil, ended up doing good. This tool-of-god Satan was still monotheistic before things began to crack in the face of the Jews' struggles to survive.

Satan the Tempter was later added to the Scriptures by editors; and "P" writers placed him in the Garden of Eden.[792] Satan and the serpent of the Garden of Eden merged only in the first century BCE.[793] We should also remember that the influence of followers of Zarathustra in Persia may well have played a role in shaping these concepts because of the distinction made between Ahura-Mazda, the Wise Lord, and Angra Mainyu, the destructive one. This resulted in tension between an ideal of monotheism and the realities of evil in the world, along with the human need to believe in a benevolent divinity watching over humanity or, at least, those chosen for special favor.

The image of Satan arose with such force in those early centuries precisely because it reflected the dark side of the church itself and its ruthless determination to control humankind in thought, word, and deed. The desire of church leaders to rule the earth and subdue the faithful was projected onto Satan, thus creating a personification of their own evil. Also, identifying Satan with the gods of people they conquered gave blessing to book-burning, torture, oppression, and genocide.

Furthermore, as the sexual aberrations of church leaders became entrenched in the institution, Satan, vaguely like Lilith before him, became increasingly material so that he could copulate with humans. The more the church became invested in its own worldly power, the more concrete and material became its imagined nemesis, shaped by priests' own dark ambitions and fantasies.

Chapter 45

The Dark Ages

The Dark Ages are generally given as the time of European decline from the 5th to 10th centuries but, if we continue our critical religious view of history, they lasted at least until the Renaissance of the 15th century – if not to the present.

Once the Roman church became secure in its own survival and had successfully made a niche in the temporal world, it turned to physical battles as well as religious ones in its pursuit of land, power, wealth, and souls.

Fifth Century

Nominal monotheism led the attack on all non-approved spiritual beings, calling them devils, demons, or false gods. As soon as the slate was wiped clean, however, the church began to establish its own pantheon of personified godly beings. Thus, during the fifth century, the veneration of saints became common. Saints had their special functions and holy days – and they filled the various roles of the old Pagan deities. Their bones and clothing were kept as miraculous relics.[794]

In fact, some "saints" are recycled Pagan deities. The assumption of already-existing powers into the new Christian cult served several purposes. First, Christianity would be more palatable to its Pagan subjects. Second, the new church could claim any powers or benefits derived from the old deities rather than becoming their competitors. In addition, the difficulty that many people have in worshiping either an abstract high god or a divine perfect savior is alleviated if they can relate through a more human intermediary. In this way, the mother of Yeshua took on the role of the Great Goddess and became the Queen Mother of Heaven, depicted in regal dress by artists of the time[795] (and decidedly European looking).

As barbarians laid waste to Roman civilization, churchmen distinguished themselves by becoming slave masters. They justified slavery as the mercy of God for those not fit to govern themselves – and starved and mutilated them.[796] The seeds of Dark Age corruption had been sown in the church by its greed for control over land and ideas – in short, for domination over all that it encountered.

The new church did not limit itself to spiritual battles. By 800 the church was the greatest single landowner in Europe, achieved mainly through "gifts" for prayer, and Mass after death. The papacy became an object of political struggle because of its tremendous temporal advantages. In the last two thirds of the 9th century there were 20 Popes. This was known as the "Rule of the Harlots" in which the children of "celibate" Popes were made successors to the Papacy. Assassination, fighting, prostitution, and bribery were common. Reform came in 962 to 963 when Otto the German cleared out this papal line, installed a new Pope, and claimed the right of papal nomination for himself and his successors.[797] Thus, secular authorities stopped this particular religious corruption – but set themselves up as church authorities as well.

These religious struggles were primarily a male sport. Women lacked any significance in the male homosexual structure of the papacy and its priestly line. What's more, the misogynist fanaticism begun by the Hellenic Paul and consolidated by Augustine and other church "fathers" came to a head in debates about whether women even had souls. That question was finally decided in 900 at Macon when an ecumenical council decided, with a one-vote margin, that women do, indeed, have souls.[798]

Religious Prejudices and Distortions of History

The very designation of "Dark Ages" is an ethnocentric perspective that ignores what was happening in the rest of the world. The darkness of the "Dark Ages" prevailed in the "Christian" world only. The level of commerce, culture and education in Moorish Spain was in sharp contrast to that of the rest of Europe. Paved roads, raised sidewalks, and streetlamps adorned the Moorish city of Cordova hundreds of years before London or Paris. There were numerous public baths at a time when Christian culture in Europe considered bathing to be diabolical. While 99 percent of Christian Europe was illiterate, education was universal in Moorish Spain. Naturally, European illiterates had no need for libraries, while Spain boasted more than 70 – one said to house 600,000 manuscripts. While Europe had only two universities of consequence, Spain supported seventeen, along with associations for the preservation and promotion of crafts and learning.[799]

This is not to say that Islam has not been subject to the same devolutionary forces as others. Although the movement of Islam is outside of the scope of this work it, nevertheless, reflects many of the same dynamics seen elsewhere. Begun as the revelation of a scripture for the Arab world and motivated by its Prophet's drive for reform, it became in many ways a tool of political forces rather than allowing its principles to shape its society.

For example, the Prophet gave women rights they did not yet have in Arabic society and sought to protect the innocent – revolutionary concepts for his time. However, the spirit of what he was attempting to provide was lost by adherence to the letter of the revelation despite changing times. To be specific, at a time when women had no recognition in court and no rights, his declaration that two women could equal the testimony of a man was an unheard-of boon.[800] Its continuation into modern times, however, betrays the original intent.

Similarly, the revelation that allowed a man four wives, now seen as license, was intended by the Prophet to be a limitation – and that allowable only if the husband could treat all his wives equally. If he could not, he should limit himself to one wife.[801] Women, as well as children and orphans, were among the most vulnerable of the society and it was Mohammed who gave them a value far exceeding what they had at the time, with a clear intent that women were to be treated with egalitarian respect. His intent was toward justice and equality.

Without any knowledge of the principles of Islam, along with a dose of racism, many Westerners have attributed all reprehensible behavior of Arabs to Islam. (This is like assuming all Christians are like torturous Inquisitors.) For example, not only does Islam prohibit the mistreatment of hostages, but expects captors to provide for them and to help them gain their freedom – considerations yet unheard of in many "modern" societies.

The Isle of Saints and Scholars

The island of Ireland was another area that escaped the Dark Ages of Catholic and Barbarian Europe. In its conquest of Europe, Rome began withdrawing its forces from the British Isles before it reached Ireland. Thus, the island continued its traditional Irish/Celtic practices. It was neither Romanized nor centralized and, thereby, escaped the fate of Continental Europe. (Historian Thomas Cahill's book, *How the Irish Saved Civilization*, gives a more detailed description of that process.)

When Christianity came to Ireland, it took the shape of Irish traditions. It was first centered around monasteries that might include men and women. These monasteries were local institutions and reflected the people's appreciation of the natural world that could be described as "mystical." Thus, Christianity was absorbed into the hospitable, decentralized, heroic, and word-loving culture of this land. Nature was part of God's blessing to humanity, and literacy became a "central religious act."[802]

The legendary "Saint" Patrick, a Briton, had been taken as a slave around the age of 16 to Ireland and put in service for six years as a shepherd until his escape and return home. But, responding to his inner call to return to Ireland to teach, he did not embody the rigid, legalistic, and stilted Catholicism of Augustine's Rome. Thus, he brought a de-Romanized Christianity to Ireland, [803] probably more in line with his lowly experiences as a rural servant than an elite urban priest.

At that time, Irish Christianity was not a top-down institution from a distant centralized authority. It spread first through the "Green Martyrdom" in which Irish monks left their homes and villages and went into secluded places to pray and study. In their privations, they found companionship not only from whatever literature they brought and visions they had, but also from animals, trees, stones or, in other words, nature. Nature was a companion in their quest, not an enemy to it. As these holy men and women were discovered, others came to learn from them, and small monastic settlements gathered around them. It was likely their devotion and personal embodiment of scriptural *principles* that drew people to them rather than dogma.

Even after Eurocentric Roman Catholic customs were imposed at the Synod of Whitby in 664, Irish devotion to multiple sources of literature and learning continued as it had before. Thus, in the fifth century, as Roman territories descended into chaos, Irish culture was making its transition toward a prolific written literate culture, centered around monasteries and their scribes. Before that time, oral literature dominated, kept by poets, bards, and Druids.

The Irish were as hospitable to language, writings, and words as they were to visitors. They copied both Christian and Pagan classics and did not confine themselves to approved Church writings. These monks collected and copied Greek, Latin, Irish and some Hebrew texts, learning the languages along the way.

Monasteries remained small and, when they grew, devotees were sent out to establish their own. In what is known as the "White Martyrdom," monks set sail into the white dawn and traveled eastward to the land of the Picts and on into Europe. These White Martyrs, (dressed like Druids, Cahill says) fanned out across Europe.[804] This reached its peak in the second half of the seventh century.[805] These traveling Irish monks were recognized as an elite class of learned scholars and they seeded a renewal of literature, language, and learning. An Irish hand became the common script of the Middle Ages.[806] In this way, Irish missionaries were, in addition to the Islamic world, preserving knowledge that would have been lost in the decline of the Roman Empire.

The difference between Augustine's Roman and Patrick's Irish Christianity is another example in which what one *teaches* is overshadowed by what one *is*. The personhood of the teacher becomes embedded in the teaching. This one fact could explain much of the diversity of religious interpretation and be fertile ground for a psychoanalysis of religious dogmas based on whose minds it has passed through – themselves shaped by their land, culture, and time.

We still see Roman attitudes in the suppression of indigenous people, women, literature, science, and education in areas that fall under fundamentalist control today, regardless of the religion. There seems to have always been a struggle for external control and political influence that displace the original calls for personal repentance, transformation, direct access to the Divine, and caring for our neighbors. And, like many leaders today, church and state officials found ways to distract from their corruption through persecution, wars, and crusades of various kinds.

Chapter 46

Crusades and the Growth of Papal Authority

The Church's greed for power, land, and wealth spread like a cancer over its European subjects. It was shaken, however, when Jerusalem was taken over by the Turks in 1071.[807] For reasons hardly spiritual, the first Crusade was called in 1095 by Pope Urban II. Crusaders were recruited through material and spiritual rewards. Not only did they escape restrictions at home, but they were freed from interest on their debts, and were forgiven tithes and taxes.[808] Because the Crusade served as penance, Crusaders were assured of heaven, and excused from atrocities they committed along the way.

As Crusaders moved through Europe toward the holy land, their arson, torture, and butchery of both Jews and fellow Christians resulted in some of them being destroyed by the Hungarians long before they were able to fight the Muslims. The First Crusade arrived in Syria in 1097. In the summer of 1099, Jerusalem was captured, and the Christian crusaders celebrated with pillage, arson, and slaughter. Jews were herded into synagogues and burned while thousands of Muslims – regardless of age or sex[809] – were butchered in the Holy Area of the Dome of the Rock.[810] Also, as a result of the Crusaders' victory, Coptic, Jacobite, Armenian, Georgian, and Orthodox Christians lost the freedom of worship they had enjoyed under the Muslims.[811] It had been a crusade for Roman Catholicism, not for Christianity.

A second Crusade followed in 1146 but, in 1187, Saladin took back Jerusalem for the Muslims. In contrast to the behavior of the "Christian" crusaders before him, Saladin was so noted for the scrupulousness of his word and his chivalry that town after town surrendered to him. The third Crusade was launched and Richard the Lionhearted marched. When he took Acre from the Muslims in July of 1191, Lionheart beheaded nearly 3,000 Muslim captives. As the third Crusade ended, Saladin and Richard signed a treaty that gave Christians coastal cities while Muslims held the area from Libya to the Tigris.[812] The eighth and final Crusade was in 1270. Christians were eventually expelled from the Holy Land in 1291, ending the period of the Crusades.[813]

These Crusades had unexpected consequences on church and government. Kings became stronger as nobles died in battle or stayed in foreign lands that were more inviting than the homes they left. With fewer nobles, a middle class arose from among the people that opposed the church's strict control. What's more, Crusaders brought back new ideas resulting in independence of thought and unorthodox beliefs.[814] Although a pious Catholic legend attributes the Rosary to a vision by Dominic during the Inquisition, it was the crusaders who brought it back with them from Islamic lands.[815] The church, of course, adapted it to its own ideology.

Overlapping the Crusades, the church in Rome also sought to suppress heresy through the office of the "Inquisition" that grew in strength from the 11th to the 13th centuries, as we'll see in the next chapter. Since "confession" was the only way a heretic's soul could be redeemed, inquisitors developed their means of "persuasion" – dietary and sleep restrictions, and torture.[816]

In 1312, Knights Templar, who had served in the Crusades, were declared heretical and, under torture, were forced to confess to the worship of something called "Baphomet" that is sometimes thought to be a bearded man's head, a skull, goat,[817] or the face of Jesus on what became the shroud of Turin.[818] It has also been suggested to be a corruption of the name Mohammed. It seems that this idolatrous object or name that had been created from torture had a most unclear identity – or was pure fantasy.

The last grand master of the Templars was burned outside of Paris in 1314. His name was Jacques DeMolay and a fraternal order for young men exists in his honor.[819] When I was a teenager, I was a member of the Order of DeMolay. One of my Catholic friends was told by his priest that, if he joined the order, he'd be excommunicated. He joined anyway.

Twelfth Century

While the church was fighting its political and bloody land battles, the evolution of its dogma and mythology continued. In popular imagery, Mary assumed the status of the bride of Christ.[820] We've seen through the course of history that many previous religions had their trinities containing a feminine element. However, the Church continued to eliminate the feminine from the Godhead, continuing the traditions of Greek, Roman, and Jewish ideology. Nevertheless, something of the Feminine Divine persisted, even if often relegated to the fringes of society. The early designation of Mary as the Ever-Virgin Mother of God kept alive humanity's collective realization that life requires birth and mothering. The archetype of the Queen of Heaven was thus carried over even into the Church's blatant misogyny. After all, half the population was female – probably more when men were lost in war.

But the status of women, man's relation to her, and their sexual nature continued to be an issue. Debate arose once more among priests about marriage: was it simply to control human weakness or was it a sacrament? This question was not settled until 1563.[821]

Meanwhile, Pope Innocent III, 1198-1216, enjoyed the height of papal power. He showed his contempt for the world by dominating it. He claimed to be overlord of the Christian world and, in 1215, the Lateran congress established the claim that "the Pope was the final ultimate earthly authority..."[822]

Chapter 47

Inquisition into Heresy

The shadows of the Church loomed darkest in the struggle between heresy and orthodoxy. All sense of holiness, religious purpose, compassion, and the social values of their savior were abandoned in the church's greed for land, wealth, and power. The Church and its followers were absorbed into their narrow worldview and demonstrated in horrific ways the inherent danger of unchecked fanatic religious fervor.

Along with the crusade for land, Church warlords turned against women as well. Their actions against women, justified by accusations of heresy, took the form not of religious debate, but highly sexualized inquisitions and torture.

Cathars

We've seen the possible influence on Augustine of Manichaeism and its dualism. In the 11th and 12th centuries, dualism took a peculiar character and emerged as Catharism. This duality was the Hellenic concept of the good spiritual world over the inferior material world. The god of evil was again identified with Yahweh while the god of good was revealed in the New Testament. To them, Christ was purely an exemplary spirit.[823]

The popularity of this "heresy" was stoked by its high ethical ideals and its stance against the immorality of the clergy. The Cathar sect and their Albigensians were hard-working and prosperous, and thereby attracted the envy of Rome to become another victim of its violent persecution. Two elements made the Cathars especially repulsive to the church. One was the fact that women, in equality with men, could become one of the "Perfect," and the other was the Cathar idea that casual fornication was less reprehensible than institutionalized sex in marriage which, by promoting children, perpetuated bondage to loathsome earth.[824] It was in response to the celibacy of the "Perfect" of the Cathars that prompted the imposition of strict celibacy on the Roman priesthood. Furthermore, the Roman rite of extreme unction followed the Cathar rite of consolamentum.[825]

In 1209, the Pope declared a crusade against the Albigenses which drove this movement underground.[826] In a military attack that same year, the Abbot of Citeaux was asked how the heretics were to be distinguished from the loyal. He gave his infamous reply "Slay them all, the Lord will know his own".[827] 1244 marked the end of this sect when 200 Cathars – mostly women – were burned alive.[828]

Inquisition

One of the chief purposes of the Roman church's Dominican Order – later active in the Inquisition – was to oppose the Albigenses.[829] From *Domini canes* or the hounds of God, the Dominican Order was founded about 1220 to fight heresy and to teach. The Inquisition was staffed with their Black Friars.[830] Drunk with its power, distorted by its celibacy and hatred of women, oppressed by its own philosophies, the church's satanic shadow then took shape in its witch hunts and life-negating theologies.

With the Christian doctrines of Original Sin, work was no longer valued in its own right but became punishment for humankind's sinful nature.[831] This world was the "Devil's excrement," our flesh the home of Original Sin, and life an evil to be despised.[832] Since the church had defined human life as sin, it was free to set itself up as the agent of divinely appointed "correction".[833] Murderous acts were first directed against lepers. The King of France in June of 1321 issued an edict that lepers who confessed to being part of a conspiracy were to be burned and those who refused to confess were to be tortured and, once confessing, to be burned. Then came the plague of 1347. It was blamed on the Jews who were then massacred in various cities.[834]

In 1184, Pope Lucius III had invoked a passage in John[835] to justify the burning of heretics. That passage reads, "If a man abides not in me, he is cast forth as a branch and is withered; and men gather them, and cast them into the fire, and they are burned."[836] To concretize a metaphor is disastrous for both its victims and the original idea it was trying to illustrate.

To medieval theologians, Jews, infidels, and heretics had no rights to be violated. According to Augustine, the individual had no right to dissent.[837] In the Inquisition's handling of heresies, the property of every person who was burned became the Church's. Children were forced to watch their parents burn and were themselves whipped for being children of the accused. They were then set free to wander as beggars or remanded into "Christian" orphanages.[838]

Between the 15th and 18th centuries, estimates range that somewhere between one and nine million people were burned as witches.[839] Most of them were women but, between 1120 and 1741, ninety domestic animals were also tried in court for murder and witchcraft.[840]

Under the authority of the Inquisition, people were officially persecuted and killed as "heretics" between 1200 and 1484. Then, in 1484, a Papal Bull against witchcraft was made by Pope Innocent VIII.[841] Two years later in 1486, two Dominican monks wrote their *Malleus Maleficarum*. This work asserted that it is the nature of women to be agents of the Devil. Although *heretics* were burned on "relapse," from the 15th century onward "*witches*" were burned upon first conviction.[842]

The truth of this medieval madness is obscured by the stranglehold the church held on writings and public policy. In fact, witchcraft, as it is commonly known, and Satanism were both *invented* in the church's fevered obsession with destroying competitive ideas, along with people that it could not control. Our modern popular image of the evil witch is based on Inquisition trial records of the 16th to 18th centuries. These evil witches were accused of such horrid things as healing, hygiene, and relieving the pain of childbirth. In the Christian Middle Ages, life was "supposed to be diseased, wretched, and painful" and was God's "punishment for human sin." Therefore, all those who tried to alleviate suffering were agents of the Devil. Thus, midwives and herbalist doctors were targeted and often rejected as social outcasts. During an epidemic, a woman in Scotland was burned alive for being a witch. Her crime was bathing children. And, in 1486, it was officially declared that "No one does more harm to the Catholic faith than midwives".[843]

To this Church, it was godly to judge, torture, and burn alive – and devilishly sinful to alleviate suffering. This idea of a pact with the devil came from the minds of theologians.[844] The Church, as the state of Rome had done centuries earlier, accused its enemies of godlessness and cannibalism. If Jesus/Yeshua had returned during the Middle Ages to heal and to teach forgiveness along with the immanence of the Kingdom of God, he would, no doubt, have been declared a heretic and be burned by his church.

A Grain of Truth?

Under priestly and papal fabrications, under civil intrigues for power and land, under popular hysteria used to control the masses, was there anything beyond the fantasies of celibate, misogynist misanthropes in the priesthood? More than one author has gone to great lengths to prove that something called "witchcraft" existed prior to the Inquisition and, in so doing, show the existence of a Green Man and cults devoted to the goddess Diana. Of course, Pagan festivals preceded later Christian celebrations. What's more, Pagan rebels, at least into the fifth century, were "dedicated to the worship of the goddess Diana".[845]

Ginsburg points to the *Benandanti* – or "Good Walkers" – in 16th and 17th century Italy as evidence of actual witch-like activities on behalf of the community. These Benandanti were women who made nighttime spiritual flights to do battle with malevolent witches to preserve the fertility of the land. He described them as headed by a nocturnal goddess. Among these various groups, the one thing they had in common was their ecstatic nature and their relationship with a mistress of the animals, like Artemis.[846]

Even granting the existence of genuine competitors to the church's authority, its efforts were directed indiscriminately against any sign of deviation from its authority for any reason. One church apologist claimed that the essence of witchcraft is to defy Church and society "on behalf of the power of evil".[847] Of course, to oppose the church was automatically evil, as was the alleviation of suffering. It was not necessary, however, for those accused to worship or even believe in any devil. It was enough that they defied the Church's authority.

Accusations, Torture and Death

Everyday vagaries in the unpredictability of life were demonized so that an evil force was assumed to be behind them. And there was someone to be blamed for all deviance from the Church's dogma – usually a woman. Anything that aroused suspicion could be "the signature of the Devil in her flesh" – including jealousy that *others* felt toward her, too much success, attractiveness, etc. A wart, mole, freckle, or skin blemish on a woman was a "sign" that she had been "kissed by Satan." The sexual obsession of Christian witch-burners is legendary. The church's new inquisitor's bible, the *Malleus Maleficarum* or Witch-Hammer, constantly equated the Devil with sexual activity.[848] This is a natural outgrowth of a poorly conceived rule of celibacy for priests and philosophical judgments against all things material.

Under clerics, inquisitorial rules required there be no conviction without a confession and then went on to define what kinds of torture could be used in order to extract one.[849] Torturers could not only rape and abuse women in their chambers, but priests blessed the instruments of torture before they were used.[850]

Women were exposed in public and, regardless of any trial, death was the outcome of being accused.[851] The only control the victim could exercise was how much torture she or he would suffer before death, depending on how soon the "confession" was rendered.

Church-approved torture could include such things as:

> eye gouging;
> branding irons;
> metal forehead tourniquets;
> spine rollers with sharp metal protrusions;
> thumb screws;
> leg vices;
> boards with spikes to kneel on (for hours);
> "the pear" (heated to red hot, inserted in the victims' mouth, anus or vagina and then spread);
> feathers dipped in burning sulpher to be clamped in the armpits or groin;

> scalding baths of water and lime;
> stretching on the rack;
> suspension by the thumbs – with weights on the ankles, along with other means of separating joints of the body;
> cutting off of hands, tongues, noses and ears;
> tearing women's breasts with red-hot pincers.[852]

Under such torture, girls as young as nine or ten "confessed" to sexual relations with the Devil.[853] Even after people had confessed, been sentenced, and were waiting to be burned, they could still be subjected to random torture. Such was the mercy of the Church of Rome, wedded to civil authorities.

Good and helpful witches were viewed as more dangerous than obviously evil ones, and helping their neighbors was proof that a woman had a pact with the Devil. It was not 'wickedness' that the church wanted to destroy but the witch's effectiveness.[854] Even dreamers were to be stoned.[855]

Modern and scholarly treatment of the witch hunts sometimes falls under the spell of church propaganda. One writer, for example, mouths Augustine's perversion about inherent evils of humankind and argues that events such as the Inquisition are understandable and sane, although disgraceful.[856] Denying the influence of forced confessions under torture, he credits the practice of witchcraft with creating popular hysteria despite the fact that nothing was known by the populace other than what the Inquisitors claimed. He even claims that the lack of any popular resistance indicates "widespread support for the persecution"[857] ignoring the fact that those who objected could be accused as well.

The "Satan" referred to by Inquisitors would hardly have been recognized by earlier Christians. This goat-like being was not to be found in Zoroastrian, Judaic or early Christian mythology. It was not until Christian missionaries spread into the rest of the world where various horned fertility deities were found that Satan was given this image. It was this horned god that threatened the foreign totalitarian Church and its invasion.[858]

In the end, damage done by Church dogma and domination created a morbid world of alienation, fear, and repression. Anything outside of Biblical canon as defined by Church authority was automatically evil and therefore bereft of any rights or values – as was anyone who defended such deviations. Thus, the Dark Ages and Inquisition were a direct consequence of the cancer of absolute Church authority infecting state and personal life with no check on its self-righteous monolithic totalitarianism. We see the echoes of this insidious disease in some right-wing "conservative" movements of today.

The control of information has always been a means of manipulation by authoritarian institutions, whether by burning books, killing priests and priestesses of other traditions, or simply leaving out elements of history. In sharing early versions of this manuscript, I was surprised to find that some graduates of Catholic schools, despite intensive Church history, never heard of the Inquisition or its atrocities.

Chapter 48

Reformation and The Bible

No doubt Church excesses during its brutal witch hunts contributed to an eventual loss of power as people sobered from the intoxication of hysterical accusations, fear, propaganda, and burning flesh. The Church became so corrupt and deficient that its totalitarian hold on the beliefs of those under its shadow could not hold. It had run its course from a spiritual movement to political power and eventually to a self-serving institution. Thus, Henry VIII declared his "Act of Supremacy" that made *him* head of the Church in England.[859] Protestant movements arose that then included their own massacres and religious warfare.[860]

Most people no longer saw the Roman Church as the sole infallible source of connection with the Divine. To what could people turn? They sought access through the only other commonly known source of Christian knowledge – the Bible. The Bible had been kept away from common people, thus ensuring that the Church would remain *the* source of Christian doctrine. Biblical writings had been reserved for clergy. By the 14th century, the only public English writings, for example, were parts of the Ten Commandments, Beatitudes, and the Lord's Prayer. In the 11th and 12th centuries, two popes (Gregory VII and Innocent III) declared that the writings of faith should not be provided to the public for fear of misunderstanding. By the 14th century, the Bible had become linked with "social insurrection".[861]

Under John Wycliff, who denounced the powers of the Church in favor of the common people, an English Bible was produced. He was called an anti-Christ for his efforts and a provincial council in the 15th century decreed excommunication to anyone who translates or reads a Bible in English.[862]

Born at the end of the 15th century, William Tyndale also struck at the heart of the Church's monopoly on biblical writings. Because he could not execute his plans in England, he moved to the continent where he was forced to stay ahead of spies. He eventually had fresh translations of the New Testament printed. Smuggled into England, they were confiscated and burned by the authorities. Meanwhile, more copies were printed, and he translated parts of the Old Testament as well. In 1535 he was seized and imprisoned. Declared a heretic, he was first strangled to death and then burned at the stake on October 6, 1536.[863]

Obviously, these efforts by the authorities failed. Distrust of the Church because of its abuses, the Protestant revolution, public desire for knowledge, and the invention of the printing press all contributed to dissemination of The Word, free from priestly control but not clerical interpretation. These efforts were less revolutionary than they appear, however. While they attempted to wrestle power away from the established church, they did little to reform underlying beliefs that led to the initial abuses and oppression. Stern reformers, for example, now opposed cults of Mary, at least in part, because she was merciful.[864]

One group that was relatively accepted yet outside of the mainstream was the Religious Society of Friends, often called "Quakers." The Quaker movement was initiated by George Fox (1624-1691). To him, Christianity was not of laws, doctrines, and sermons but an experience of the inner light – an echo of Gnosticism. The "Word of God" was not confined to scriptures or professional clergy. God's voice could be heard through anyone God chose to inspire – man or woman. All people were to be treated as friends. War, slavery, and swearing of oaths were violations, and church sacraments were acts of idolatry.[865] They did not quite fit the mold of respectable citizens. In 1660 a woman was tried in Massachusetts for witchcraft. She was acquitted but then convicted of being a Quaker and was thereby banished from the colony.[866]

At this point, we see three primary sources of religious authority: the institution of the Catholic Church with its claim of apostolic succession, the frequently edited and translated Scriptures, and contemporary revelations of the voice of God.

We often admire, if with amusement, early Puritans, as we are told of their idea of forging their own religious communities in a free world where they could worship as they pleased. There's a dark side to this optimistic picture. Part of their legacy was their own religious tyranny and exclusiveness: the rights they claimed for themselves they would not extend to others. Thus, it was not just for religious liberty that they left their native European countries but the fact that civil authorities would not allow them to persecute others as they wished.

Salem, Massachusetts became the arena for one of the worst episodes of satanic behavior in the North. Beginning with the strange behavior of a minister's daughter and niece, it was a physician in February of 1692 who attributed his own helplessness to the possibility that the girls' behavior was caused by witchcraft. The "afflictions" spread to several other girls between the ages of 12 and 19 and, on February 29, 1692, warrants were sent out for the arrest of three women who were accused by the girls, but only after intense "questioning" by adults.[867]

More women were accused in March. They were "tested" by being brought near the afflicted girls. If the girls reacted with hysteria, the accused was jailed. One of the accused "witches" was a four-year-old girl who remained in prison in irons for nine months before being set free. It was not until April that the first man was accused – a former minister. On June 10, the first execution was carried out and a woman named Bridget Bishop was hanged. On July 19, five more women were executed as witches. More convictions came in August and, on September 23, more were condemned to die. Those who confessed, however, were set free. Those who did not, died. One was crushed to death with heavy weights piled on his body.[868]

Accusations and "tests" continued. Bodies of the accused were examined in detail in search of the "witch's teat" from which the devil might suck. Or a challenge to recite a prayer might be made. If there were any errors, it was "proof" that the individual was in league with the devil – even if, as happened in one instance, the condemned were to perfectly recite the prayer on the gallows. He was hanged anyway.[869]

Eventually, the Massachusetts governor forbade further imprisonments for witchcraft because of the questionable nature of the accusations and tests. By February of 1693, the remaining prisoners were released. One hundred and forty-two individuals had been formally accused – and in some cases an accuser was also accused. It took the action of civil authorities to curb the rabid religious fanaticism that was only satisfied by the sacrifice of innocents.

None of these sad deaths had to occur. In another community in 1734, similar behavior of some girls was interpreted as an outpouring of God's spirit.[870] People of that village were converted instead of condemned.

Doubtless there were complicated social, religious, and personal forces at work that resulted in Salem's witch accusations, but the questions will always remain: what kind of religious institution inspires and guides such shameful chapters in history, and what sort of god do they carry in their hearts? Perhaps a more important question of our time would be: what would it take to restore primacy to love, healing, forgiveness, and mercy?

Chapter 49

New Order of the Ages

In America's 1992 presidential campaign, a failed presidential candidate (Pat Buchanan) opened the Republican convention by referring to the values on which America was founded as the Judeo-Christian tradition. The phrase "American values" is often used by the religious right who lump fundamentalist biblical admonitions with America and its "founding fathers."

The "rigid Puritanism of Protestant fundamentalism can be traced to the biblical Old Testament".[871] In fact, the Hebraic styled Puritans tried to establish a new tyrannical Bible community on this continent but were checked by the "founding fathers" who sought to strictly limit the power of the church. This was a critical issue to individuals attempting to establish a safe nation free of the excesses, tyrannies, and abusive power under which many had already suffered.

A careful look at what some of these men wrote and believed should clarify that part of what America was created for was to limit religious domination of any kind. Early writers, though devout in their own way, had seen the abuses perpetrated by politically powerful religious devotees. Therefore, they distrusted the ability of any group that claimed to speak for God to monitor its own behavior and not become a menace to the rest of society.

Thomas Paine echoed the ancient Gnostics when he wrote:

Whenever we read the obscene stories, the voluptuous debaucheries, the cruel and torturous executions, the unrelenting vindictiveness, with which more than half the Bible is filled, it would be more consistent that we call it the word of the demon than the word of God. It is a history of wickedness, that has served to corrupt and brutalize mankind; and for my part I sincerely detest it, as I detest everything that is cruel.[872]

Thomas Jefferson asserted that, since the introduction of Christianity, there have been millions of innocent men, women and children burnt, tortured, fined, and imprisoned in the church's efforts at uniformity. The only result, however, has been "to make one half of the world fools, and the other half hypocrites".[873]

The founding fathers of the United States, men with purpose and education, showed curious esoteric roots in their affiliations and symbols. The words *Novus Ordo Seclorum* (meaning "New Order of the Ages") were made part of the Seal of the United States, which revealed their expectation that a new age had been born. That order was to establish a secular institution that would protect their right to worship within their own traditions – largely Rosicrucian and Masonic. They knew only too well the dangers when church and state combine.

These are not just historical oddities. James Watt, Ronald Reagan's first Secretary of the Interior, told Congress that protection of natural resources was not important given the imminent return of his Jesus. "After the last tree is felled, Christ will come back," he is quoted to have said.[874] Even without this religious insanity, we have been on a path of self-destruction as we resist what scientists have tried to tell us about our future if we don't change how we treat our environment. Conservative religious political regimes seek to suppress science and education.

Invocations of modern politicians and moralists aside, what is most in line with American values are those of the esotericists and dissenters: freedom of thought and belief, freedom from religious persecution, and a say in one's destiny. The American Constitution and Bill of Rights were established to *prevent* the very thing leaders of religious supremacist movements invoke it to support: an archaic and incestuous marriage between church and state that would again justify persecution, censorship, the denigration of women, and destruction of the natural world.

It's a telling statement that the population at large is only gradually coming to understand what it truly means to have individual freedom, and how backward some people still are, controlled by religious dogma and their own inadequate education. Women are still subordinated not only to men, but even to the children they bear. And any group might be targeted by "True Believers" for persecution.

America has seen the election of a national leader who, despite obvious character defects, moral shortcomings, and illegal and abusive acts, inspires the devoted support of a significant portion of the population. Many of these people *want* an authoritarian leader who promises them the glory of a mythical past and illusory future, gives them someone else to blame for their troubles, encourages them to act out pathological psychosocial defects, and sets up boundaries between "them" and "us." This is the same propaganda and behavior we saw used against early Christians and then used by the Christian establishment when it became a political power. It eliminated its competitors and put the common people into various forms of servitude.

This, it seems, is an American tradition. The tendency we saw for religious partisans to claim as their own the ideas and practices of the people they sought to suppress also occurred in founding the United States of America. Most of us were taught that (white) European ideas of democracy and freedom, perhaps originating in ancient Greece, were imported into this land of "savages." This myth belies the degree to which the American confederation was derived largely from the League of the Iroquois and their Great Law of Peace.[875] As Hieronimus puts it, "Indeed, centuries before Columbus arrived in the New World, democracy was alive and well, just waiting for the founding fathers to discover it".[876] But when Europeans adopted these ideas, they applied them only to white, male landowners.

As recently as the 1990s, political partisans tried to dismiss these historical realities,[877] apparently trying to hold to their mythical notion of the superiority of white European culture. Like religious partisans, these political partisans claim a white nationalist supremacy over the conquered people's ideas that our founders copied.

Thus, we see the survival of old ways of conquest as various factions struggle not just for power but for domination and erasure of the knowledge of the foundations on which the "new" good news was built. It has happened in religion, in secular rulers' consolidation of power, and in nationalist movements. The biblical warning about putting new wine into old skins could be talking about religious institutions, political establishments, social movements, or the psyche of everyday people.

The Taboo against Knowing

In the Judeo-Christian tradition, a battle over knowledge and the process of knowing began in the Garden of Eden when the creator-god tells the couple not to eat of the fruit of the tree in the middle of the garden because they will die on that day. But the serpent, we remember, contradicts this god and says, "this will open your eyes and you will see what god sees." Since that time, there have been various punishments for both knowledge as well as the means of knowing throughout Western religious history. We have been pressed not only to deny the foundations on which our modern institutions were built, but also to protect their mythical origins. Ignorance and mythologies keep devoted fanatics under enchantment. The library of Alexandria was destroyed; Roman Catholic and Protestant churches suppressed publication of the Bible; healers, herbalists and midwives were persecuted and burned; and books have been banned and burned. Evolution and a heliocentric solar system were denied because they conflicted with Church dogma. After the discovery of mind-altering drugs, rather than exploring their healing and noetic properties, the U.S. government crafted misleading campaigns and unethical experiments to scare people away from practices that indigenous shamans have used for eons for healing and enlightenment. Fortunately, that seems to be changing with studies of therapeutic effects of psilocybin in various populations.

No one seems to have taken Jesus seriously when he said, "the truth shall free you." But truth seems to have been – and continues to be – the enemy of a corrupt Church and State rather than their foundation.

Chapter 50

Conclusions – Is Past Prologue?

Cherish those who seek the truth but beware of those who find it. – Voltaire

At this point, I'd like to offer some perspectives on this history, summarize the patterns we've seen, note some of the primal wounds we've endured because of it, confess my own expectations of religion, encourage readers to use this information to do their own reading and to deepen their religious thought and practice, and to offer some thoughts about the future.

Three Perspectives, Three Realities

First, one could find in this history the persistent politicization and corruption of religious institutions in their own development, and in their ambition for secular power. Second, one could also see this history as a series of recurring religious revolutions, each one attempting to better answer the needs of the time than its predecessor had done. Third, one could also view it as a story of recurring spiritual emergence with an ineffable spiritual impulse that sparks inspiration and social change.

My own judgment is that all three are true. There is something in the heart of humanity that yearns for spiritual experience, an expansion of perspective, and to feel fully integrated and supported in the arms of powers here and beyond. There is always an intuition that there is something beyond the senses, beyond our thinking, and beyond the ideologies that would be imposed upon us. We revere those individuals who can inspire us with extraordinary experiences, who give meaning to our existence and, perhaps, show us the way forward. Groups may then bond around common perceptions of those meaningful ideas. This, in turn, gives rise to not only religions, but also spiritual and educational movements, mystery schools, and inspiring independent teachers. We've seen inspired charismatics such as Akhenaton, Moses, Yeshua/Jesus, and Mohammed, along with the various mystics of those traditions. History has also shown us the development of religious practice, ideology, and institutions that arise around their mythical stories – all subject to endless human frailty. In that human frailty, we find regular patterns in the life cycle of religious movements.

Prophets to Priests, Revelation to Heresy

The pattern that became evident in my research and that I will summarize here seems to be a function of two overarching forces. First, humanity is a social creature and prone to seek those of like mind where we can find some degree of protection and belonging. This tendency orients us toward the outside world and toward conformity to, or rebellion against, the actions and ideas of others. In addition, there is something in the human spirit that yearns to give voice to what is *inside* of *us*, especially numinous and expansive experiences that take us beyond the social and sensory world. We see the interplay of these two forces in the life cycle of religious institutions: emergence, crystallization, orthodoxy, decline, reformation, and new revelation. Let's take these one at a time.

Emergence

Some Unknown Mystery inserts itself into the experience of an individual that manifests in visions, revelations, or Otherworldly contact. Religious figures, along with saints and mystics, become icons and way-showers as we celebrate their numinous experiences and expansive ideas. Their importance centers around *their* numinous experience of the Divine – something ineffable and beyond common experience.

Crystallization and Externalization

These experiences of prophets and shamans are first exalted and then gradually codified under the authority of a priesthood. Direct experience is thereby supplanted by dogma and theology. Thus, numinous experience is followed by attempts to communicate what that experience was and what it means. It is in this meaning-making that theology and dogma arise – a meaning that is rooted in the cultural context of the time. This is where a profound experience is reduced to fit into linguistic and social containers. They inspire the people even as they threaten political and religious structures. They will naturally attract those who have been failed by the prevailing tradition or who seek greater realization. When there is a charismatic power in the teachings, they may also be used as a tool of political and militaristic colonization.

Orthodoxy and Heresy

Orthodoxy requires codification, defined theologies, and boundaries around identity. This determines who belongs and thereby receives benefits and privileges, and those who do not. The establishment of orthodoxy naturally creates heresy and various kinds of "others" that must be defended against by the "true believers." Once "the truth" is found, further "revelation" is curtailed. Those who continue searching for it become heretics. Also, once a movement adopts some revelation, it then moves to discredit the *process* of revelation itself to guard against the next such revelatory emergence that might compete with it. So, the writer of each new revelation declares it to be the last and final revelation and then, through the actions of his or her followers, creates a human – and therefore corruptible – establishment that makes an eventual new revelation necessary.

A central part of the problem is that these religions have not been able to integrate the totality of human functioning. Unaccepted qualities of humanity are exiled and then coalesce into fringe religions, mystery schools, esoteric movements, hostile disbelief, or pockets of social chaos. When they are persecuted, they go underground, and re-integration into the dominant ideology is even less likely. Their traditions, however, leave footprints in secret societies and such organizations as the Theosophical Society, Liberal Catholic Church, Rosicrucians, Freemasons, and some Christian and ecumenical denominations. If Christian, they often celebrate a Cosmic Christ as a divine presence available to all. Mainstream churches generally consider them infidels and heretics, or worse.

Decline

Institutional structures may endure but they lose their numinous qualities and fail to inspire the kind of devotion triggered by the original emergence. The inspiration toward personal transformation and social reform that were a part of the movement's birth are lost in its struggle for survival, acceptance, and/or political power. In place of struggles of character that should be waged within oneself, the battle is externalized against those people and ideas that that have been defined as "not belonging." Eventually, it decays until a new revelation emerges to fill the void left in its emptiness. A new source of revelation or inspiration arises – and the cycle begins once more.

Reformation and revelation

Human religious institutions, having crystallized into orthodoxy, no longer answer to the needs of the ever-changing human condition. As the old structure cracks, new light leaks through and is embraced by those dissatisfied or left behind. Given the state of our world with its climate crisis, religious intolerance, dysfunctional social structures, rampant hostility, and inhumane wealth discrepancies, we may be ripe for the emergence of one or more spiritual movements that will have the potential to spawn something new – perhaps something not even recognizable as religion. We see major religious institutions struggling to deal with sexual abuse within their own ranks, with scientific discoveries, with climate and political refugees, and other serious social problems. Some people have turned toward feel-good churches for comfort while others seek out institutions that attempt to honestly minister to the needs of humanity in these times.

In summary, our need to identify with something greater than ourselves, and to be part of social institutions that reflect our perceptions and values combine to manifest in a religious impulse that is subverted when it becomes channeled into political and secular arenas. These institutions are fraught with all the foibles of humanity and psychological dynamics of anxiety, neurosis, and projection. Once the spiritual spark gathers a social circle, it becomes a religion. Once the religion moves toward gaining political power for itself, it has begun its decline into corruption. Then, in the face of social disruption or new revelation, the enchantment of the old institution is broken. Meanwhile, "secret societies" who have carried "heresies" outside of the religious enchantment, work *sub rosa* to maintain their lineage of knowledge from earlier times. They can emerge and nudge the culture's spiritual environment toward evolution. They, too, can be subject to corruption, of course, but are less likely to fall prey to secular ambition because of their exile from the mainstream. They, too, can lose the spark of their spiritual inspiration and become empty traditions, but they are more likely, because of their practices, to keep their spiritual garden prepared for new seeds that may be blown in from the Great Mystery.

Three primal Wounds

Humanity has suffered three primal wounds in our religious evolution. One wound is to our relationship with the spiritual resources within us and our ability to access them. The second wound is to our relationship with the natural world around us. And the third wound is to gender relationships. Let's look at these wounds one by one because our future – both religious and secular – will be shaped by our response to them.

Our Relationship with Our Deeper Self and Its Spiritual Expression

This is a wound I have been discussing throughout this work: the way that a spiritual impulse gets defined, confined, and distorted within religion, and then is further shaped to serve political objectives. Shadows are cast when we put a human mask on the face of God and put words to the nameless. We abandon the realm of spirit when we take the truth of *a* time and try to make it a Truth for *All* Time. Nor does a spiritual impulse do well when we try to homogenize the diversity of humankind, centralize religious authority, fear experiences we don't understand, take ownership over the spiritual experiences of others, or impose previously existing meanings on new experiences. Humility is required in the face of numinosity.

Something deeply human is hurt when any internal experience is judged and interpreted by reductionist external explanations. The delicate balance between the inner world of each unique individual and the external world of cultural consensus and tradition must be respected.

This is more than a philosophical point. Most of humanity has a sense of an Otherworld, and many people have had direct experiences with it through spiritual, paranormal, or other conditions of altered states. Some of these experiences could, of course, be illusory, psychological, or self-generated, but to judge all experiences by such detours is an affront to true science. Indigenous shamans, when "discovered" by Western explorers, were subjected to changing cultural judgments that depended on the Western observers' cultural perspectives. Initially, shamans were judged as being possessed by demons. When Western culture began to lose its belief in demons, shamans were judged to be crazy or tricksters.[878] Only in the last few decades did anthropologists and other scientists begin to seriously study it and themselves experience shamanic realities.[879] Today, it is scientifically acceptable to view shamanic experiences as the result of changes in brain rhythms or brainwave states. All these judgments, however, are only looking at the external expression of these experiences, and not their origin, content, or the usefulness of their revelations.

The real work of spiritual exploration is being done by mystics, shamans and mystery schools that have escaped the destructive ramifications of Augustine's Original Sin and can provide a safe container for internal and transcendent experiences to unfold in their own right.

Our Relationship with The Natural World

The second primal wound is our alienation from nature, especially in men who are more likely to perceive the world as "Other." Women and nature are thereby objectified, manipulated, and reduced to commodities rather than relationships.

Women can also fall prey to the materialistic cultural enchantment that fosters alienation from nature, but it seems that most women (as well as some men) readily recognize the value of relationship. They also have access to empathic data that surpass cold objectivity. This "empathic data" may seem like anthropomorphizing nature. Nevertheless, it can lead us to better perceive the impact of human activity on the natural world when we can put ourselves in the place of nature's experience of us.

Fortunately, various sciences are waking up to the interrelationships within ecological webs that could return humanity to its conscious and rightful place in the natural world, if it can escape oppression by economic, religious, and political pressures.

The Shared Gender Wound

The third wound is shared by both genders. It has resulted in gender discord, distrust, and struggles for dominance. In almost every era, one gender has been favored over the other. It may have been in subtle ways or in the blatant persecution that we've seen in patriarchal institutions. In these histories, it seems that, as soon as humanity began to organize, one of the genders was perceived as superior and dominant, depending on what qualities were needed for survival in their time and place. This hierarchy may not always have been oppressive, but institutional inequality means that one side enjoys its status at the expense of the other. No matter how well-meaning, it is always destructive.

Our modern popular myth is that we once enjoyed nurturing matrifocal societies that were taken over by various forms of patriarchy. The term "patriarchy" has become a shorthand for all manner of male privilege, domination, abuse, and technological excess. The word *patriarchy* means "rule by the fathers," but what I see happening under this title is rule by warring tribal adolescents caught in various pissing contests, many of whom have yet to grow beyond a toddler's stage of self-centered greed. No healthy father would treat his children the way people have been treated by these "patriarchal" institutions. A real father sacrifices his own well-being and resources so that those under his care can blossom in their own right. He takes pleasure in seeing them go beyond his own achievements and knows when to step back and let them assume control. He is concerned about the world his grandchildren and their children will inherit rather than his own power and status.

The term *patriarchy*, although a convenient shorthand for many of the excesses we've seen, nevertheless perpetuates the gender wound in two ways. First, it lowers the standard of what it means to be a father. Second, it implies that hierarchies are exclusively male while history shows us female-dominant hierarchies as well. There were certainly differences between them, but *hierarchical dominance* is the overriding issue – not just the realities of dysfunctional male power.

My Expectations of Religion

I was not an objective observer of these histories. I had visceral reactions to what I read, horrified at the wanton destruction, torture, and genocide in the name of religion. It has colored how I view religious traditions. The bright, well-dressed façade of our dominant religions hides their dark secrets – the times when they violated their professed values for their own benefit and claimed that their god put them up to it. And then, there is the willingness of ordinary people to follow them. A religious enchantment allows people to bypass their critical faculties and usual moral standards.

It wasn't until after I had written most of this that I realized I should examine my own expectations of religion because of my personal reactions. I questioned whether my expectations of religion have been too high, but I first had to define and examine them. I'll leave others to decide whether they are reasonable.

What, then, might we expect of religion?
- Bring people together with a shared set of values and purpose and support one another in their efforts to transform themselves and the world.
- Live out the values they profess, holding their leadership to the highest standards.
- Foster the best of human behavior, bringing compassion, forgiveness, mercy, and love into every relationship among people, other creatures, and with the land.
- Encourage personal and direct experience of the divine.
- Provide a safe foundation and container for purposeful or accidental spiritual experience.
- Be of service to others without expectation of conversion or reward. Otherwise, it's just another form of colonization and marketplace barter.
- Foster respect for the sources of life, which means keeping poisons out of our water, air, and land; and protecting women and children.
- Balance personal "salvation" and transformation with efforts toward social justice: caring for the poor, sharing wealth, offering forgiveness, granting mercy, and withdrawing judgmentalism for all – not just their own.
- In religious education, balance information and ideology with direct personal experience and service. Information can be a good foundation for growth but becomes a barrier when it's frozen into monuments.

The fruits of any religious institution should be truth, beauty, empowerment, and self-realization of the individual, with reciprocity and mutual respect among all involved. A true ministry develops adherents who become their own spiritual authority within wholesome relationships – with their communities, with nature and, of course, with the Divine. This is more than a self-focused personal conversion. The spiritual impulse should be treasured and explored, and not be put in service to political or secular ambitions. This is not to say the adherents of these movements should not be *involved* in the political arena, but their ideologies should not *become* the political arena. Public political activity should serve the entire community – not any one ideology or sect.

Don't Turn Away – Go Deeper

It can be unsettling to be faced with unsavory elements in the history of something we hold dear. By what I have written, one might assume that I take a dim view of religion. This is not the case. However, I have a very dim view of religious institutions that betray the values taught by their founders and who use those founders as a mascot rather than an example to be emulated. I do not ask for the abandonment of religion but for its refinement. Perhaps we need to heed what the word "religion" means – *re+ligare* – "to bind back," back to its beginning. To do this, we must get beyond the intervening theologies and dogmas to recover what is at the heart of each religion. Then we can judge if it is in harmony with what's in our hearts and true to its own professed original values. It's the responsibility of every one of us to refine those institutions that have carried the promise of better lives, and to hold them accountable so we can be a part of them and yet remain in spiritual sovereignty and integrity. Religion is not a spectator sport and its true foundation is in the spiritual experiences of individuals.

My emphasis here has been on the shadow side of religious institutions created when they abandon spiritual principles for temporal power. However, it also behooves us to give credit for their many gifts. We might become thereby religious alchemists where the dross is burned away, and we discover the gold hidden in the heart of their – and our – spiritual natures.

The Future of Religion

What do our existing religions have to offer us in this age of the Internet, when our military powers could destroy life as we know it, when lies have become an accepted political currency, when the warming climate has reached crisis and is still denied at all levels of society, when our air, water, and soil are being poisoned for corporate gain, when women and minorities are still treated as second-class citizens, when religious institutions can no longer police their clergy to keep them from abusing vulnerable parishioners, when religious and other forms of bigotry have been normalized, when terrible things are done in the name of saviors and prophets? And would we *want* them involved when they are the same religions that brought us to this point?

Perhaps another perspective is in order. Humankind has been created wonderfully diverse, as creatures of both unique individuality and common ground, with pleasure in both outward belonging *and* internal exploration. We still belong to the land like we belong to our genetics and communities. Multiple languages were not a punishment. (We've seen where that myth came from.) Multiplicity is but one example of the riches given to us by the Creator, for each language is its own landscape that reflects the land and culture in which it developed and thereby is an expression of human experience. This diversity is a beautiful thing. The religion that cannot celebrate our diversity and foster human self-realization will have little to offer the people of today.

As religion brings people together around a common set of experiences, ideas, beliefs, theology, rules, and practices, it must also be open to its own self-reflection, growth, and evolution. Individuals can then be a part of something greater than themselves that also gives them value, and in which they can find meaning for their lives and direction for their actions. It can be a way to express collective values (which is where things get complicated). When those values are universal human values such as love or caring for others, they are life supporting, but when they include status, conquest, colonization, and domination, they have become a military and political organization and are no longer religions. What's more, the diversity of humankind requires a diversity of religious expression. This can mean many religions, or it could mean one religion with many facets. It could also mean the rise of non-religious movements that, nevertheless, allow people to come together around shared numinous experiences, practices, values, and social service.

The End and the Beginning

My dream is that spiritual experiences be fostered and be untainted by limiting concepts, generalizations, interpretations, or pre-existing meaning. In the end, we must remember that every monument, organization, and theology casts its shadow, even as it spreads the light that gave it birth. We have always yearned for the Divine to have a human face but, over and over, we have shaped that face to look like us – or like those in power. I hope we can find ways to enjoy our own identification with the Divine in our own way, without needing to impose it on others.

Wouldn't it be wonderful if we could join with our neighbors to take an honest look at the problems around us and what we might do about them, rather than engaging in puerile discussions about religious purity, social conformity, fruitless blame, and unquestionable theological "truths?" Of course, we might also blithely consume ourselves to death, destroy our environment and our relationships with each other while our governmental players, corporations, and religious institutions act like ancient mythological Titans locked in their own battles for power and dominance. Fortunately, there are individuals and groups that seek to connect us with our spiritual depths and steer the world toward a healthy environment free of chemical and social toxicity. The best of them promote healthy and constructive relationships among people, with the environment, and with the Divine.

Some 2,000 years ago, Magi from Persia (modern Iran) entered the Christian narrative to commemorate the end of the age of Aries and the arrival of the avatar of the Piscean age. I remain hopeful that some good star will yet call forth wise ones who will restore the gifts of our human depths with their potentials for further evolution. May they inspire us to return to our hearts' deepest yearnings for spiritual experience and, perhaps, even bring to fruition the mythical ideals of the approaching Aquarian age: friendship, egalitarianism, and expansion of consciousness. Perhaps those wise ones are already among us.

Perhaps, too, the time will then come when the prophecy of Jeremiah will be fulfilled:

> "... I will set my law within them and write it on their hearts; ... No longer need they teach one another to know the Lord ..."

Appendix A

Of Mind and Heart

First, I would warn any reader of the danger of taking anything I have written at face value. Better to consider it simply as a journal of my travels through what I could find of human history. I claim no truth but my own, and hope readers will do the same for themselves. If our respective truths are thoughtfully shared, we ourselves might be refined toward our wholeness, and a still greater truth realized.

Reality of the Psyche

I could not put this manuscript to rest until I explicitly acknowledged that the shaping of the spiritual impulse, people's reaction to it, ability to understand and implement it are subject to the same psychodynamics as every other impulse – high or low, personal or social, creative or destructive.

Thus, what follows are essays rooted in the reality that everything we experience occurs within the confines of the mind. Everything from the Word of God to love and hate, to lust and desire takes shape in the mind. This does not change when ideas are set down in writing. Writing is itself an externalization and objectification of the contents of the psyche. The beauty of the written word is that we can look at it, contemplate it, refine it, and reabsorb what is worthy and dispense with what is not. This is the power of personal journals as well as great philosophical tracts and Scriptures. They can be reviewed, tested, and further refined, if not written in stone, as the saying goes.

A Return to Soul – Living from the Heart

There is something creative in each of us – divine if you will – that seeks to realize itself and find manifestation in the world. These impulses may be facilitated, twisted, or crushed by the context in which individuals find themselves. They too often get lost in the engineered distractions of our current social and economic systems. While recognizing the realities of the world around us, we need to recover the deep yearning that makes the heart come alive. If there's truth in the idea that there is something divine in each of us, we err if we confine ourselves to only look to others to show the way. Their path may or may not serve us or speak to our experience of our world. Our way is made by living it. As Carl Jung admonished, we must each go our own way.[880]

I am reminded of the Gospel of Thomas that quotes Jesus in Verse 70 as saying,

*"When you bring forth that which is within you,
that which you bring forth will save you.
If you do not bring forth what is within you,
what you fail to bring forth will destroy you."*[881]

This idea is resurrected 2,000 years later by the late 21st century Sami Shaman Ailo Gaup who wrote,

*"The problem is actually not that we set ourselves too high targets and miss them,
but that we have low targets and hit them.
Unused possibilities and abilities are constantly beckoning us.
If we do not make use of them,
they turn sour and start to consume us from within.
Many an inner void has arisen in this way."*[882]

Appendix B

Substance and Shadow

Nothing here is meant to impugn the intentions of saints, saviors, gods, or advocates of these religions, nor the teachings held dear by their followers. It is a call to go deeper into their truths. It has unfortunately been the predicament of religions and other institutions to gaze only at their own light but others' shadows. It's time we attend to both light and shadow in ourselves and our institutions.

Anything of substance casts a shadow. It is a destructive folly to ignore or deny it. What is needed is to recognize the shadow, wrestle with the discomfort of it, make amends for its violations, and to zealously work to reduce its adverse outcomes. Then, we may find whether light is hidden in its heart, or if it is just an illusion – or both. This is more than control of outward behavior and public relations. It requires a constant returning to the Source and letting *its* light guide its contemporary manifestations.

What we deny does not go away. It hides inside of us and emerges unexpectedly at inopportune times, or we project it onto others. This fragments us and leaves us at the mercy of larger forces that will try to compensate for our blind spots in its own way. *Having* a shadow is not bad, but its denial generates adverse outcomes. This splitting and projection are, to my mind, the greatest psychological perils of our time. On the other hand, to care-fully explore it can reveal a hidden source of light and power that could support us. This takes courage, honest self-reflection, and integrity in both individuals and organizations. It can be difficult work and there is much aligned against it. As Carl Jung said in *Psychology and Alchemy*, "People will do anything, no matter how absurd, in order to avoid facing their own souls. One does not become enlightened by imagining figures of light, but by making the darkness conscious."[883] If that weren't enough, many of our relationships and social structures depend on us not making changes that might disrupt the status quo.

The measure of any religious movement is not its rituals, theology or saints, saviors or gods, or its shadow, but the degree to which it transforms its adherents into worthy vessels in which the divine source of life can find a hospitable home – a place to work its magic through their – or your – wholeness.

Appendix C

"The Fall" and the Psyche's Original Sin

The struggles I've described throughout these pages don't originate in the "natural" world. The ultimate problems we face arise from within us – individually and collectively. They are psycho-social problems that are triggered by needs for the survival of personal and collective identity, relationships with other people, and our relationship with the land from which we draw life.

I'd like to return to some of the ideas presented in the very first chapter with regard to early humanity's *participation mystique* and our early embedded relationship with the world around us. In the beginning, everything was alive, had soul, and we were a part of it. Nature responded to our thought and behavior and spoke to us. Those who could read these messages became their people's wise leaders. Even as we developed the idea of a centralized Spirit, we were still a part of it all. Then something in our consciousness changed: The Fall.

The Fall

This "fall" was not a theological event, decision, or action, but a change in consciousness. It was our loss of identification with nature, a fall from when we lived an integrated and interdependent life within the natural world. This loss of the *participation mystique* has made us aliens in our homeland, strangers to ourselves, and manipulators of people. While it has brought advances in technology, health, and nutrition, our failure to develop beyond it has cost us dearly.

The Original Sin – Fruits of the Tree of Knowledge of Good and Evil

Objectification was part of a process that separated us from our place in the greater world. But it also gave us self-consciousness and choice, along with the illusion of being independent from the landscapes around us and within us. However, it allowed for the *objectification* of other people and the elements of nature. In so doing, it reduced everything to a commodity with a drive for privatization and ownership of everything possible (or profitable). With that came the sale and abuse of women, men, and children; the unsustainable exploitation of the land, trees, and animals; and the crippling of our capacity for empathy and respect for living things. It is a suicidal path of fragmentation and contraction.

As our "science" became focused on ever smaller units and withdrew from larger questions, our consciousness also began to fragment. We came to value abstract ideas and collective beliefs over individual experiences. This left us not only having to defend beliefs but also face an increasing number of people and ideas that we perceive as "alien." Perfection according to an external ideal replaced integration and wholeness; and our efforts to conform further fragmented us into one-sided neuroses. We became as exiled from parts of ourselves as we were from the world outside. Through this alienation, the Savior we have been given is a relentless devouring beast who would crush all that does not conform or turn a profit. The Savior we *need* is the person, force, or institution that can re-integrate our fragmented consciousness.

Like the Tree of the Knowledge of Good and Evil, objectification is a double-edged sword. It does take us to a place of conscious choice. Also, seeing an objective other brings opportunity for genuine relationship, to behold something beautiful, to establish a conscious relationship with it and to realize our uniqueness as well as our unity with the other. It *could* ennoble rather than diminish us. Thus, objectification is an evolution of consciousness but, when it loses connection with our internal and external natures, it traps us in fragmentation, abuse, and war. When re-integrated into our wholeness, however, it places us on the threshold of revelation, where being *with* and being *one* can occur simultaneously. This is the mystics' goal of unity in multiplicity.

When we lose identification with the larger world (nature), we are left to identify with our own narrow perspectives and individualistic impulses: we make everything around us (including people) the object – or victim – of those impulses. It's not all psychological, of course. There *is* a real world that is both separate from us and of which we are a part. But we've created our own alien otherness because we are ourselves broken. Thus, the condition of the psyche is primary in any consideration of human activity because we perceive, experience, interpret, and communicate any reality through that psyche. There is no other way.

Re-Interpreting the Biblical Fall

If we view the Garden of Eden story as an allegory, it becomes a telling representation of this objectification. In our loss of the *participation mystique,* we "fell" into awareness, choice, and individuality, along with alienation wrought by this objectification.

Feeding the Shadow

Striving for externally determined perfection of religious ideals seems like virtue until its fruits are found in its wounds to the psyche. Our religious institutions show us an *ego ideal* through their image of an exceptional person, along with the teachings of that person's immediate disciples. We *project* what we believe to be the best of humanity onto those individuals and their teachings. As an ideal to which all should strive, we attempt to conform to those ideals but, of course, we all fall short. Our actions do not always follow our intention. Unacceptable habits don't go away because we no longer want them. We have impulses and doubts contrary to the ideal. These less desirable features of our being – and our *consciousness* of them – are *repressed* into an individual and collective *shadow*. After all, most of us are loath to face our failings and faults. Rather than claiming responsibility for the shadow elements of our personalities, we *project* them onto a real or imagined satanic being, malevolent demonic forces, or onto other individuals or groups.

But this projection onto others does not end the struggle because we are always threatened with the painful discovery that these are our own faults and shortcomings. We build defenses while we search for confirmation that it is the *other* who carries these faults. As for the collective shadow, any vulnerable population can be the target of our personal and collective projections. Thus, what should be an internal "holy war" is externalized with the resulting need for battles against people, events, things, and ideas. If we put it out there in the world, we can condemn it, fight it, and absolve ourselves of responsibility for its existence. We feel moral, righteous, justified and, in this too, we are diminished. Our power over our own shortcomings is lost. This external focus helps to keep us from knowing who we are and to keep us engaged in judgment and fragmentation rather than consciousness, transformation, and integration. There are genuine external battles to be fought. However, if we don't clear the moat from our own eye, we won't have much success dealing with the splinter in another's.

I should note here that the shadow is not always "negative." It contains whatever we and our culture *believe* to be unacceptable and is, therefore, relative to cultural needs. In a warrior culture, tenderness will naturally be suppressed. In a conquering culture, empathy for the oppressed is unacceptable. In a punitive culture, forgiveness is sinful. In a compassionate culture, harm to others is condemned.

This is not a new revelation. It is found in all those religions and philosophies that have their version of the "Golden Rule" asking us to give other people as much value as we expect for ourselves. What's more, the sayings of Jesus assert the principle that *everyone* is our neighbor, that whatever we do to another we do to him, and whatever we withhold from another, we withhold from the God he embodies.

So, What Is to Be done?

If we would move toward a genuine liberation (promised by almost every tradition), I suspect the following items would be worth considering for us all.
- Shift efforts from perfection according to external standards toward a condition of wholeness. Find the exiled parts of yourself, invite them back home, and forge a wholesome relationship with them.

- Give up the escape of blaming others – women, heretics, priests, minorities, politicians, televangelists, etc. – for our troubles. Instead, recognize your own contribution to what you perceive. Even if the other warrants your judgments, you are still responsible for your judgments.
- Re-establish intimacy with nature in whatever way you can – its cycles, beauties, and wounds – with awareness of the human impact on it. Remember that it's nature that supports life and is where our children will live.
- Build a new relationship with what is inside of you, untainted by consumerism, social pressure, and attention-grabbing diversions. This means 1) identifying the core values that make your heart come alive, 2) discovering parts of soul that have been lost in your efforts to gain skills, position, and security and, 3) bringing into the world the gifts you have as an individual, whether a skill, hobby, or a deep yearning that has always been with you.

The more whole we are, the more thoughtful, effective, and rewarding will be our actions and relationships – and the more effective our efforts at addressing the problems we face.

Appendix D

Revelation, Fragmentation, and Integration

We live in a spiritual wasteland of electronic devices, two-dimensional access to a world-wide web of information (and misinformation), swift and shiny means of transportation, the availability of almost instant communication, highly efficient weapons that could destroy us all, and more information than we can digest. With all this largesse, people are restless, insecure, empty, hungry, yearning, and searching.

In that void, we see a resurgence of interest in shamanism and indigenous cultures that attribute selfhood, intelligence, and communication to animals, objects, and events. We also see it in religious, spiritual, and self-help movements that seek to calm our gluttonous, fragmented, and manufactured desires in favor of unitive experiences. It appears on the edges of science in the Gaia hypothesis, in the realization of our impact on ecosystems and world climate, and in the strange behavior of subatomic particles. We find it in medicine where objective statistical realities and precise chemical measurements fail to provide the physiological foundation for health and wellness that gratitude, positive emotions, and supportive relationships provide. We find it in the field of psychology with a shift toward "Positive Psychology" and a focus on human strengths. And then there's Carl Jung's formulation of a psychology that can embrace the full spectrum of human experience from the mundane to the spiritual. We should remember, too, the drug experimentation of the 1960s in which psychoactive substances were used not just for recreational purposes but also to explore experience itself and gain perspectives beyond conditioned boundaries of perception. Ironically, it may be these fringe movements that could eventually direct us back toward the Center.

On a personal note, I found myself in recent decades turning not to psychological researchers but to poets who could articulate a personal, alive, and subjective relationship with the world. Artists and poets often grant sentience, perception, and consciousness to the objects of the world. I often turned to the writings of John O'Donohue, David Whyte, Mary Oliver, and Rainer Maria Rilke, among others. Memorizing their poetry brought insight and comfort.

Traditional shamans, it seems, have generally recognized the selfhood of natural elements, both animate and inanimate. They may have conversations with their spirits, as well as trees, stones, mountains, winds, bodies of water, etc. This was not so unusual in early cultures that we generally consider "primitive." Because of our modern objectification, however, people who feel a shamanic calling are faced with overcoming the conditioning that would confine intelligence and personhood to within their own skulls.

Children can still do this. Often seen as a stage of development, they have conversations with all manner of "others." Children's early experiences have been an open secret in their conversations with "imaginary friends," memories of apparent past-life experiences, and seeing things that others don't see. Rather than just immature development, however, these perceptions are a function of theta brainwave states that are strong in preschool children. This is a phase of brain development that we pass through but may return to at will for various purposes. Thus, childhood states are not just phases to move beyond on our way to a stress-filled beta-brainwave adulthood. Rather, they are demonstrations – practice, if you will – of inner resources we might access at will when we understand their value.

Modern attitudes, of course, encourage externally-focused beta brainwave states to the degree that people must relearn to produce at will the deeper alpha and theta states – the first providing relaxed alertness while the other facilitates visionary experiences. But, as Celtic shaman Tom Cowan has noted, ". . . our society generally discourages private visionary experiences in favor of mass-produced fantasies such as movies, video games, and comic books."[884] In short, our brain development and Western culture encourage extraverted, externally dependent modes of perception and behavior that erode our potential for perceptual and spiritual autonomy. There is no room for inspiration, let alone revelation, unless we make a space for it.

Introverts in this European-American culture are often portrayed as deficient or socially awkward. However, introversion is a gift of perception into personal landscapes not easily visible to extraverts. This distinction was explored by Carl Jung[885] in the last century and by those in this century waking up to its advantages.[886] These are often gifted people who can stand on the thresholds of consciousness and, at will, look both inward and outward, to the personal and the impersonal.

The growing interest in neo-shamanic practice, meditation, neurofeedback, and the therapeutic use of entheogens reflects a societal attempt to counterbalance our pathologically extraverted, externally dependent obsession with the outer material world. Imagine the advantages to both individuals and society if we were all trained in the development of our imaginal faculties where we could change perception and perspective at will. Of course, some will have more natural aptitude for such things than others.

I do not suggest that we all become neo-shamanic, ghost whispering, drug taking, trance mediums or visionaries, but we could at least get beyond the religious and cultural straightjackets that truncate a true science that could help us explore the possibilities. If we could do that, we might restore the value of people who have these aptitudes, provide a safe context for them to explore their gifts, and allow them to serve the larger community. We would all benefit.

The Psyche's Salvation

The salvation of humanity's fragmented consciousness and communities rests in those able to effect various forms of re-collecting the soul and re-integrating our communities into a functional whole. In the end, we are each individually responsible for the shape of the mask we put on the face of the Divine – and for its shadows. No matter our intention or degree of devotion, we are responsible for the fruits of our ideas and actions, and whether those fruits support life – or poison our people, land, and our relationship with the Divine.

Acknowledgements

Many people – friends and clients – have contributed to my observations by sharing their experiences, enduring my questions, forwarding information they thought might be relevant, or simply encouraging my efforts. They included not only people of traditional Christian faiths, but Shamans, Druids, Native Americans, Rosicrucians, Swamis, Sufis, and New Thought teachers.

Two friends read parts of the manuscript and gave valuable feedback for which I'm grateful. They were Tom Cowan and Cindy Leigh McGinley.

Three patient individuals read versions of the manuscript and helped shape it into a more readable account of what I was trying to say. I did not always take their advice so the responsibility of whatever was written here remains mine. Nevertheless, their encouragement and good humor helped me endure my attempts to communicate my ruminations. They are:

Carol Kniskern who was a (mostly) patient partner as I spread materials out on the dining room table for days on end. She provided valuable feedback from her biblical background that far exceeds mine.

Steve Walker who was subjected to a lumbering and wandering manuscript with tangents and endless parenthetical phrases. His feedback helped me to re-focus on the task at hand and take more direct routes through my thoughts to my conclusions.

And, Jami Shoemaker who helped put a professional touch on an otherwise amateur production.

Through their feedback, I learned about my own thought processes and ways to make their content more comprehensible – to myself and to others. Thank you.

References

Achterberg, Jean, *Imagery and Healing: Shamanism and Modern Medicine*, Shamballa, Boston, 1985

Albright, William Foxwell, *Yahweh and the Gods of Canaan: A Historical Analysis of Two Contrasting Faiths*, Eisenbrauns, Winona Lake, IN, 1990

Aldred, Cyril, *Akhenaten: Pharaoh of Egypt - a new study*, McGraw-Hill, NY, 1968

Armstrong, Karen, *Mohammed: A Biography of the Prophet*, HarperCollins, San Francisco, 1992

Ashe, Geoffrey, *Dawn of the Dawn: A Search for the Earthly Paradise*, John MacRae, NY, 1992

Baigent, Michael, Richard Leigh and Henry Lincoln, *Holy Blood, Holy Grail*, Delacorte Press, NY, 1982

Barstow, Anne, "The Prehistoric Goddess" in *The Book of the Goddess Past and Present: An Introduction to Her Religion*, Carl Olson, ed, Crossroad, NY, 1990

Barthel, Manfred, trans and adapted by Mark Howson, *What the Bible Really Says: Casting New Light on the Book of Books*, Quill, NY, 1983

Batzel, Beth and Karl Schlotterbeck, *Lion of Satan, Lion of God*, published by the authors, 1993

Berry, Gerald, *Religions of the World*, Barnes & Noble, NY, 1968

Bloom, Harold and David Rosenberg, *The Book of J*, Grove Press, NY, 1990

Bowie, W. Russell, "History of the English Bible," in *The Encyclopedia Americana, International Edition*, Vol. 3, Americana Corporation, NY, 1972

Breasted, James Henry, *The Dawn of Conscience*, Charles Scribner's Sons, NY, 1933

Brusher, Joseph, *Popes Through the Ages*, Neff-Kane, San Rafael, CA 1980

Budge, E.A. Wallis, *Egyptian Magic*, Dover Publications, NY, 1971

Burkert, Walter, *Ancient Mystery Cults*, Harvard Univ. Press, Cambridge Mass., 1987

Cahill, Thomas, *How the Irish Saved Civilization: The Untold Story of Ireland's Heroic Role from the Fall of Rome to the Rise of Medieval Europe,* Anchor Books, 1995

Cain, Susan, *Quiet: The Power of Introverts in a World That Can't Stop Talking,* Crown Publishers, 2012
Casson, Lionel, *Ancient Egypt,* Time, Inc., NY, 1965

Cavendish, Richard, ed., *Legends of the World,* Schocken Books, NY, 1982

Clark, R.T. Rundle, *Myth and Symbol in Ancient Egypt,* Thames & Hudson, NY 1959

Cotterell, Arthur, *A Dictionary of World Mythology,* Putnam's Sons, NY 1979

Cowan, Tom, *The Book of Séance: How to Reach Out to the Next World,* Contemporary Books, 1994

Cross, Fran, "Frank Moore Cross: An Interview," in *Bible Review,* Vol. VIII, No. 4, August 1992

Cumbey, Constance, *The Hidden Dangers of the Rainbow: The New Age Movement and Our Coming Age of Barbarism,* Huntington House, Shreveport, LA, 1983

Doane, T.W., *Bible Myths and Their Parallels in other Religions,* University Books, 1971

Douglas-Klotz, Neil, *Prayers of the Cosmos: Meditations on the Aramaic Words of Jesus,* Harper and Row, San Francisco, CA, 1990

Eisler, Riane, *The Chalice and the Blade: Our History, Our Future,* Harper and Row, NY, 1987

Enlightenment from the Aramaic: Selected Passages from the Khabouris Manuscript, An Ancient Text of the Syriac New Testament, Yonan Codex Foundation, Atlanta, GA, 1974.

Errico, Rocco, *Let There Be Light: The Seven Keys,* DeVorss & Co., Marina del Rey, CA, 1985

Errico, Rocco, *Treasures from the Language of Jesus,* DeVorss, Marina del Rey, CA, 1987

Feuerstein, Georg, *Sacred Sexuality: Living the Vision of the Erotic Spirit,* J.P. Tarcher, Los Angeles, 1992

Frankfort, Henri, *Ancient Egyptian Religion,* Harper and Row, NY, 1948

Franzius, Enno, *History of the Order of Assassins,* Funk & Wagnalls, NY, 1969

Friedman, Richard, *Who Wrote the Bible?* Harper & Row, NY, 1987

Gardiner, Sir Alan, *Egypt of the Pharaohs*, Oxford Univ Press, NY, 1961

Gardner, Joseph L., ed., *Reader's Digest Atlas of the Bible: An Illustrated Guide to the Holy Land*, Pleasantville NY, 1981

Garraty, John and Peter Gay, eds., *The Columbia History of the World*, Harper & Row, NY, 1972

Gaup, Ailo, *The Shamanic Zone*, Three Bears Publishing, Kindle Edition, 2014

Ginsburg, Carlo, trans. by Raymond Rosenthal, *Ecstasies: Deciphering the Witches' Sabbath*, Pantheon Books, NY, 1991

Godwin, Joscelyn, *Mystery Religions in the Ancient World*, Harper and Row, San Francisco, 1981

Graves, Robert & Raphael Patai, *Hebrew Myths: The Book of Genesis*, Greenwich House, NY, 1983

Gray, John, *Near Eastern Mythology*, Peter Bedrick Books, NY, 1982 revision

Gray, William, *Western Inner Workings*, Samuel Weiser, Inc., York Beach, Maine, 1983

Guidici, Frank, *Overview of the New Testament*, (undated audiotape), Unity Village, MO

Guidici, Frank, *An Overview of the Old Testament: A Historical and Metaphysical Perspective*, (audio tape set, undated), Unity Village, MO

Guillaumont, A, Henri-Charles Puech, Gilles Quispel, Walter Till, Yassah 'Abd Al Masih, *The Gospel According to Thomas: Coptic Text Established and Translated*, Harper & Row, NY 1959

Hall, Nor, *The Moon and the Virgin: Reflections on the Archetypal Feminine*, Harper & Row, NY, 1980

Hall, Robert, "Epispasm: Circumcision in Reverse," in *Bible Review*, Vol. VIII, No. 4, August 1992

Harner, Michael, *The Way of the Shaman: A Guide to Power and Healing,* Harper and Row, 1980

Harner, Michael, *Cave and Cosmos: Shamanic Encounters with Another Reality*, North Atlantic Books, 2013

Hieronimus, Robert, with Laura Cortner, *Founding Fathers, Secret Societies: Freemasons, Illuminati, Rosicrucians, and the Decoding of the Great Seal*, Destiny Books, 2006

Highwater, Jamake *Myth and Sexuality*, Meridian, NY, 1988

Hoeller, Hans, "God the Father, God the Mother; Gnostic Spiritual Feminism" (undated audiotape), BC Tapes

Hoeller, Hans, "Paul the Gnostic Apostle" Hoeller, undated audiotape, BC Recordings

Hoeller, Stephan A., *The Gnostic Jung and the Seven Sermons to the Dead*, Quest Books, 1982, Wheaton, Ill.

Hoeller, Stephan, *Secret Sayings of Jesus*, #GG4, BC Recordings, Los Angeles, CA

Ions, Veronica, *Egyptian Mythology*, Hamlyn Publishing Group Ltd, Middlesex, 1968

Jackson, John, *Man, God and Civilization*, Citadel Press, NJ, 1972

"Jerome," in *Encyclopedia Americana*, Vol. 16, Encyclopedia Americana Corp, NY, 1972

Jonas, Hans, *The Gnostic Religion*, Beacon Press, Boston, 1958. (GR)

Jones, Tom, "Constantine I," in *Encyclopedia Americana*, Vol. 7, Encyclopedia Americana Corp, NY, 1972

Jung, C.G., *Psychological Types*, in *The Collected Works of C.G. June*, Volume 6, Princeton University Press, 1971

Jung, C.G., *Psychology and Alchemy*, in *The Collected Works of C.G. Jung*, Volume 12, Princeton University Press, 1968, pp. 99-100

Jung, C. G., "*The Red Book: Liber Novus – A Reader's Edition*, edited by Sonu Shamdasani, W.W. Norton and Company, 2009

Kersten, Holger, *Jesus Lived in India: His Unknown Life Before and After the Crucifixion*, Element Books, Ltd, Dorset, England, 1986

King, C.W., *The Gnostics and Their Remains, Ancient and Mediaeval*, Wizards Bookshelf, MN, 1973 (originally publ. in 1887)

Kramer, Samuel, *History Begins at Sumer*, Doubleday, NY, 1959

Kramer Samuel, *The Sacred Marriage Rite*, Indiana University Press, 1969, p 63

Lamsa, George, *The Holy Bible from Ancient Eastern Manuscripts*, A.J. Holman Co, Nashville, TN, 1957

Lamsa, George, *Idioms in the Bible Explained: A Key to the Holy Scriptures*, Holman Bible Publishers, Nashville, TN, 1971

Lamsa, George, *Old Testament Light: The Indispensable Guide to the Customs, Manners, and Idioms of Biblical Times*, Harper and Row, NY, 1964

Leloup, Jean-Yves, *The Gospel of Thomas: The Gnostic Wisdom of Jesus*, Inner Traditions (Kindle Edition), 2005

Lewis, H. Spencer, *The Symbolic Prophecy of the Great Pyramid*, Supreme Grand Lodge of AMORC, San Jose, 1936

Lyons, Arthur, *Satan Wants You: The Cult of Devil Worship in America*, The Mysterious Press, NY, 1988

Mabry, John, *The Way of Thomas: Insights for Spiritual Living from the Gnostic Gospel of Thomas*, The Apocryphile Press, Kindle Edition, 2007, location 560

MacGregor, Geddes, *Gnosis: A Renaissance in Christian Thought*, Theosophical Publishing House, Wheaton, IL, 1979

Mason, Herbert, *Gilgamesh: A Verse Narrative*, Mentor Book, NY 1970

Mehr, Farhang, *The Zoroastrian Tradition: An Introduction to the Ancient Wisdom of Zarathustra*, Element, Rock Port, Mass, 1991

Mellaart, James, *Catal Huyuk: A Neolithic Town in Anatolia*, McGraw-Hill Book Co, NY, 1967

Mertz, Barbara, *Temples, Tombs and Hieroglyphs: A Popular History of Ancient Egypt*, revised edition, Peter Bedrick Books, NY 1990

Mitchell, Stephen, *The Gospel According to Jesus: A New Translation and Guide to His Essential Teachings for Believers and Unbelievers*, HarperCollins, NY, 1991

Metzger, Bruce and Roland Murphy, eds., *The New Oxford Annotated Bible, New Revised Standard Version,* Oxford University Press, NY, 1994

Montet, Pierre, *Eternal Egypt*, Mentor, NY, 1964

Narby, Jeremy and Francis Huxley, eds., *Shamans Through Time: 500 Years on the Path to Knowledge,* Jeremy P. Tarcher/Putnam, 2001

Neumann, Erich, *The Great Mother: An Analysis of the Archetype*, Bollingen Series XLVII, Princeton University Press, 1955, 1963

The New English Bible, Cambridge University Press, 1970

The New English Bible: New Testament, The Delegates of the Oxford University Press, and the Syndics of the Cambridge University Press, 1961

Nigosian, Solomon, *Judaism: The Way of Holiness*, Aquarian Press, Great Britain, 1986

Noss, John B., *Man's Religions*, Macmillan Co., NY, 1963

Pagels, Elaine, *Adam, Eve, and the Serpent*, Random House, NY, 1988

Pagels, Elaine, *The Gnostic Gospels*, Vintage Books, NY, 1979

Palo, John, "Women of Ancient Egypt" in *The Rosicrucian Digest*, Vol. 66, No. 1, Jan/Feb 1988

Parrinder, Geoffrey, ed., *World Religions from Ancient History to the Present*, Hamlyn Publishing Group Ltd., Newnes Books, 1971

Parrinder, Geoffrey, ed, *World Religions from Ancient History to the Present*, Facts on File Publications, NY, 1983

Perera, Sylvia Brinton, *Descent to the Goddess: A Way of Initiation for Women,* Inner City Books, 1981

Potter, Charles Francis, *The Story of Religion*, Garden City Publishing Co, Garden City, NY 1929

Pritchard, James, ed., *Ancient Near Eastern Texts Relating to the Old Testament*, Princeton Univ Press, 1955

Qualls-Corbett, Nancy, *The Sacred Prostitute: Eternal Aspect of the Feminine*, Inner City Books, Toronto, 1982

Rainey, Anson, "The 'Apiru Problem," in *Biblical Archeology Review*, Nov/Dec 1991, p. 59

Robinson, Herbert Spencer and Knox Wilson, *Myths and Legends of All Nations*, Rowman & Allanheld, NJ, 1976

Rothgeb, Carrie Lee, *Abstracts of the Standard Edition of the Complete Psychological Works of Sigmund Freud*, Jason Aronson, NY, 1973

Rudolph, Kurt, *Gnosis: The Nature and History of Gnosticism*, Harper and Row, San Francisco, 1984

Russell, Jeffrey Burton, *Witchcraft in the Middle Ages*, Cornell Univ Press, 1972

Sjoo, Monica & Barbara Mor, *The Great Cosmic Mother: Rediscovering the Religion of the Earth*, Harper & Row, San Francisco, 1987

Smith, George, *Chaldean Account of Genesis*, Wizards Bookshelf, MN, 1977 reproduction of the 1876 edition

Smith, Morton, *Jesus the Magician*, Harper and Row, San Francisco, 1978

Smith, Morton, *The Secret Gospel*, the Dawn Horse Press, Clear Lake, CA, 1973, 1982
Stone, Merlin, *When God Was a Woman*, Harcourt, Brace, Jovanovich, NY, 1976

Strachan, Elspeth and Gordon, *Freeing the Feminine*, Labarum Publications, Ltd., Dunbar Scotland, 1985

Szekely, Edmond Bordeaux, *The Essene Jesus: A Revaluation from the Dead Sea Scrolls*, Academy Books, San Diego, CA, 1972

Tompkins, Peter, *Secrets of the Great Pyramid*, Harper & Row, NY, 1971

Ulansey, David, *The Origins of the Mithraic Mysteries: Cosmology and Salvation in the Ancient World*, Oxford University Press, NY 1989

"Valentinians", in *Encyclopedia Americana*, Vol. 27, Encyclopedia Americana Corp, NY, 1972

Vanderkam, James, "Implications for the History of Judaism and Christianity", in *The Dead Sea Scrolls After Forty Years*, Biblical Archeological Society, Wash, DC, 1991

Walker, Benjamin, *Gnosticism: Its History and Influence*, Aquarian Press, Northhamptonshire, 1983

Walsh, Michael, *An Illustrated History of the Popes: Saint Peter to John Paul II*, St. Martin's Press, NY, 1980

Warner, Marina, *Alone of All Her Sex: The Myth and the Cult of the Virgin Mary*, Vintage Books, NY, 1976

Weddeck, Harry, and Wade Baskin, *Dictionary of Pagan Religions*, Philosophical Library, NY 1971

Whiston, William, *The Works of Josephus, Complete and Unabridged*, Hendrickson Publishers, MA, 1987

Wolkstein, Diane and Samuel Noah Kramer, *Inanna: Queen of Heaven and Earth, Her Stories and Hymns from Sumer*, Harper & Row, 1983

Wooley, C. Leonard, *The Sumerians*, Norton & Co, NY, 1965

Used but not referenced:
Koltuv, Barbara Black, *The Book of Lilith*, Nicolas-Hays, Inc., York Beach, ME, 1986.

Sanders, James, "Understanding the Development of the Biblical Texts", in *The Dead Sea Scrolls After Forty Years*, Biblical Archeological Society, Wash, DC, 1991.

Shanks, Hershel, James Vanderkam, P. Kyle McCarter, Jr., James Sanders, The *Dead Sea Scrolls After Forty Years*, Biblical Archeological Society, Wash, DC, 1991.

Barton, Bruce, *The Man Nobody Knows*, Collier Books, NY, 1925.

Breasted, James, *A History of Egypt*, Charles Scribner's Sons, NY, 1909.

Edwards, I.E.S., *The Pyramids of Egypt*, The Viking Press, NY, 1972.

Goedicke, Hans, *Man & God in Ancient Egypt,* course notes, the Johns Hopkins University, 1969.

Endnotes

[1] *The New English Bible: New Testament*, 1961, p. 293
[2] Sjoo and Mor, pp. 151 & 153
[3] Highwater, p. 50
[4] Sjoo and Mor, p. 10
[5] Sjoo and Mor, p. 184
[6] Batzel and Schlotterbeck
[7] Genesis 11:30-31
[8] Genesis 12:1
[9] Noss, p. 499
[10] Garraty & Gay, p. 55
[11] Gray, John, p. 40
[12] Wooley, pp. 39, 126
[13] Garraty, pp. 57-58
[14] Wooley, pp. 29, 33
[15] Garraty & Gay, p. 60
[16] Gray, John, p. 55
[17] Cavendish, p. 94
[18] Robinson & Knox, p. 10
[19] Kramer, 1959, p. 29-30
[20] Garraty & Gay, p. 62
[21] Garraty & Gay, p. 62
[22] Wooley, p. 103
[23] Wooley, p. 120
[24] Wooley, p. 106
[25] Wooley, p. 146
[26] Wooley, p. 107
[27] Cotterell, p. 16
[28] Gray, John, p. 53, 56
[29] Strachan & Strachan, p. 37
[30] Qualls-Corbett, p. 24
[31] Cotterell, p. 16
[32] Qualls-Corbett, p. 24
[33] Kramer, 1969, p 63
[34] Wooley, p. 119
[35] Kramer, 1959, p. 78, 79
[36] Jackson, p. 84; and Smith, George, p. 58
[37] Kramer, 1959, p. 90
[38] Smith, George, p. 59
[39] Kramer, 1959, pp. 105-106
[40] Gray, John, p. 25
[41] Kramer, 1959, p. 79
[42] Kramer, 1959, p. 77
[43] Parrinder, 1983, p. 118
[44] Robinson & Knox, p. 11, 12
[45] Parrinder, 1983, p. 118
[46] Kramer, 1959, p. 104
[47] Kramer, 1959, p. 77
[48] Kramer, 1959, p. 101-103
[49] Barthel, p. 46
[50] Wooley, pp. 124

[51] Gray, John, p. 50
[52] Garraty & Gay, p. 52
[53] Barthel, p. 69
[54] Stone, p. 4
[55] Wolkstein & Kramer, p. 42
[56] Stone, p. 23
[57] Hall, Nor, p. 10
[58] Perera, p. 9-10; and Gray, John, p. 36
[59] Mason, p. 118
[60] Mason, p. 43
[61] Mason, p. 45
[62] Noss, p. 945-496
[63] Genesis. 35:2
[64] Nigosian, p. 66; and Potter, p. 56
[65] Noss, p. 497
[66] Albright, p. 87
[67] Rainey, p. 59
[68] Cross, p. 30
[69] Albright, p. 74-75
[70] Albright, p. 84, 108
[71] Noss, p. 498, 500
[72] Albright, p. 65
[73] Genesis 12:10
[74] Lamsa, 1964, p. 40
[75] Genesis 11:12-13
[76] Genesis 13:14-15
[77] Genesis 16:13
[78] Genesis 17:11
[79] Genesis 18:16-33
[80] Genesis 19:5
[81] Genesis 19:8
[82] Genesis 19:11
[83] Genesis 19:26
[84] Genesis 19:31-38
[85] Genesis 20:1-18
[86] Genesis 26:7-11
[87] Genesis 32:22-31
[88] Genesis 34:2-4
[89] Exodus 2:1-10
[90] Breasted, 1933, p. 24
[91] Gardiner, p. 27
[92] Garraty & Gay, p. 69
[93] Gardiner, p. 27
[94] Aldred, p. 164
[95] Aldred, p. 22
[96] Pritchard, p. 31
[97] Montet, p. 55
[98] Aldred, p. 20
[99] Ions, p. 11
[100] Breasted, 1933, p. 25
[101] Clark, p. 41

[102] Frankfort, pp. 15, 13, 10
[103] Frankfort, pp. 16, 18
[104] Clark, p. 29
[105] Clark, p. 36
[106] Clark, p. 87
[107] Pritchard, p. 371
[108] Pritchard, p. 371
[109] Ions, p. 37
[110] Ions, p. 95
[111] Frankfort, p. 63
[112] Breasted, 1933, p. 20
[113] Ions, p. 115
[114] Clark, p. 266
[115] Clark, pp. 236, 219, 242
[116] Ions, p. 127
[117] Clark, p. 73
[118] Frankfort, pp. 69, 73, 77
[119] Frankfort, p. 126
[120] Ions, p. 61
[121] Jackson, p. 123-124
[122] Breasted, 1933, pp. 109, 113
[123] Berry, p. 10
[124] Pritchard, p. 35
[125] Breasted, 1933, p. 34
[126] Breasted, 1933, p. 37
[127] Breasted, 1933, pp. 34, 38
[128] Budge, p. 6
[129] Budge, p. 7-10
[130] Budge, p. 23
[131] Budge, p. xii-xiv
[132] Budge, pp. 20, 21
[133] Montet, p. 57
[134] Ions, p. 14, 27
[135] Montet, p. 59
[136] Ions, p. 16
[137] Aldred, p. 25
[138] Frankfort, p. 63
[139] Frankfort, p. 30
[140] Ions, p. 17
[141] Clark, p. 30
[142] Aldred, p. 29-30
[143] Aldred, p. 30
[144] Garraty & Gay, p. 74
[145] Casson, p. 35
[146] Stone, p. 36
[147] Highwater, p. 20
[148] Casson, p. 79
[149] Stone, p. 38
[150] Palo, p. 12-13
[151] Aldred, p. 23
[152] Garraty & Gay, p. 76

[153] Breasted, 1933, p. 27
[154] Garraty & Gay, p. 71
[155] Lewis; Tompkins
[156] Breasted, 1933, p. 275
[157] Aldred, p. 35
[158] Breasted, 1933, p. 280
[159] Mertz, p. 217
[160] Aldred, p. 52
[161] Mertz, p. 217
[162] Breasted, 1933, p. 280
[163] Aldred, p. 190
[164] Aldred, p. 188-189
[165] Aldred, p. 52
[166] Mertz, p. 232
[167] Aldred, p. 194, 258
[168] Mertz, p. 324-235
[169] Aldred, p. 52
[170] Aldred, p. 260
[171] Garraty & Gay, p. 81
[172] Garraty & Gay, p. 79
[173] Ashe, p. 117
[174] Aldred, p. 37
[175] Gardiner, p. 356, 203
[176] Breasted, 1933, p. 349
[177] Potter, p. 42
[178] Parrinder, 1983, p. 22
[179] Budge, p. 5
[180] Breasted, 1933, p. 351
[181] Potter, p. 57
[182] Exodus 4:25-26, *The New English Bible*
[183] Exodus 14:2
[184] Lamsa, 1964, p. 125 - 127
[185] Graves, p. 145
[186] Ginsburg, p. 38
[187] Garraty & Gay, p. 141
[188] Stone, p. 121
[189] Friedman, p. 82
[190] Exodus 22:30
[191] Exodus 24:8
[192] Noss, p. 506, 506
[193] Friedman, p. 36
[194] Kersten, p. 48-49
[195] Exodus 21:23,24
[196] Noss, p. 505
[197] Exodus 23:16 and again in 34:26
[198] Noss, p. 506, 507
[199] Noss, p. 507
[200] Acts 7:22
[201] Breasted, 1933, p. 353
[202] Num. 5:22, and Deut. 27:15
[203] II Kings 18:4

[204] Breasted, 1933, p. 354, 357
[205] Breasted, 1933, p. 360, 364-365, 371
[206] Pritchard, p. 10
[207] Rothgeb, p. 250
[208] Jackson, p. 132-133
[209] Sjoo & Mor, p. 268
[210] Stone, p. 124
[211] Breasted, 1933, p. 351
[212] Stone, p. 124
[213] Gray, John, p. 109
[214] Barthel, p. 118
[215] Sjoo & Mor, p. 155
[216] Stone, p. 117
[217] Stone, p. 64
[218] Stone, p. 118
[219] Albright, p. 111
[220] Gray, John, p. 64
[221] Gray, John, p. 64
[222] Albright, p. 120
[223] Gray, John, p. 68 - 70
[224] Albright, p. 121
[225] Albright, p. 124
[226] Gray, John, p. 69
[227] Gray, John, p. 64
[228] Albright, p. 124-125
[229] Gray, John, p. 72
[230] Albright, p. 126
[231] Gray, John, p. 70
[232] Gray, John, p. 87, 113
[233] Albright, p. 134
[234] Gray, John, p. 60, 70
[235] Eisler, pp. 12 & 27
[236] Sjoo & Mor, p. 19
[237] Eisler, p. 2
[238] Eisler, pp. 27 - 42
[239] Eisler, p. 42
[240] Eisler, p. 4,5
[241] Eisler, pp. 10, 23, 66-67
[242] Sjoo & Mor, p. 99
[243] Eisler, pp. 18, 20
[244] Sjoo & Mor, pp. 100-103
[245] Sjoo & Mor, p. 177
[246] Sjoo & Mor, p. 49
[247] Sjoo & Mor, p. 271-272
[248] Hall, Nor, p. 11
[249] Strachan & Strachan, p. 56-57
[250] Strachan, E & G, p. 57
[251] Stone, pp. 201, 212
[252] Strachan, E & G, p. 41
[253] Strachan, E & G, p. 89
[254] Noss, p. 67

[255] Strachan, E & G, p. 55
[256] Eisler, p. 18
[257] Stone, p. 4
[258] Stone, p. 15
[259] Mellaart, p. 20
[260] Sjoo & Mor, p. 19
[261] Sjoo & Mor, p. 213
[262] Qualls-Corbett, p. 22
[263] Qualls-Corbett, p. 23
[264] Qualls-Corbett, p. 34
[265] Qualls-Corbett, p. 37
[266] Qualls-Corbett, p. 30
[267] Qualls-Corbett, p. 34
[268] (https://www.nationalgeographic.com/archaeology-and-history/magazine/2019/march-april/early-agricultural-settlement-catalhoyuk-turkey/?cmpid=org=ngp::mc=crm-email::src=ngp::cmp=editorial::add=History_20190401::rid=727657)
[269] Ashe, p. 6
[270] Eisler, p. 44
[271] Sjoo & Mor, p. 219
[272] Eisler, p. 44
[273] Sjoo & Mor, p. 220
[274] Stone, p. 23
[275] Eisler, p. 57
[276] Sjoo & Mor, p. 201
[277] Numbers 31: 32-35
[278] Eisler, p. 44, 49
[279] Eisler, p. 53
[280] Eisler, p. 46
[281] Eisler, p. 45
[282] Ashe, p. 30
[283] Eisler, p. 48
[284] Barstow, pp. 12, 13
[285] Stone, p. 23
[286] Eisler, p. 74
[287] Stone, pp. 132, 133
[288] Joshua 10:40-41
[289] Noss, pp. 509-511
[290] Joshua 23:16
[291] Weddeck &Baskin, p. 45
[292] Gray, John, p. 83
[293] Cavendish, p. 140
[294] Gray, John, pp. 87, 113
[295] Gray, John, p. 103
[296] Graves, p. 69
[297] Friedman, p. 39
[298] I Samuel 27: 7-10
[299] I Samuel 27:10-12
[300] 1 Samuel 28:3-4
[301] I Samuel 28:6
[302] I Samuel 28:13-20
[303] I Samuel 14:43-46

[304] Graves, p. 175
[305] II Samuel 1:10
[306] II Samuel 5:3
[307] Barthel, p. 172
[308] Friedman, p. 39-40
[309] II Samuel 5:10
[310] II Samuel 12:10
[311] Friedman, p. 38, 40
[312] Friedman, p. 41, 42
[313] Friedman, p. 44
[314] Friedman, p. 49
[315] Berry, p. 32-33
[316] Friedman, p. 43, 46-48
[317] Friedman, p. 87
[318] Bloom & Rosenberg, p. 186
[319] Bloom & Rosenberg, p. 43, 47
[320] Friedman, p. 61
[321] Friedman, p. 75, 83
[322] Friedman, p. 87
[323] Bloom & Rosenberg, p. 7
[324] Friedman, p. 79, 80, 83
[325] Friedman, p. 66, 75
[326] Friedman, p. 88
[327] Nigosian, p. 150
[328] Noss, p. 516
[329] Nigosian, p. 77
[330] Noss, p. 514
[331] Noss, p. 514-515
[332] Nigosian, p. 80
[333] Nigosian, p. 80
[334] Noss, p. 517
[335] Noss, p. 523
[336] Noss, p. 526
[337] Berry, p. 33
[338] Friedman, pp. 91-92
[339] Friedman, p. 95
[340] Friedman, p. 96-97
[341] Friedman, p. 97
[342] Friedman, p. 103
[343] Friedman, pp. 105, 113
[344] Friedman, p. 120
[345] Friedman, p. 102
[346] Noss, p. 528, and Garraty & Gay, p. 161
[347] Friedman, p. 124
[348] Friedman, p. 146-147
[349] Noss, pp. 528-529
[350] Nigosian, p. 137
[351] Noss, p. 535
[352] Friedman, p. 98
[353] Friedman, p. 99
[354] Noss, p. 536

[355] Jeremiah 44:17-18
[356] Friedman, p. 154
[357] Noss, p. 538
[358] Noss, p. 537
[359] Gray, John, pp. 28-29, 32
[360] Strachan, E & G, p. 42, 43
[361] Pritchard, p. 383
[362] Pritchard, p. 384
[363] Berry, p. 12
[364] Jackson, p. 243
[365] Berry, p. 14
[366] Ashe, p. 76
[367] Doane, pp. 34-35
[368] Ashe, pp. 30, 46, 82
[369] Noss, p. 478
[370] Friedman, p. 155
[371] Barthel, p. 23
[372] King, p. 32
[373] Friedman, p. 158
[374] Noss, p. 541
[375] Noss, p. 543
[376] Noss, p. 547
[377] Friedman, p. 158
[378] Noss, p. 546
[379] Friedman, pp. 158-159
[380] Noss, p. 546
[381] Noss, pp. 456-547
[382] Noss, p. 549
[383] Friedman, pp. 190-191
[384] Friedman, p. 217
[385] Friedman, p. 192
[386] Friedman, p. 197
[387] Numbers 25:13
[388] Friedman, p. 203
[389] Friedman, pp. 159-160
[390] Friedman, pp. 218, 219, 223
[391] Friedman, pp. 226-227
[392] Jeremiah 8:8
[393] Friedman, p. 209
[394] Noss, p. 466
[395] Mehr, p. 5
[396] Noss, p. 468
[397] Berry, p. 37
[398] Noss, p. 479
[399] Mehr, p. 50
[400] Mehr, p. 55
[401] Mehr, pp. 15, 64
[402] Nigosian, p. 167
[403] Mehr, p. 97
[404] Parrinder, 1971, p. 178
[405] Noss, p. 483

[406] Berry, p. 37
[407] Noss, p. 476
[408] Noss, pp. 487-488, and Berry, p. 37
[409] Noss, p. 478
[410] Mehr, p. 51
[411] Noss, p. 483
[412] Mehr, p. 97
[413] Parrinder, 1971, p. 181
[414] Noss, p. 485
[415] Berry, p. 37
[416] Highwater, p. 32
[417] Nigosian, p. 138
[418] Noss, p. 559
[419] Noss, p. 559
[420] Nigosian, p. 138
[421] Noss, p. 559
[422] Nigosian, p. 85
[423] Strachan, E & G, p. 115
[424] Eisler, p. 78, and Highwater, p. 67
[425] Feuerstein, pp. 65, 66
[426] Highwater, p. 27, 56
[427] Highwater, p. 80
[428] Feuerstein, p. 86
[429] Strachan, E & G, p. 120
[430] Strachan, E & G, p. 122
[431] Highwater, p. 75
[432] Feuerstein, p. 78
[433] Hall, Robert, pp. 52, 53, 55
[434] Noss, p. 559
[435] Nigosian, p. 138
[436] Noss, p. 559
[437] Noss, p. 559
[438] Nigosian, p. 87
[439] Exodus 3:14
[440] Graves, pp. 27, 13
[441] Lamsa, 1964, p. 91
[442] Graves, p. 27
[443] Lamsa, 1964, p. 111
[444] Deuteronomy 32:8
[445] Gray, John, p. 132
[446] Lamsa, 1964, p. 11
[447] Deuteronomy 33:8-11
[448] Nigosian, p. 153
[449] Friedman, pp. 51, 59
[450] Friedman, pp. 197, 217
[451] Nigosian, p. 168
[452] Parrinder, 1971, p. 401
[453] Nigosian, p. 45
[454] Nigosian, p. 32
[455] Isaiah 45:6-7
[456] Deuteronomy 22:28-29

[457] Eisler, p. 97
[458] Stone, p. 56
[459] Numbers 31
[460] Eisler, pp. 98, 100
[461] Eisler, p. 102
[462] Graves, pp. 65-68
[463] Graves, p. 68
[464] Psalms 72: 1-4, 6, 7, 12-14, 16
[465] Psalms 2:8-12; 21:4; 72:5,8-11
[466] Nigosian, pp. 55-56
[467] Noss, pp. 95, 100
[468] Burkert, p. 11
[469] Noss, p. 105
[470] Noss, p. 106
[471] Berry, p. 57
[472] Rudolph, p. 290
[473] Rudolph, p. 290
[474] Stone, p. 146
[475] Godwin, p. 111
[476] Parrinder, 1971, p. 176
[477] Walker, p. 111
[478] Parrinder, 1971, p. 176
[479] Noss, p. 105
[480] Stone, p. 146
[481] Godwin, p. 98
[482] Burkert, p. 7
[483] Parrinder, 1971, p. 187
[484] Berry, p. 56
[485] Parrinder, 1971, p. 187
[486] Berry, p. 71
[487] Noss, p. 106
[488] Parrinder, 1971, p. 175
[489] Barthel, p. 312
[490] Barthel, p. 312
[491] Weddeck &Baskin, p. 401
[492] Sjoo & Mor, p. 284
[493] Vanderkam, p. 22&36
[494] Sjoo & Mor, p. 285
[495] Sjoo & Mor, p. 287
[496] Kersten, pp. 99, 106-107
[497] Graves, p. 90
[498] Whiston, p. 477
[499] Gardner, p. 298
[500] Barthel, p. 303
[501] Kersten, p. 85
[502] Barthel, p. 303
[503] Barthel, p. 306-307
[504] Mitchell, p. 129
[505] Errico, 1987, p. 3
[506] Mitchell, p. 23 and Barthel, p. 308
[507] Parrinder, 1983, p. 14

[508] Gray, John, p. 126
[509] Warner, p. 19
[510] Guidici, Frank, *Overview of the New Testament*
[511] Matthew 12:47-48 and 13:56; Mark 3:31 and 6:3; Luke 8:19-21
[512] Matthew 1:25
[513] Kersten, p. 93
[514] Noss, p. 595
[515] Matthew 17:12-13
[516] Luke 7:34
[517] Mitchell, p. 15
[518] Pagels, 1988, p. xxii
[519] Barthel, p. 200
[520] John 18:30
[521] Smith, Morton, 1978, p. 33
[522] Smith, Morton, 1982, p. 106
[523] Gardner, p. 181
[524] Gray, William, p. 29
[525] Sjoo & Mor, p. 286
[526] Gray, William, p. 30
[527] Smith, Morton, 1982, p. 103
[528] Kersten, p. 17
[529] Kersten, pp. 84, 95, 200, 208
[530] Cotterell, p. 4-5
[531] Rothgeb, p. 18
[532] Matthew 7:1-2
[533] Matthew 5:45-46
[534] Errico, 1987, p. 85
[535] Mitchell, p. 15
[536] Barthel, p. 309
[537] Matthew 5:16
[538] Noss, p. 607
[539] Matthew 5:22, 28
[540] Matthew 5:17
[541] Noss, p. 610
[542] Matthew 9:13
[543] Matthew 4:17, 10:7 and 12:28
[544] Matthew 11:12 and 23:13
[545] Leloup, 240 of 257
[546] Parrinder, 1983, p. 12
[547] Hoeller, Hans, "God the Father"
[548] Noss, p. 606
[549] Noss, p. 604
[550] Mitchell, p. 10
[551] Hoeller, Stephan, *Secret Sayings of Jesus*
[552] Guidici, Frank, *Overview of the New Testament*
[553] Barthel, p. 292
[554] Barthel, pp. 319, 320
[555] Smith, Morton, 1978, p. 145
[556] Matthew 10:5-6
[557] Smith, Morton, 1978, p. 26
[558] Barthel, pp. 347, 330-331

[559] Barthel, pp. 370, 347
[560] Errico, 1987, p. 69
[561] Mitchell, p. 146
[562] *Enlightenment from the Aramaic*, p. 4
[563] *Enlightenment from the Aramaic*, p. 8
[564] Errico, 1987, p. 74
[565] Douglas-Klotz, p. 3
[566] Douglas-Klotz, p. 3
[567] *Enlightenment from the Aramaic*, p. 6
[568] *Enlightenment from the Aramaic*, p. 45
[569] Kersten, p. 95
[570] Errico, 1987, p. 24
[571] Errico, 1987, p. 15
[572] Matthew 5:44
[573] *Enlightenment from the Aramaic*, p. 8
[574] Douglas-Klotz, p. 85
[575] Song of Songs 5:4
[576] Isaiah 63:15
[577] Errico, 1985, p. 29
[578] Matthew 6:22-23
[579] *Enlightenment from the Aramaic*, p. 19
[580] Errico, 1985, p. 18
[581] Matthew 7:6
[582] Lamsa, 1971, p. 70
[583] Errico, 1985, p. 26
[584] Errico, 1987, p. 4
[585] Lamsa, 1957
[586] Lamsa, 1971 and Errico, 1985, for example
[587] Douglas-Klotz, p. 41
[588] Kersten, p. 108
[589] Guillaumont, p. 57
[590] Luke 10:1; Luke 10:17
[591] Smith, Morton, 1982, p. 90
[592] Smith, Morton, 1982, p. 113-114
[593] Hoeller, Stephan, *Secret Sayings of Jesus*
[594] Hoeller, Stephan, *Secret Sayings of Jesus*
[595] Smith, Morton, 1982, p. 122-123
[596] Mark 9: 38-39; Luke 9:49-50
[597] Matthew 20:26-28
[598] Noss, p. 618
[599] Acts 6:1-6
[600] Noss, p. 619
[601] Guidici, Frank, *Overview of the New Testament*
[602] Acts 8:1
[603] II Cor 12:1-18
[604] Smith, Morton, 1978, pp. 122, 148
[605] Smith, Morton, 1982, p. 131
[606] Kersten, p. 29
[607] Barthel, p. 384
[608] Nigosian, p. 88
[609] Noss, p. 620

[610] Acts 8:2-3
[611] Acts 9:1-2
[612] Acts 9:10-16
[613] Metzger & Murphy, pp. 160 & 47
[614] Noss, p. 622
[615] Kersten, p. 28
[616] Acts 13:6-12
[617] Mitchell, p. 88
[618] Mitchell, p. 41
[619] Barthel, p. 379
[620] Noss, p. 623
[621] Rudolph, pp. 300-301, 368
[622] King, p. 9
[623] Feuerstein, p. 103
[624] I Corinthians 15:50
[625] I Corinthians 15:3
[626] Mitchell, p. 41
[627] Barthel, p. 379
[628] Mitchell, p. 151
[629] Hoeller, Hans, "Paul the Gnostic Apostle"
[630] Noss, p. 627
[631] Noss, p. 627
[632] Nigosian, p. 88
[633] Nigosian, p. 89
[634] Nigosian, p. 87
[635] Pagels, 1979, p. 92
[636] Highwater, p. 109
[637] Garraty & Gay, p. 219
[638] Pagels, 1979, p. 102
[639] Smith, Morton, 1978, p. 50
[640] Pagels, 1979, p. 41
[641] Pagels, 1979, p. 179
[642] Noss, p. 627
[643] Pagels, 1979, p. xxxviii
[644] Garraty & Gay, p. 207
[645] Hoeller, Stephan, 1982, p. 11
[646] Pagels, 1979, pp. 16, 17
[647] King, pp. 9, 42
[648] Jonas, p. 6
[649] "Valentinians", p. 860
[650] Godwin, p. 85
[651] Pagels, 1979, p. 44
[652] Walker, p. 47
[653] Pagels, 1979, p. 58
[654] Pagels, 1979, pp. 61, 37
[655] Jonas, p. 44
[656] Walker, p. 32
[657] Jonas, p. 288
[658] Gen. 2:18
[659] Gen. 3:4-5
[660] Hoeller, "God the Father

[661] Pagels, 1979, p. 36
[662] Pagels, 1988, p. 65
[663] Hoeller, Stephan, 1982, p. 83
[664] Hoeller, Stephan, 1982, p. 36
[665] Rudolph, p. 322
[666] Jonas, p. 44
[667] Rudolph, p. 292
[668] Walker, pp. 107, 113
[669] Jonas, p. 72
[670] Pagels, 1988, pp. 71, 94
[671] Hoeller, Stephan, 1982, p. 98
[672] Hoeller, Stephan, 1982, p. 82
[673] MacGregor, p. 42
[674] Hoeller, Stephan, 1982, p. 11
[675] Rudolph, p. 55
[676] MacGregor, p. 19
[677] Pagels, 1979, p. 155
[678] Pagels, 1979, p. xviii, xix, xx
[679] Pagels, 1979, p. 161
[680] Pagels, 1988, p. 72
[681] Walker, p. 46
[682] Mark 4:10-12
[683] Jonas, p. 139
[684] Walker, p. 76
[685] Rudolph, p. 159
[686] Walker, p. 77
[687] Rudolph, p. 161-162
[688] Walker, p. 104
[689] Pagels, 1979, p. 20
[690] MacGregor, p. 1
[691] Rudolph, pp. 216, 205
[692] Pagels, 1988, p. 60-61
[693] Rudolph, p. 318
[694] Pagels, 1988, p. 61
[695] Pagels, 1979, p. 43
[696] Rudolph, p. 206
[697] Pagels, 1979, p. 45
[698] Rudolph, p. 226
[699] Walker, p. 148
[700] Rudolph, p. 246
[701] Walker
[702] King, p. 81
[703] Walker, p. 143
[704] Rudolph, p. 315
[705] Walker, p. 144
[706] Jonas, p. 144
[707] Rudolph, p. 317
[708] Rudolph, p. 263
[709] Hoeller, Stephan, 1982, p. 81
[710] Pagels, 1979, p. 3
[711] Pagels, 1979, pp. 30, 49

[712] Pagels, 1979, p. 174
[713] Hoeller, Stephan, 1982, pp. 13, 14
[714] Pagels, 1979, p. 64
[715] Pagels, 1979, pp. 72, 80
[716] Godwin, p. 86
[717] Noss, p. 638
[718] Pagels, 1979, p. 53
[719] Pagels, 1979, p. xxxviii
[720] Pagels, 1979, p. 68
[721] Pagels, 1988, p. 63
[722] Sjoo & Mor, p. 275
[723] Feuerstein, p. 109
[724] Walker, p. 112
[725] Sjoo & Mor, p. 292
[726] Burkert, pp. 6, 83
[727] Godwin, p. 99
[728] Berry, p. 71
[729] Weddeck &Baskin, p. 78
[730] Berry, p. 56
[731] Godwin, p. 99
[732] Berry, p. 57
[733] Godwin, p. 99
[734] Berry, pp. 56, 57
[735] Burkert, p. 7
[736] Rudolph, p. 290
[737] Burkert, p. 42
[738] Berry, p. 57
[739] King, p. 122
[740] Parrinder, 1971, p. 187
[741] King, p. 124
[742] Berry, p. 71
[743] Godwin, p. 99
[744] Parrinder, 1971, p. 187
[745] Burkert, p. 42
[746] King, p. xviii
[747] Matthew 16:18
[748] Berry, p. 57-58
[749] Ulansey, p. 107
[750] Ulansey, p. 83
[751] King, p. 122-123
[752] Stone, p. 194
[753] Jones, p. 649
[754] Garraty & Gay, p. 231
[755] Jones, p. 649
[756] Baigent, pp. 339-341
[757] Garraty & Gay, p. 231
[758] Baigent, p. 341
[759] Jones, p. 649
[760] Walker, p. 112
[761] Smith, Morton, 1978, p.
[762] Baigent, p. 342

[763] Baigent, p. 342
[764] Garraty & Gay, p. 231
[765] Eisler, p. 131
[766] Walsh, p. 43
[767] Baigent, p. 340
[768] Noss, p. 638
[769] Brusher, p. 72
[770] Barthel, p. 305
[771] Pagels, 1988, p. 94
[772] Warner, p. 73
[773] Noss, p. 644
[774] Noss, p. 646
[775] Pagels, 1988, pp. xxv, xix
[776] Noss, p. 646
[777] Berry, p. 77
[778] Pagels, 1988, p. 150
[779] Pagels, 1988, pp. 146, 150
[780] Berry, p. 74
[781] Pagels, 1979, p. xviii
[782] Walker, p. 158-159
[783] Stone, p. 194
[784] Jackson, p. 258
[785] Eisler, p. 143
[786] Pagels, 1979, p. 126
[787] Pagels, 1988, pp. 40, 41
[788] Walker, p. 149-150
[789] Warner, p. 64-65
[790] Gray, John, p. 132
[791] Graves, pp. 12, 58
[792] Noss, p. 557
[793] Bloom & Rosenberg, p. 181
[794] Berry, p. 82
[795] Feuerstein, p. 107
[796] Jackson, p. 261
[797] Berry, pp. 83-84
[798] Sjoo & Mor, p. 292
[799] Jackson, p. 272-273
[800] Armstrong
[801] Armstrong
[802] Cahill, Location 2089, Kindle edition
[803] Cahill, Location 1871, Kindle edition
[804] Cahill, Location 2497, Kindle edition
[805] Cahill, Location 2646, Kindle edition
[806] Cahill, Location 2120, Kindle edition
[807] Franzius, p. 89
[808] Berry, p. 97
[809] Franzius, pp. 90, 93
[810] Nigosian, p. 141
[811] Franzius, p. 93
[812] Franzius, pp. 115, 118, 119
[813] Berry, p. 99

[814] Berry, p. 87
[815] Warner, pp. 308, 305
[816] Berry, p. 81
[817] Lyons, p. 31
[818] Kersten, p. 39
[819] Lyons, p. 32
[820] Feuerstein, p. 107
[821] Warner, p. 145
[822] Berry, pp. 85, 86
[823] Berry, p. 79
[824] Warner, p. 144
[825] Walker, p. 172
[826] Berry, p. 80
[827] Walker, p. 172
[828] Walker, p. 172
[829] MacGregor, p. 61-62
[830] Warner, p. 146
[831] Sjoo & Mor, p. 294
[832] Eisler, p. 205
[833] Sjoo & Mor, p. 297
[834] Ginsburg, pp. 34, 63
[835] Berry, p. 6
[836] Russell, p. 151
[837] Russell, p. 148
[838] Sjoo & Mor, p. 302
[839] Sjoo & Mor, p. 298
[840] Lyons, p. 33
[841] Sjoo & Mor, pp. 298, 299
[842] Russell, p. 151
[843] Eisler, pp. 203-204
[844] Russell, p. 57
[845] Russell, p. 57
[846] Ginsburg, pp. 165, 211
[847] Russell, p. 101
[848] Sjoo & Mor, p. 300
[849] Russell, p. 153
[850] Sjoo & Mor, p. 301
[851] Sjoo & Mor, p. 302
[852] Sjoo & Mor, p. 304
[853] Sjoo & Mor, p. 304
[854] Sjoo & Mor, pp. 305, 306
[855] Leviticus 20:27 and Deuteronomy 13:3-5
[856] Russell, pp. 30, 288
[857] Russell, pp. 152, 286
[858] Lyons, pp. 23, 25
[859] Berry, p. 101
[860] Lyons, p. 33
[861] Bowie, p. 716
[862] Bowie, p. 716
[863] Bowie, p. 716
[864] Warner, p. 330

[865] Noss, p. 690-691
[866] Lyons, p. 65
[867] Achterberg, pp. 2, 3
[868] Achterberg, pp. 5, 7, 8
[869] Achterberg, p. 13
[870] Achterberg, p. 29-30
[871] Sjoo & Mor, p. 336
[872] Sjoo & Mor, p. 333
[873] Sjoo & Mor, p. 333
[874] https://www.beliefnet.com/news/2005/03/environmental-armageddon.aspx#5WovoZHqHPUPJbsZ.99

[875] Hieronimus, pp. 5-22
[876] Hieronimus, p. 11
[877] Hieronimus, p. 16
[878] Narby & Huxley
[879] Harner, 1980 and 2013
[880] Jung, 2009, p. 125
[881] Mabry, location 560
[882] Gaup, location 3695
[883] Jung, 1968, pp. 99-100
[884] Cowan, p. 50
[885] Jung, 1971
[886] Cain

www.ingramcontent.com/pod-product-compliance
Lightning Source LLC
Chambersburg PA
CBHW081227080526
44587CB00022B/3853